Hot Groups

Hot Groups

---

*Seeding Them, Feeding Them, and
Using Them to Ignite Your Organization*

Jean Lipman-Blumen
Harold J. Leavitt

New York   Oxford
Oxford University Press
1999

Oxford University Press

Oxford   New York

Athens   Auckland   Bangkok   Bogotá   Bombay
Buenos Aires   Calcutta   Cape Town   Dar es Salaam   Delhi
Florence   Hong Kong   Istanbul   Karachi
Kuala Lumpur   Madras   Madrid   Melbourne
Mexico City   Nairobi   Paris   Singapore
Taipei   Tokyo   Toronto   Warsaw

and associated companies in
Berlin   Ibadan

Published by Oxford University Press, Inc.
198 Madison Avenue, New York, New York 10016

Oxford is a registered trademark of Oxford University Press

Library of Congress Cataloging-in-Publication Data
Lipman-Blumen, Jean
Hot groups : seeding them, feeding them
and using them to ignite your organization /
by Jean Lipman-Blumen and Harold J. Leavitt
p.   cm.   Includes index.
ISBN 0-19-512686-6
1. Organizational effectiveness. 2. Group decision making.
3. Industrial efficiency. I. Leavitt, Harold J. II. Title.
HD58.9.L42   1999   658.4'036—dc21   98-8524

1 3 5 7 9 8 6 4 2
Printed in the United States of America
on acid-free paper

For
Gene Webb
Dear Friend, Wise and Generous Colleague
1933–1995

Contents

Foreword

In a traditional industrial company—circa 1975—the ratio of stock market value (in dollars) to hard assets might run about one-to-one. Near the end of 1998, the equivalent ratio at Microsoft was 212-to-one.

Yikes!

Microsoft. Extreme? Yes. Yet indicative of the new age stars. Microsoft…a floating crap game of hot folks…working on hot projects. Period.

And that's precisely what makes Jean Lipman-Blumen and Hal Leavitt's book so timely…important…and, yes, hot.

Hot Groups! Yes! Yes! Yes!

I can honestly say my hands frequently shook as I read this book (and I hope yours do too).

The global dance led by the new technologies is ripping up the old economy to shreds and replacing it with the new one at, literally, the speed of light. Old firms are merging and consolidating and disappearing at a record clip. New firms are racing to the foreground. (At a record clip.) A Netscape is born, changes the world, and dies (bought out by America On Line), all in the space of two years. Oh yes, America On Line; last time I looked, its stock market value was about one-and-a-half times greater than that of General Motors.

As I said, yikes!

It is an age of speed. An age of impermanence. An age as never before of rapidly applied brainpower. (The chief of giant ABB [Asea Brown Boveri] recently described his firm as 300 tons of applied brainpower.)

There is a raft of books on Internet strategies. And a whole industry of books on information technology in general. And some cool, new magazines—*Fast Company* comes immediately to mind—which herald the new, peripatetic employee. But what's missing is the work itself! What is it? (The *new* it.) How does it get done?

And now, I believe, we have a brilliant first draft of an answer. I am a pretty good student of the new-economy literature, popular and academic; and when I say this book is unique, well, I think I'm right. Hot Groups are passionate, task-obsessed. They are the meat and the potatoes of what an organization needs in order to fling itself productively at this shifting, wild, woolly economy.

Good news: Hot Groups are now necessary, but they're not new. As the authors say, they've always been around: the Hot Group of scientists that broke the code and discovered the double helix; the amazing group of impressionists who reinvented art in Paris in the 1870s, etc. So we don't have to reinvent the wheel. To mix a metaphor, what we need to do is turn up the heat and learn quickly how to seed and feed and weed Hot Groups in sufficient numbers to keep pace with the unforgiving times.

Lipman-Blumen and Leavitt do not provide a standard how-to treatment. (There's too much lingering uncertainty for that.) But they do give us a brilliant, detailed, and pretty darned complete roadmap. They tell us what a Hot Group is and is not. (E.g., it ain't a team or task force.) They tell us exactly how Hot Groups work. (They love the task, not necessarily one another. Touchy-feely this is not.) They explain the Hot Group leadership challenges. (Hot Groups tend to make a lot of enemies!) And for the big cheese, they offer advice on preparing fertile soil in which Hot Groups will grow in record number. (For one thing, you've got to have a sky-high tolerance for ambiguity.)

I've already hinted at my hope: I hope this book changes your life! It is crystal clear to me—and damned few things are!—that Lipman-Blumen and Leavitt's *Hot Groups* is about the way things will work in the years ahead. Effective, perpetually renewing organizations-as-shifting-collections-of-Hot Groups is it. Master the discipline-strategy now, or else. That's the way I see it.

I recently chatted with the chief of one of the largest white-collar unions in America. I told him I thought the new information tools would transform white-collar jobs in the next ten or so years as much as blue-collar jobs have been transformed in the last one-hundred years. I said I expected it would make re-engineering of the past decade look like small change and that ninety-percent of his members, or more, should be prepared to see their jobs as they are today evaporate.

I believe what I said. And at the same time I am modestly, or more, optimistic. We coped with the traumatic changes on the farm and in the factory. And I think we'll cope with this one too. But we need a whole new bag of tricks—to re-invent work and organizations fast. I think what I'll call the Hot Group Solution is a marvelous start down the trail toward surviving, even thriving, and, not so incidentally, having fun along the way.

Good reading and good luck!

Tom Peters

23 January 1999
West Tinmouth, Vermont

Preface

———

The time is ripe for large, hierarchical, well-ordered organizations to make room for small, egalitarian, disordered hot groups. That is the first thesis of this book. Hot groups should not, however, be confused with teams, task forces, panels, boards, or committees. Any of those might become a hot group, but few do. A hot group is not a name for another kind of structural unit. It is a task-obsessed state of mind, an attitude shared by a group's members. Organizations need many such groups to help them confront the near chaos of their rapidly changing environments.

Although our book has come to praise the passionate, productive mentalities that are the hallmarks of little hot groups, it has not come to bury large, well-ordered organizations. Large and even larger organizations are certainly in our future, but they will not be the stolid, monolithic pyramids of the past. They will be designed by a radically new breed of architects. The information revolution has shrunk not only the spatial world, but the temporal one as well. This new world is small and growing smaller, and it is fast and going faster, forcing slow-moving large organizations to become much more innovatively proactive and much more quickly reactive. Hot groups are a tool, perhaps a necessary one, for helping organizations do both. They are extremely innovative, and they react rapidly in urgent situations.

The book's second and ultimately more important thesis is that hot groups are not good just for organizations. They are also good for people. They offer individuals opportunities to find meaning and ennoblement through their work. In our fast and impermanent new organizational world, those who work in organizations—and that includes most of us—both expect and deserve such opportunities.

Hot groups are not an alternative to large, disciplined organizations, but they can help loosen and dis-organize them, so that those organizations can better confront their volatile milieux. It is said that Henry VIII found it easy to destroy the large and powerful Catholic abbeys of sixteenth-century England precisely because they were so tightly organized and closely controlled from the top. When he beheaded the abbot, the whole rigidly linked structure began to crumble.

Yet somehow, the parent of those abbeys, the Church of Rome, also hierarchical and strictly controlled, has managed to survive for a very long time. The Catholic Church has had its own hot groups, too, many of them unintended and unwelcomed. Sometimes, the Church viewed such groups as threats and tried to kill them off altogether. At other times, however, Rome used hot groups effectively, which is precisely what today's large organizations ought to do.

In our new century, one that will surely be marked by much more speed and innovation, such old, top-down designs will have an even harder time of it. Organizations will need fast, creative mechanisms like hot groups, mechanisms that, in the past, were usually seen as difficult or even dangerous. Now, organizations will have to find active ways to propagate just such hot groups. They will have to figure out how to change themselves so that hot groups can flourish within their loosened boundaries. In our new millennium, we do not believe that cosmetic, peripheral organizational changes will be enough to accomplish all that.

Size, in itself, is not the enemy. The devil is in the ponderous and anti-human rigidity that so often accompanies large organizational size. That size can also be beautiful has been demonstrated again and again by a few large yet flexible and adaptive companies. Indeed, it has been demonstrated for better than two hundred years by the flexibility and innovativeness of our American democracy.

Our book, then, is about the fundamental role of hot groups in large, modern organizations. It is about the nature of hot groups, and it is also an unabashed paean to their usefulness. It describes hot groups' most prominent characteristics and the organizational conditions most likely to encourage their development. This book also confronts some down-to-earth issues: If you want to generate more hot groups in your organization, how can you do it? What kinds of leaders do hot groups need? What are some effective and some ineffective ways of leading hot groups? What are the political and social traps that leaders of hot groups are likely to encounter? For individual members of hot groups, what are the benefits and what are the costs?

We believe the answer to that last question is clear. Hot groups are fundamentally good for people. They provide opportunities to stretch ourselves, to move beyond even our own personal bests. That organizations are now beginning to value hot groups is, we believe, a positive sign for the future of work. Perhaps, finally, we shall see, if not an end to the era of work as drudgery, at least a beginning of an era of work as enrichment and ennoblement.

Our book is not based on any program of systematic research, but draws heavily on our own and others' research, as well as on a mélange of other sources. Both of us have been interested in hot groups since the early 1980s, although we didn't label them "hot" until about 1987. Our work on small groups in general goes back a long time before that. We have run formal experiments with small groups, observed hot groups in our consulting practices, participated in them in our own academic research and elsewhere, and studied others' work in the abundant literature on small groups, teams, and general management. We have also conducted a number of formal and informal interviews with leaders and members of hot groups.

Hot groups, it should be added, are by no means a phenomenon of modern organizations. They have probably been around as long as human beings have inhabited the earth. Nor are they limited to the narrow sector of the best and the brightest. Neither are hot groups the sole property of adults, of Americans, or of white males. And they are nothing at all like conformist cults.

The hot group state of mind can occur anywhere and anytime, wherever and whenever people come together to do something they believe is worth doing. Yet, these ideal conditions don't occur often. Most of us can feel lucky if we have had the chance to participate in one or two really hot groups in our lifetimes. Why they

have been so rare, especially in the world of work, we shall discuss
in the early chapters of our book. How we can seed, feed, and har-
vest many more of them, we save for later chapters.

JEAN LIPMAN-BLUMEN
HAROLD J. LEAVITT

Pasadena, California
August 1998

I

HOT GROUPS:
WHAT THEY ARE AND WHY
THEY'RE HOT

1

The Hot Group State of Mind:
What Is It? Where Is It?
Why Does It Matter?

A hot group is a special state of mind. It's not a name for some new kind of team or task force or committee. The hot group state of mind is task-obsessed and full of passion. It is always coupled with a distinctive way of behaving, a style that is intense, sharply focused, and full-bore.

Any group can become a hot group—if it can get itself into that distinctive state of mind. A few groups currently called teams manage to do that, but the great majority don't. Some task forces and other variously labeled groups also heat up, but most don't. It is not the name, but that contagious single-mindedness, that all-out dedication to doing something important, that most distinguishes a hot group from all others.

To catch the flavor of a hot group, consider this case recently recounted to us by retired Naval Officer Alan Lerchbacker. Six years out of the Naval Academy, Lt. Lerchbacker received a challenging assignment: To manage the overhaul of the USS Dale and transform it into a guided missile cruiser in only twelve months. What made the task seem quite impossible was the simple historical fact that the U.S. Navy had never completed a complex cruiser overhaul within that time frame. Moreover, Alan had never even been inside a shipyard before. The assignment was daunting.

> I was twenty-eight, and they gave me 1200 people to work for me every day. Isn't that incredible? It was just a phenomenal opportunity. Here was a shipyard that had not finished a ship on time, or under cost, or even *at* cost, in five years. This was a pretty big ship, . . . At the time, she had guns, so she wasn't a guided missile cruiser. They were going to tear off all the guns, tear the whole ship apart, and install guided missiles, fore and aft. That type of overhaul had never been done in less than fourteen months, and the Navy said that the Naval Shipyard in Charleston, South Carolina—which hadn't finished a ship in five years—was going to do it in twelve months. And they gave it to me, because I was a young lieutenant, and they knew it was going to fail, and then I'd get the ax. So who better to fire than somebody who had nothing to risk. So they said go do it. And so we did.
>
> When I came in they had it scheduled for twelve months, and the one thing I'd learned in my short time in the Navy was that if you scheduled something for twelve it'll finish in thirteen at least. So we revamped the whole schedule for eleven. We were going to finish it thirty days early rather than on schedule. I figured that was the only chance we had. And we finished it exactly thirty days early, in eleven months and broke the Navy record by 3 months.
>
> Everybody came down when it was done. I mean, there were admirals out of Washington to see how we had done it. I was too stupid to know we couldn't. I just told the team, "Let's just do it."

Lerchbacker's management group consisted of nine military people and four civilians. This hot group, excited by a virtually impossible challenge, did something the Navy had never before been able to accomplish.

> That small group was totally committed to making it happen. I had master chiefs and a senior chief and two enlisted personnel who had been in shipyards and on ships their whole life. . . . They were really excited, because this was the first officer that had come in to say, "We're going to succeed." Before, everybody had said, "We can't do it, but let's give it a shot." . . . And we simply made up our minds that we were going to do it, and they just got really excited about it.

We then went to all the civilian leadership, the general foremen and foremen. They would usually have weekly meetings, but we made it daily. So we would get together for at least half an hour and discuss how we were going to execute the events of the day. We . . . had all of the supervisors on board the ship. Usually, they'd sit in their offices. So we moved all the meetings to the site where we were working. . . .

[The meetings] were either right on board the ship, or we'd set up a trailer. It usually got pretty loud on board, . . . with all the pounding and welding and everything that was going on. So we set up the trailer right next to the ship, so everyone at least had to come down to the trailer. And as soon as we finished the meeting we'd take them on board the ship. I think this was the first time the workers had ever seen their leadership on the site.

The management group then turned its attention to the engineers, whose clean, comfortable offices were a safe quarter mile from the noise and turbulence of the waterfront. Lerchbacker recalls:

Actually, we had engineers who had never [left their offices before]. We called [their quarters] "the Crystal Palace." There was this huge building—it was beautiful. You know what a waterfront looks like, it's all nasty and dirty and filthy—and then there was this impeccable building, and that's where all the engineers and senior managers were.

So we made them come out of that building and down to the waterfront to see where we were. I remember, we had this electrical engineer who I don't think [had ever been on a ship]—I mean, he used to wear suit coats and ties! And we were having a problem—we couldn't get a generator test to run. We couldn't make it work, and so I went up there, and I said, "You're going to come down and see what we're doing." The minute he got down there he said, "Oh, it's the wrong generator." We had the wrong technical manual. We'd been working for three days to try to test these generators, and we couldn't because the procedure he'd written was for the wrong generator. We'd have never known that; we would have sat there for weeks, and that's just the kind of thing that used to go on all the time. Nobody in the Crystal Palace knew what was going on with the people down on the waterfront. They just sat in that concrete building with its beautiful windows, so they could see us, but they never came down to the ship.

The major event in getting a ship through an overhaul is the "Light Off Exam" (LOE) that has to be passed before actually firing up the boilers and turning on the equipment. As the time approached for the examining team to make its visit, the tension mounted.

> The team comes from Norfolk, and they are experts in every system that you have in propulsion: all the air-conditioning, steam propulsion, etc. . . . They bring a team of about forty people down, and they inspect every part of that ship to make sure that it's safe to light off, to strike the boilers.
>
> And if you fail that exam, you'll lose four weeks at least, because they have their schedule. They have so many inspections going on all over the East Coast . . . that they have to work you back into their schedule. A lot of times they'll come on board, and they'll leave the same day they get there, because they'll just look at the ship, and they'll go, "You're not even close." And they'll just walk off.
>
> So one week before that exam, I went down, and there were seven major pieces of equipment that hadn't even been installed. They were not even on board.

Lerchbacker's group was already working at full capacity. Still they knew that that wasn't good enough. Driven by their own excitement, the group made one critical decision that eventually led to other key steps—a general meeting would be called late that night, during the swing shift.

Lerchbacker described what happened:

> I called a meeting for about 10 o'clock that night of all the supervisors, and they all had to come back into the shipyard. I called the shipyard commander and said, "I've got to have them back here. Get those civilians. We'll pay 'em, but they've got to be back here." So they came back in and I told them, "I'm not going to leave here or take a shower or go to sleep until we pass this inspection." I was terrible. For that week, I was pretty hard to get near. But I didn't care, and our team, all thirteen of them, stayed right there. And we slept for about 15 to 20 minutes in chairs, and we stayed there that whole week to get ready for that exam.
>
> They all stayed. Actually, they started to go home on Monday, and when we called the meeting that late—it was so late at night—they said, "Let's just stay through the night." The next day at the end of work, we were having our end-of-the-day talk about what's going to

go on tomorrow. . . . I started to ask really hard questions like: "What has to happen tomorrow? What has to happen this hour—and we started by the hour—what has to happen (the next) hour?" That's how close things were.

And the day before the exam—there are two main engine rooms, and there's two boiler rooms. At 1 o'clock in the morning—and the [examination] team was going to be there at 8 o'clock in the morning—we had over 500 people in those spaces. And you're not supposed to have anybody . . . because you're supposed to be done! And we still had 500 people on board! . . . You're not supposed to have anybody. It's supposed to be like you're just taking a dustmop and sweeping things up and making it look pretty.

At 7:30 [in the morning] we got everybody, all those people, off the ship, and it was ready to go. Actually, we still had about probably fifty people doing some minor little tweaks around, trying to fix it up. So when the [exam] team came on board, rather than go down into the spaces, we told them they had to have breakfast. So we had coffee and doughnuts in the ward room. We stalled them there for another hour and then they went down. And thank goodness we were ready. And we passed!

That bonded the team so much that there was nothing we couldn't do after that. They were going to go home and go back to our regular schedule, and I told them, "Do whatever you guys need to do." Part of the team stayed there with me. We had shifts, and that shipyard ran twenty-four hours a day, seven days a week. We set it up so that there would be two people on . . . the graveyard and two people on the swing shift. There would be ten people on the day shift. Sometimes, even until the end, the people on the day shift were so committed that they didn't go home either.

What did they get for their efforts? A big party and some very nominal, token rewards. Lerchbacker explained,

All you can do is give civilians a small award, and so you write them a letter. For all the senior people, all the general foremen, and all the foremen, I wrote over 180 letters, and those letters only get people a small . . . monetary award, because it is the government. You can get them anywhere from $50 to $200. We had a big awards ceremony for the whole 1200 in this huge auditorium. We gave them the letters, and I thanked everybody. Then we had a cookout after that. A big pig roast is what they do in Charleston.

It was not the money that drove that management group and their 1200 people. It was the challenge, the enormous sense of excitement that erupted from a task seemingly beyond reach. It was the sense of pride in doing something that had never been done before. That state of mind spurred the dedication of their leaders, who did not simply demand sacrifice from the employees, but also willingly made sacrifices themselves, actions that inspired the rest. Ultimately, the men and women involved felt they had stretched themselves beyond any performance level previously achieved.

That obsession and commitment radiated out from the small, hot Lerchbacker group to the civilian general foremen, the foremen, even to the engineers in the Crystal Palace. The LOE deadline—a real deadline, not a phony one—further increased everyone's sense of urgency. It catalyzed the round-the-clock crisis mode of the last week, lighting another kind of fire, a human fire that kept the operation hot enough to finish the job thirty days ahead of schedule.

Following a success like that, one might think the Navy would try to keep that hot little group together. They did not, and they may well have been right. They sent those hot group members on their separate ways. Hot groups, as we shall see, do not maintain their heat indefinitely. Lerchbacker and his senior staff, most of whom were promoted, were split up. Lerchbacker made lieutenant commander and was transferred to several special operations schools before he went on to join the Navy Aquanaut Team.

The challenge of the task and the sense of mission that accompanies it are always characteristic of the hot group state of mind. The words of some hot group veterans communicate that state of mind far better than we can, so we offer a few quotes from members of several different kinds of hot groups.

This is Bill Gates's description of the programming group he belonged to before the birth of Microsoft:

> We didn't even obey a 24-hour clock. We'd come in and program for a couple days straight, we'd—you know four or five of us—when it was time to eat, we'd get in our cars and kind of race over to the restaurant and sit and talk about what we were doing. Sometimes I'd get (so) excited about things, I'd forget to eat. Then we'd go back and program some more. . . . Those were also the fun days.[1]

Here is an aerospace executive, as he recaptured the culture of a project team he worked on in the mid-1990s:

> We even walked differently than anybody else. We felt we were way out there, ahead of the whole world.[2]

This is Emmy award-winning actress Barbara Babcock recalling the working atmosphere during the production of the 1980s hit television series *Hill Street Blues*:

> "Everybody was involved in that show," she said, her eyes almost tearful, "We actors didn't just read our lines. We worked on the whole show with the writers and directors. . . . We knew we were doing something wonderful, something innovative and important."[3]

This is the way John Sculley described the Macintosh design group as he first encountered it, just after he joined little Apple Computer in the early 1980s:

> It was almost as though there were magnetic fields, some spiritual force, mesmerizing people. Their eyes were just dazed. Excitement showed on everyone's face. It was nearly a cult environment.[4]

And here is Robert Kennedy's description of the working style of the "ExComm," the ad hoc crisis group advising President John Kennedy, in October 1962, during the tense thirteen days of the Cuban missile crisis:

> During all these deliberations, we all spoke as equals. There was no rank, and, in fact, we did not even have a chairman. . . . As a result, with the encouragement of McNamara, Bundy, and Ball, the conversations were completely uninhibited. . . . Everyone had an equal opportunity to express himself and to be heard directly. It was a tremendously advantageous procedure that does not frequently occur within the executive branch of the government, where rank is often so important.[5]

Those excerpts provide a pretty good picture of the nature of the hot group state of mind—spirited, intensely motivated, and task-obsessed. No matter how trivial it may look to outsiders, hot groups always see distinction and meaning in their undertakings. Their tasks completely captivate their members, temporarily monopolizing their hearts and minds to the exclusion of almost everything else. And hot groups do great things at an exhilarating pace.

Hot groups can be highly diverse. They need not be composed of intellectual giants, although there is certainly nothing to prevent such virtuosi from participating—so long as their egos do not blow the group to pieces. Members' IQs are simply unrelated to a group's heat. So are social rank, professional status, race, gender, and political affiliation. A street corner gang of school dropouts could be a hot group, while a set of Nobelists in economics might be ice cold.

- Lerchbacker's shipyard group was a military/civilian mix, with both officers and enlisted men in the military set. Some were young, some old. Some were novices, some had long experience.

- The Gates group was a turned-on collection of deeply committed, bright youngsters, confident that they were on the trail of something great. And they were.

- The aerospace team was quite homogeneous: a set of engineers and technologists with more or less similar backgrounds working inside a large bureaucratic organization.

- The *Hill Street Blues* group was a temporary assemblage engaged in a common task; a company composed of actors, directors, producers, and camera people who had come together to engage in a specific, relatively short-term undertaking. It was a highly diverse group. Some members were probably brilliant and some were not. Some were bigger shots in the entertainment industry than others. Some thought first about art, others about money.

- The Mac group consisted of a gaggle of bright, brash young Northern California nerds—working in a struggling new enterprise.

- President Kennedy's ExComm was intentionally hetero-geneous, though all its members were experienced senior public officials working within the context of a much larger bureaucracy.

Those groups differed sharply from one another. Their members characteristically varied in age, intelligence, occupation, race, education, status, and gender. Some of them were quite autonomous; others worked within the confines of governmental or industrial bureaucracies. They went by different names. The Navy group was simply the set of managers in charge of an overhaul project. The aerospace group was called a "team." The ExComm was a "committee." The *Hill Street Blues* group was a "company" in the original sense of that word—a temporary group gathered to do a piece of work. The Gates and Macintosh groups had no special names. They were simply working groups of imaginative young people. Yet, all those groups represent only a narrow sample of the wide range of sizes, shapes, times, and places in which one can find hot groups.

All those examples share these core characteristics of the hot group state of mind:

- Each group felt itself engaged in an important, even vital, and personally ennobling mission.

- In each, the task itself dominated all other considerations. The process was simultaneously arduous and intoxicating. Contrary to some fundamental tenets of organization development theory, interpersonal relationships played only secondary roles.

- All those hot groups were relatively short-lived, yet each is remembered nostalgically and in considerable detail by its participants.

One more important point: The fact that several individuals have worked together as a hot group at one moment does not mean that similar heat, excitement, and accomplishment will always accompany their joint ventures. President Kennedy's Excom was a hot group that happened to be made up of experienced veterans of politics and diplomacy. Nonetheless, a not-at-all hot group, composed of many of those same individuals, had stumbled disastrously in the earlier Bay of Pigs operation.[6] The *Hill Street Blues* company also heated up, but many of the same participants, working together in other productions, did not strike any particular sparks.

A hot group, we repeat, is not a name for another kind of organizational unit. A hot group is not to be confused with a team, task force, panel, board, or committee. It is a state of mind, shared by a group's members. Nor is a hot group a collection of people tagged with a macho label like "tiger team" or "red raiders." Any group, whatever its title, could turn into a hot group—but few do. In fact, many of the hottest groups have no names at all. Others have simply been labeled by outsiders for convenience, dramatic effect, or, occasionally, to express awe or resentment. Moreover, hot groups are not limited to organizations. Many, if not most, grow entirely independently of large organizations.

To illustrate the difference between a hot group and the recent organizational interest in "teams," consider this all-too-familiar case summary of a new "team program" as it was introduced into a Canadian company and reported by Rob Duimering of the University of Waterloo. He studied "a large Canadian manufacturer [that had] recently instituted a corporate program for implementing a team-based management approach throughout its operations"[7] and describes what happened. [The italics are ours, to emphasize the differences between groups put together by managers and stamped with the label "team" and a genuine hot group.]

> Employees were trained in team concepts; a team facilitator was appointed and given an office in the middle of the factory; meetings were held among factory employee "teams"; new performance measures were instituted for managers; and several teams developed process improvement suggestions that they formally presented to higher management. . . .
>
> [To document and evaluate the program,] two research reports were generated. The first report described in detail the workings of one team that was generally regarded as being successful and exem-

plary. . . . *It had been implemented as a self-managing work group prior to the "rolling in" of the official corporate team program. Before the team program began, the group had received very little recognition by others in the factory and was more or less tolerated along with its overzealous manager. With the new program giving her group some legitimacy within the organization, the manager began to refer to them as a "team" and soon earned some formal recognition for her efforts. . . .*

The second report described the implementation of the team program in general . . . and concluded that the program as a whole had more or less failed . . . [and] resulted in a great deal of time spent in meetings with little to show for it. . . .

The *first* report [on the single team] was widely circulated by management. Several people associated with the team program were given promotions, including the team facilitator. . . . The university researchers' . . . contract was renewed. . . . *On the evidence of the first report, the team program was generally regarded by corporate management as highly successful.*

The second report [on the total program] was carefully filed away . . . as if it had never been written. . . . The corporation was [already] beginning to "roll out" the team program in favor of a new program that emphasized "continuous improvement" and "business process reengineering."

That case says a lot. The single "team" described in the first report is a classic hot group. It began spontaneously, before the official team program even started. It operated under the aegis of an "overzealous" manager. That it was initially tolerated, though largely ignored, has also been a common experience of hot groups that have had the temerity to sprout through the cracks in organizational concrete. Moreover, as in this case, formal team programs, instigated by management, are often entirely unrelated to anything resembling a hot group. They are this year's—or last year's—human resources' pet.

Looking Ahead: The Structure of This Book

Although this is not a how-to book, it will take us into many practical issues: What kind of leadership do hot groups need? What danger signals do leaders have to watch out for, both inside a group and outside? What can leaders of hot groups do to mesh their wide-open operating styles with the necessarily restrictive control systems of a large organization? What happens when a hot group overheats? How can a manager in a large organization seed and feed hot groups? How can organizations grow successive crops of such groups? What, if any, changes in its culture and core values must any particular organization make to accommodate hot groups? And, perhaps most important, what will membership in a hot group do for you? What risks and what rewards are involved for the individual? To get at such questions, we have structured the rest of this book into four parts:

- The first four chapters constitute Part I, which draws a general picture of hot groups—the what, why and how issues. Chapter 2 tries to answer the question: Why now? Why does the world need hot groups more this year than ever? Why should organizations, which have traditionally despised hot groups, now embrace them? Chapter 3 lays out a list of the characteristic thinking styles of hot groups; Chapter 4 does the same for their working styles.

- Part II consists of three chapters examining the leadership of hot groups. Chapter 5 describes three quite distinct varieties of hot group leaders. Chapters 6 and 7 offer some counsel for nascent leaders of such groups. What skills do they need? What and where are the signals of impending trouble inside the group? How can one deal with such troubles? And what red flags do both leaders and members have to watch for *outside* the group, in the larger organization as well as the world beyond? Where are the booby traps and land mines?

- Part III focuses on the operations of hot groups and their internal design. That's where we examine the tenuous relationships between hot groups and their parent organizations. Chapter 8 considers the internal design of hot groups, their nonhierarchical, loose, temporary structures. Chapter 9 explores the often troubled relationship between wide open, egalitarian hot groups and rather closed, hierarchical organizations. In Chapter 10, we offer some unrequested advice about how that relationship can be improved without either partner having to abandon its core beliefs and values. Chapter 11 looks at the downsides of hot groups, at some of the most frequent causes of their failures, and at the effects of such unhappy endings. When a hot group comes up empty, what happens to its people and to its parent organization?

- Chapter 12, still in Part III, focuses on the individuals inside hot groups. What do hot groups do for their members? And what are the costs of membership? Not surprisingly, we argue that such groups offer rare opportunities for their members to find some of the personal meaning and even ennoblement that all of us seek. We also, however, suggest some of the bills that must be paid for such all-out dedication to a group task.

- Chapter 13 is the first of two chapters about the organizational and other settings that help and hurt the growth of hot groups. Chapter 13 concerns three organizational conditions that hot groups need if they are to prosper. Chapter 14 examines some more unusual and perhaps unexpected conditions that can also promote hot groups.

- Part IV deals with what we think lies ahead. Chapter 15 spreads its wings to consider differential rates of change in the world, organizations, and people. There, we argue that those differential rates augur well for all concerned. Chapter 16 then considers why freer individuals, working in small, impermanent hot groups are almost ideal instruments for accomplishing things in the impermanent institutions of our new world.

In Summary

In this opening chapter, we have described that impassioned, collective state of mind we call a "hot group." We believe hot groups will and should become a key structural aspect of future organizations. We use the word "aspect" because hot groups cannot properly be called structural "units" or "elements." They are too flexible, forever changing and reshaping themselves, unlike the solid, fixed organizational building blocks of the past.

We have also laid out a brief chapter-by-chapter description of the structure of the book, so selective readers can see what they are likely to find in the sections that follow.

Thus far we have said very little about what hot groups do for people, or about how hot groups work, think, and feel, or about their attitudes, prejudices, and interpersonal relationships. In the next chapter, we begin to look inside hot groups, at several of their special and unusual characteristics and their working styles.

2

Hot Groups: Why Now?

Hot groups are not new. They are probably as old as the human race. Why do organizations or society in general need more hot groups? And why begin fussing about them now? Is this year really so different that we suddenly need what some will surely dismiss as another gimmick called a "hot group"?

Why Do We Need Hot Groups?
Aren't Hot Individuals Enough?

We should remember that not too long ago "hot" individuals were also unwelcome in many large organizations. They, too, were frequently treated as misfits and poor team players. Such "zealots," "weirdos," and, yes, "entrepreneurs" were often hidden away in isolated organizational woodsheds. Thanks in part to Gifford Pinchot, who relabeled these mavericks "intrapreneurs" and highlighted their important contributions, hot individuals are now much more in demand.[1]

Well before that, however, a few farsighted corporate leaders appreciated the value of such individualistic "wild ducks." One such leader was Thomas J. Watson, Jr.

> When Watson was leading IBM, the legend goes, he was intrigued with an essay written by the nineteenth-century Danish philosopher, Søren Kierkegaard. The essay described how, in winter, wild ducks migrated into Denmark from the North, to remain there until spring. The local people welcomed the visitors. They fed and cared for them. The people were so nurturant that when the time arrived for the spring northward migration, most of those ducks, now fat and happy, stayed on, refusing the arduous journey. A few, however, could never be seduced into the soft life. When the time came, true to their natures, they always migrated back to the North.

Watson saw the lesson hidden in that essay and carried it back to IBM. He wanted his neat, white-shirted organization to include at least a scattering of untamable "wild ducks," individuals who marched to their own internal drummers, and who, he believed, would help to stimulate the company's creative juices. From that idea, the IBM Fellows Program eventually emerged. In that program, a few unusual individuals—wild ducks—are freed from the normal organizational constraints, to do anything they think should be done.

What Watson tried to do with hot individuals is what some thoughtful managers are now doing with groups. In our era, hot individuals are not enough. They cannot go it alone. Almost every complex task typical of the new world requires at least several individuals working together to meet the challenge. Only a generous salting with hot groups will change the underlying ebb and flow of the modern organization. Still, that transition to flocks of wild ducks will not be easy.

Hot Groups and "Teams" Don't Come From the Same Planet

Over the last decade, many organizations have tried to navigate at least part of their transition into the new era by turning to "teams": self-managed teams, cross-functional teams, quality circles, skunk works, tiger teams, and a host of others. Few of those teams, however, have turned into hot groups. The biggest underlying reason is the broad and basic mismatch between the nature of hot groups and that of traditional organizations. Hot groups and organizational teams grow from entirely different rootstocks.

Corporations became interested in "self-managed teams," "empowerment," "quality circles," and the rest for two major reasons:

1. The manufacturing successes of the Japanese in the late 1970s and 1980s impressed us, scared us, and lit our fires. Those successes seemed closely related to Japanese companies' effective use of small groups—or so said several best-selling American books about Japanese management styles.[2] Consequently, many Western companies began experimenting with small-group techniques, with quality circles and other group formats.

2. The American shift toward teams was further escalated by the rediscovery of an enormous, largely untapped backlog of knowledge about small group dynamics. American and European researchers had focused intensely on the nature and behavior of small groups during the 1950s and 1960s. Twenty years later, much of that research still lay gathering dust in academic warehouses. Only the scare from Japan prompted American managers to retrieve many of those findings. It is true that the field that came to be called "organizational development (OD)," deeply grounded in small group theory, had made an impact well before Japan arrived on the American screen. It was the Japanese, though—or rather Americans writing about Japanese management— who really stimulated a renewed interest in small group methods and gave OD a very large shot in the arm.

In contrast, the recent emergence of *hot* groups had little to do with either Japan or the earlier academic research on group dynamics. Nor were hot groups born of OD. They had been around for eons before all that. It was not until the late 1970s, however, that they made any significant entry into the larger organizational world. When they did, they came in with a bang—not on a slow boat from Kyoto, but via the young, upstart start-ups of Northern California's Silicon Valley and Boston's Route 128. Many founders of those new entities—"organizations" is probably too formal a descriptor for most of them—belonged to the anti-establishment generation, the brash, organizationally naïve children of the sixties; veterans of campus unrest, Vietnam, and the sexual revolution. That was the generation that had come to distrust all large institutions, from governments to universities. They had never worn gray flannel suits and sincere ties at Procter & Gamble or General Motors. Their values were just about 180 degrees from the values of the traditional "organization man."[3] They liked technology, they liked tough challenges, and they liked freedom, ideas, and pizza.

The emergence of hot groups on the business scene thus occurred at about the same time, though quite accidentally, as the big push toward teams. The two new arrivals, however, entered organizations through entirely different gateways. Although the team approach was quickly embraced, hot groups had a much harder time of it, and still do, except in young, small, nonestablishment institutions. That's because hot groups are speedy and flexible and because speed and flexibility have been properly associated with small size and young people. Such entities haven't yet barricaded themselves behind the stolid walls of formal hierarchies. Unfettered by bulk and tradition, it is easier for youthful "organizations" to tolerate, positively exploit, and enjoy the wide-open styles of hot groups.

There may be another, more psychological reason why not-yet-well-organized little companies so often breed hot groups. Those organizational infants are all alone, naked, and needy in the big scary world. Without a stable parent to feed and clothe them, their members must cling for security to the life raft of common purpose.

We Have Entered An Era of Organizational Impermanence

The organizational revolution now begun is unlikely to end. Comforting "normalcy" is not in the cards. We are not heading toward some new equilibrium, some boundless oasis at which organizations will be able to refresh and tell themselves, "OK, we've changed what needed to be changed. Now we can get back to regular business."

The hectic game of coping with volatile, mostly unpredictable, and lightning-fast change will not decelerate. Instead, it is much more likely to accelerate. Moreover, hot groups, because they offer speed and agility, inevitably will become important components of our new organizations. In fact, hot groups will be mirrored in the basic life patterns of those new world organizations. Like hot groups, they too will be spawning, innovating, producing, and then disappearing, leaving little organizational detritus in their wakes.

The recent plethora of "team" activities has been only one small signal of that organizational revolution. Besides the structural changes we have already noted, many other innovations have promised great things. A few have even delivered on their promises. Just-in-time manufacturing made a real contribution. Total quality management (TQM) has been up and down. Quality circles seem pretty much to have faded from sight. Corporate reengineering, in retrospect, paid too little attention to people, but it certainly did its bit to help.

The enthusiasm for teams seems to be cresting, but the dependence of organizations on the hot group state of mind will not abate, even in the virtual organizations that technology is so rapidly generating. In fact, small groups imbued with that urgent, dedicated orientation will surely become even more critical. They are one of the few linchpins that will continue to connect individual human beings to massive organizations, and massive organizations to the swirling world beyond. More and more, the small group, rather than the individual, will become the basic building block of the new organizational structures—except that "block" is the wrong word. Block implies solidity and permanence. Those small groups, even the cool ones, will be neither solid nor permanent. They will be fluid and transitory, and so, too, in their fashion, will the organizations of which they are transient parts. Whatever their name tags, small hot groups will, more and more, be moving into, out of, and around organizations.

Hot Groups and Impermanence Are a Good Match

Some other likely attributes of new world organizations will also make hot groups more relevant. Among them, we expect these:

- Organizations themselves will need to become more turbulent to cope with their roiling environments. They will have to be less "organized" and less controlled by a single central brain. They will be pressed to loosen up so that they can be more rapidly responsive to their ever-changing environments. They will also have to be continuously, proactively innovative.

- The widespread trend toward interconnectedness will doubtless accelerate, with many organizations collaborating with one another at some points, even as they are competing at others.[4] Small, cross-organizational groups can be effective mechanisms of collaboration.

- Organizations will not only be more impermanent, they will also be more interactive, imposing themselves on other organizations, forming new combinations and abandoning old ones. Small, autonomous, flexible hot groups will provide an almost ideal instrument for helping such organizations to prosper amid the tumult of endless volatility.

Hot Groups, Cold Groups—What's In a Name?

The buzz word "hot groups" is just another label, and, like so many other labels, it probably will have a short half-life. Buzz words, however, are not always junk, though they are often derided as if they were. They perform a vital function. They communicate ideas briefly and transferably. Remember buzzwords like "zero-based budgeting," "management by objectives," "the managerial grid," "sensitivity training," "theory Y," and, more recently, "cross-functional teams," "reengineering," and "TQM"? Were all those just dismissable sound and fury, signifying nothing? We think not.

We agree that such labels can be short-term gimmicks, designed to snag attention. Most of their names will fade away, and the how-to-do-it books about them will disappear. Yet, on balance, they leave behind many more marks of progress than unsightly scars.

Their basic insights and many of the invented techniques that accompany them do not evaporate. They are incorporated, sometimes imperceptibly, into the core of managerial thought and action. All things considered, American organizations are better now than they were in 1980. Those buzzwords and the ideas they communicated did their part to stimulate those improvements. So if you find yourself uncomfortable with the tag "hot group," feel free to discard it. But please don't throw away the rest of the package, at least until you've unwrapped it and examined what's inside.

Hot Groups Have Always Existed, Everywhere

Hot groups, we repeat, are anything but new. Throughout history, hot groups have been there. They were to be found and can still be found in just about every imaginable setting: social, artistic, military, scientific, religious, educational, and political. Military history, for example, is full of hot groups. World War II alone produced Merrill's Marauders, Carlson's Raiders, Claire Chennault's Flying Tigers, all in the U.S. military, and many, many others in armed forces, unsung undergrounds, and resistance movements all over the world.[5]

The history of science is also replete with hot groups, groups like the "double helix" scientists[6] in the United States and the United Kingdom, as well as the group of physicists who demonstrated the possibility of nuclear fission under the stands at the University of Chicago's stadium. Many hot groups also turn up in the history of architecture, such as the Bauhaus group in prewar Germany and the little Saarinen et al. group in Finland. That dedicated set of young Finnish architects lived together for four years in a compound outside Helsinki, working continuously. From there, they daringly entered and won design competitions in parts of the world they had never even seen.

In art, too, often under the label of "schools," hot groups have flourished. The mid-nineteenth-century "Barbizon School" of landscapists was not named for any individual star, but for the French village in which the whole group worked. A little later, the Impressionists emerged. Although the members of that group are remembered for their individual works, they were indeed a hot group, learning from one another and jointly fighting for recognition from the entrenched establishment. Thus, John Rewald, in his *The History of Impressionism*, writes:

> In the spring of 1874 a group of young painters defied the official salon in Paris and organized an exhibition of its own. While this was in itself a break with the established customs, the works which these men showed seemed at first glance even more revolutionary. The reaction of visitors and critics was by no means friendly; they accused the artists of painting differently from the accepted methods simply to gain attention or pull the legs of honest folk. It took years of bitter struggle before the members of the little group were able to convince the public of their sincerity, let alone their talent.
>
> This group included Monet, Renoir, Pissarro, Sisley, Degas, Cezanne, and Berthe Morisot. They were not only of diverse characters and gifts, but also . . . of differing conceptions and tendencies. Yet born almost within the same decade, they all went through similar experiences and fought against the same opposition. Thrown together more or less by chance, they accepted their common fate and eventually adopted the designation of "impressionists," a word coined in derision by a satirical journalist.[7]

Many other hot groups' innovative ideas and products, like those of the Impressionists, have initially faced resistance from the established orders of their times. They are still too seldom welcomed— although too enthusiastic a welcome might well smother them.

Hot Groups Are for Everybody

Hot groups don't just happen to other people. Many readers can surely recall with pleasure their own participation in some very warm, if not hot, groups at different stages in their lives. Most of us have had such experiences on an athletic team or newspaper at school, or while putting together a theatrical performance or working in the academic computer center, or in a military squad fighting its way up the impossible hill. Perhaps it was on an archaeological dig or on a new product design team building the next generation of electronic pasta makers. We have even received reports of hot groups taking root in board rooms. Overall, however, hot groups remain rare, especially within traditional organizations.

We Work Group More and More, but We Still Think Individual

Although a group may do something great, we are likely to single out only the leader of the group for public attention and praise. Rewald, writing about the Impressionists, underscores a reality that applies almost everywhere, a reality we reemphasize throughout: Credit that belongs to groups is too often ascribed to individuals.

> "Perfection is a collective work," Eugène Boudin once wrote. "Without that person, this one would never have achieved the perfection he did." If this is true of any artist, it is even more so in the case of a group of painters who learned, fought, suffered, and exhibited together. Even if they sometimes acted contrary to each other's interests and were, as a group, occasionally divided by internal struggles, their works tell, almost better than their actions, how they pursued— both individually and together—the conquest of a new vision.[8]

Here's another example of the pervasive emphasis on thinking individual even where it makes little sense:

> When New Zealander Sir Edmund Hillary's team climbed Everest for the first time in 1953, the whole team agreed not to speak about which individual reached the summit first. The important thing, they decided, was that the team reach the summit. They had, perforce, to travel in single file. No individual could possibly have made it without the team.
>
> Then the journalists and nationalists in the United Kingdom and Nepal got into the act. The Nepalese feted Tenzing Norkay, the Sherpa who guided the group, parading him in a seat of honor atop the royal carriage. The rest of the team rode inside that carriage, not visible to the crowd. A UK newspaper was incensed at such behavior, insisting that Tenzing was only a servant/guide and that Hillary, the *real* leader, was the first to set foot on Everest's summit.
>
> Apparently, as a result of all the bickering about who got there first, the friendship between Hillary and Tenzing began to erode. Hillary's book[9] seemed to imply that he, Hillary, had hauled Tenzing

up the last few meters of the mountain, where he lay "flopping like a great fish." Tenzing's book[10] indicated that he had never forgotten that description and continued to resent it.

Would any of that nonsense about who made it first have occurred if the outside world had not insisted on thinking *individual*, while the team necessarily worked *group*?

A more recent example arose when a colleague suggested we look into the U.S. Navy SEALS as hot groups, and recommended the book *Rogue Warrior* by the leader of one SEAL team.[11] That book, it turns out, is almost entirely about the exploits of the group's macho, swashbuckling leader. It says almost nothing about the group. That's not new. Did Winston Churchill save Britain all by himself? Did Gandhi free India all alone? Did Lee Iacocca turn Chrysler around, and did Jack Welch rejuvenate GE, each in an incredibly brilliant solo performance? The media, and biographers as well, too often treat institutions as though only their leaders matter.

You Don't Manufacture Hot Groups—You Grow Them

It is useful to think of hot groups as more like plants than manufactured products and view organizations as potential farmers of hot groups. Most other groups in organizations are planned and manufactured. Hot groups are seldom planned and rarely manufactured, at least not in the usual sense. When the conditions are right, they sprout. Companies can manufacture lots of bicycles, but they can't manufacture even a single kernel of corn. Farmers can't manufacture corn either, but good farmers know how to grow lots of it. They do it by seeding, feeding, weeding, and fertilizing, and they water generously. That's also the way companies can grow crops of hot groups.

The hottest groups in many organizations arise quite spontaneously. A hot group may begin over lunch one day when a few friends start kicking around an idea. The excitement builds. People's imaginations begin to churn. They generate all sorts of possibilities, and thus a hot group is born. In some companies, members of such a newly forming group may feel they have to keep quiet about their idea until they've got it exactly right, for fear the people upstairs will kill it. That's a pretty clear signal that those people upstairs aren't very good farmers. If they were, the new group would seek and welcome their help.

Two Major Characteristics of Hot Groups

In later chapters, we shall consider many other attributes of hot groups. For now, though, here are just two of their most salient, identifying characteristics:

Total Preoccupation with Task

By far the most outstanding characteristic of any hot group is its dedication to a task. The dedication of hot group members obliterates mere ordinary life from their personal screens. Members always feel, regardless of the opinions of others, that what they are doing is immensely significant, demanding their complete and undivided attention. The more challenging and impossible the task, the more it grabs them. Hot groups are also quite likely, therefore, to impinge on the private lives of their members. For example, software designer Doug Muise describes the total commitment that hot group members often experience: "Having a girlfriend, having an active social life is incidental. It gets in the way of code time. Writing code is the primary force that drives your lives. Everything that interrupts that is wasteful."[12] We'll be considering that issue of friends and family more fully in a later chapter.

Hot groups' preoccupation with their tasks is accompanied by extremely high performance standards. Without exception, in our experience, hot groups shoot for the stars. They intend to do great things and do them extremely well. Their members feel they are stretching themselves, surpassing themselves, moving beyond their own prior performance limits. Hot groups, therefore, don't need to be "motivated" by the promise of bonuses or other extrinsic rewards. The challenge of the task is its own pot of gold. Indeed, offers of material rewards may have negative, even destructive effects, distracting the group and generating interpersonal competition. Passionate, committed, and sometimes charismatic leaders can, however, help generate valuable extra motivational heat.

A Sense of Ennoblement

Hot groups are not mercenaries. They believe in the wars they wage. Their members have a sense of higher purpose, of embarking on an ennobling mission. Almost always they envision themselves on a journey that is supremely worthwhile. They feel their quest is righteous, that they are breaking new ground, doing something really important. Hot groups, we therefore believe, will not only be good for organizations, they will also net out as good for us as individuals. They offer much more than the support and belonging that group membership has always provided. Hot groups also offer challenge, meaning, and ennoblement, thereby helping to fill those vacuums so common in contemporary organizational life.

Sometimes, it is a broad societal good that turns on a hot group. "Our group is determined to isolate the gene for Alzheimer's disease." Or "We are designing a business school that will educate future managers the way they should be educated." A hot group's task, however, certainly doesn't need to carry world-shaking significance, just so long as it carries such meaning for its own members.

To outsiders, a hot group's great goal may look quite limited, even trivial. "We're revitalizing customer service at our supermarket." "We're designing a new kind of eggbeater that will revolutionize the culinary world." Or, as in the case of a spontaneous hot group we encountered at Singapore Airlines, "Every restroom in every single one of our aircraft is going to be spotlessly clean and smell like a rose garden."

This dedication to a task that is self-defined as meaningful is not entirely altruistic. Although such tasks may be valued because they benefit others, they also give group members some of what all humans want—a feeling that they are doing something really worthwhile. That process is circular and self-reinforcing. It is in the nature of human beings to seek internal consistency and reduce psychological dissonance.[13] The investment of our hard work in a task serves to increase our faith in its worthiness. That increasing belief in the task's worthiness is likely, subsequently, to make us work even harder.[14] Hence, hot groups, seen from the outside, may look much like cults; like little bands of fervent true-believers, dedicated to their own private "religion." Steven Levy, in his book, *Insanely Great*, describes the original Macintosh team, the one we mentioned at the beginning of Chapter 1, in just that way: "The Mac team acted as if on a mission from God. . . . Steve Jobs had taken pains to encourage the group to think of itself as a class apart, an exalted duchy within the Cupertino campus."[15]

Not all hot groups believe they are on a mission from God, but most do exhibit an almost religious zeal. As we shall see later, however, although hot groups may look something like cults, they fall in fact, at the other end of the spectrum.

It is worth noting that these two characteristics—dedication to task and a sense of high mission—are quite similar to the salient characteristics of "hot" individuals. Most individuals undertaking a task, whether writing a book, designing a building, or beginning work on a new job, actively want their task to be worth doing. We recently talked with an investment executive who was considering taking a job as dean of a business school. Would it give him a chance to help redesign the school's management education programs as he felt they ought to be reshaped? If the job meant he could try to do something meaningful, he would willingly sacrifice the salary and other perks of his present role. Don't many of us, as we mature, begin to feel the same way?[16]

The Hard Lives of Hot Groups in Cold Organizations

The seeds of hot groups need special conditions to germinate. In most traditional organizations, where regularity, predictability, and uniformity are unbreakable commandments, those necessary conditions seldom come together. When they do, and a few hot groups begin to grow, organizations are wont to treat the emergent seedlings as weeds, messing up their neatly planted gardens. They quickly apply liberal doses of weed killer. The few hardy hot groups that manage to survive are soon spotted by the organization's sophisticated control systems and promptly eradicated.

Those tightly structured large organizations know exactly what they're doing when they try to kill off nascent hot groups. They realize that while those baby hot groups may look like innocent ornaments ready to be hung on organizational Christmas trees, they are really more like live hand grenades. From a classical bureaucratic perspective, hot groups are dangerous. They are potentially explosive and infectious, portending organizational disturbance and change. So if you should happen to encounter a little hot group somewhere inside an otherwise traditional, top-down organization, at least one of these four conditions is also likely to prevail.

1. The organization doesn't yet know the group is there. If it finds out, it will probably try to kill it. Thus, in a large government-sponsored research organization, we were told by several different project managers about how they "protected" certain of their groups' activities. They used devices like setting aside some of last year's budget to fund nonapproved, current hot projects. They found ingenious ways to keep needed people, even when they had been ordered to reduce personnel. They might, for example, lay employees off, then immediately rehire them as temporaries for the maximum of 364 days, then give them a day off, then hire them again for another 364 days. Legal? Probably. Ethical? Not so clear. It is clear, however, that they didn't do this for personal gain—they did it to get good work done. Would any large bureaucracy function if people played entirely by its often mindless rules? Remember the chaos that used to result from "work-to-rule" strikes, when employees did just what the rulebook required—and no more?

   What about the ethics of such rule-bending? What prompts it in the first place? Hot groups, at least, see such rules as unnecessary bureaucratic roadblocks to which the hierarchy has simply become inured. Sometimes, the group is right. The rules are, indeed, just useless leftovers from another age. Sometimes, however, the group is too blinded by its enthusiasm to recognize the ethical issues. Distinguishing between irrelevant irritants, necessary ones, and ethical limits is not always easy. It is to hot groups' credit, at least, that they tend to push organizations toward serious reexamination of their traditional rules and regulations.

2. The CEO or some other senior manager is the gray eminence behind the group, the patron who is supporting and protecting it from harm. Perhaps he or she simply feels it

is a promising project. Or perhaps this hot group is intentionally being used as a change agent, to awaken the whole sleeping giant. By itself, that tactic has about a fifty/fifty chance of working.

In a later chapter, we describe how a new hot group of executives, labeled by their peers as the "Military Mafia," changed the behavior of a large engineering corporation. They were able to survive long enough to get broad changes started because the Chairman/CEO protected them, even from the disapproving President/COO and most other senior executives of the company.

3. The unexpected hot group may be an important early warning, a signal that a whole new organizational way of life is struggling to emerge. The presence of a few such hot groups clearly means the giant is no longer sleeping. A structural revolution is beginning. Their presence is a sign reading "Changes in Progress."

> In a graduate school of business, three new, prestigious full professors were hired simultaneously. Though very unlike one another, they shared the belief that standards at the school were too low, that courses weren't "rigorous" enough, and that the curriculum put too much emphasis on the wrong topics. They joined forces to pressure the administration and their colleagues into a total redesign of the institution. Their status made them powerful, so they were moderately successful. Unfortunately, in our opinion, they were trying to do the wrong things. Nevertheless, they were a hot group.

4. The presence of a hot group may mean that a major crisis is at hand, so normal regulations and procedures have been temporarily put aside. In its desperation, the organization is ready to try almost anything. Small groups, at the forefront of the crisis, may then be free to confront it as they see fit. Effective crisis management teams are usually small, dynamic, task-centered, and short-lived. Very often, they are hot groups.

Hot Groups Are Right for Our Volatile New World

Hot groups are, we believe, destined for far greater prominence in the new organizational world. We have several reasons for this belief:

- Organizations are not immortal, nor should they necessarily be.[17] Both material things and organizations *could* last much longer than they used to, but they don't. We change gadgetry more and more frequently, although our gadgets are more durable than ever. The names, compositions, and ownership of companies change so fast that one can hardly tell this week's organizational players without a new scorecard. CEOs seem to be replaced faster than printer cartridges. Everything, it appears, changes quickly.

    We can no longer passively assume that our great organizations are destined to live on and on. Most of them probably won't survive as long as we individuals do, let alone live forever. Organizational graveyards are all around us. A recent *Wall Street Journal* article[18] suggests that AT&T, that bastion of stability, could easily go the way of Western Union, once another bastion of stability. Not too long ago, a *Wall Street Journal* headline read, "Woolworth to Close All 5-and-10 Stores in U.S., Ending 117-Year-Old Business."[19] The Dow Jones Industrial Average (DJIA) recently dropped four long-standing members—Westinghouse Electric Corp., Texaco Inc., Bethlehem Steel Corp., and Woolworth Corp.—replacing them with Travelers Group, Hewlett-Packard, Johnson & Johnson, and Wal-Mart Stores.[20] One need only look at the history of the DJIA, now a bit more than 100 years old, to realize how many great companies of the past have died or transmogrified during little more than the average life span of an American citizen. Consider, for example, just two of the twelve original members of the Dow, as that same *Wall Street Journal* article summarized their histories:

    American Cotton Oil [was] founded in 1889 as a successor to the American Cotton Oil Trust. . . . In 1923, it sold the cotton oil business and formed Gold Dust Corp. . . . In 1936, Gold Dust was renamed Heckler Products Corp. In 1942, Heckler acquired and took the name Best Foods Inc., which merged with Corn Products Refining Co. in 1958 to become Corn Products Co. The last name change came in 1969: CPC International Inc.

In the late 1890s, the Distilling and Cattle Feeding Co. . . . was broken up, with a handful of operations continuing under the umbrella of American Spirits Manufacturing Co. . . . American Spirits became U.S. Food Products Corp. In 1924, U.S. Food restructured, becoming National Distillers and Chemical Corp. In 1988, National Distillers . . . changed its name to Quantum Chemical Corp. . . . In 1993, Quantum was acquired by Britain's Hanson PLC. Earlier this year [1996], Hanson announced plans to split itself into four businesses.[21]

Our emphasis on transitory organizations may appear to contradict what our Stanford colleagues Jim Collins and Jerry Porras pointed out in *Built to Last*.[22] They identified a number of companies that have prospered over the long pull, companies like Ford, Procter & Gamble, and Johnson & Johnson. Each was founded near or well before 1900. They continue to live fruitful lives. Yet, one of the reasons for the continuing interest in that book is precisely because such successful, long-lived companies are fast becoming quite unusual, if not downright rare.

- To cope with environmental turbulence, organizations are trying to become much more nimble, innovative, and continuously self-modifying. They are also much more willing to combine, subdivide, form alliances, absorb pieces of one another, and spin off pieces of themselves. Hot groups, temporary and deft, are a perfect fit for such volatile conditions.

- For individuals, also caught in the whitewater of this new milieu, hot groups can provide a new kind of refuge; not the lotus blossom refuge of tranquility, but a refuge from anomie;

a refuge of challenge, opportunity, even ennoblement; and a refuge for individuality as well. Hot groups offer room for those individual eccentricities that organizations profess to want, but, in practice, so often reject.

- Individuals are rethinking their hopes and expectations. Old notions about lifelong careers in a single company, loyalty to employers, and job security no longer seem to apply. Organizations are unlikely to provide the security they once did. Nor does the new generation even appear to want what those organizations previously offered. Hot groups are a mechanism that may allow individuals to fulfill some new and some old human wants by committing themselves, at least temporarily, to a task and even to a group of like-minded colleagues.

In Summary

This chapter has described two identifying characteristics of a hot group: single-minded dedication to a task and a sense of ennoblement, of meaning. Organizations, however, have traditionally given hot groups a hard time. Their single-mindedness makes them difficult to manage—at least by traditional standards, and their love of their task makes them appear arrogant. Yet, in the volatile new world, a world causing all sorts of organizations to rethink their shapes, sizes, and philosophies, these eager, fast-paced little groups may be just what organizations and the people within them really need.

In the next chapter, the unusual characteristics of hot groups are spelled out in much more detail, with all the costs and all the benefits that those qualities entail.

3

How Hot Groups Think:
Left Brain? Right Brain?
How About Both?

This chapter is mostly about how hot groups think. The next one is about how hot groups work. We want, however, to begin this duet by emphasizing how hot groups do *not* think and how they do *not* work. The sculpted figure may emerge more clearly when the surrounding material has been chipped away. These are a few of the larger chips:

- ***Hot groups are not "touchy-feely." Hot group members love their task, but they don't necessarily love one another.***

If you're looking for deep, lasting relationships, you're not likely to find them in a hot group. Members of hot groups usually do come to trust and respect one another. They also take care of one another while the task lasts. They seldom, however, develop intimate, empathic relationships with one another. The task is too eclipsing. In fact, hot groups are likely to be internally confrontational, challenging, and critical, all with the aim of improving their work. Members rarely engage in ad hominem attacks or personal arguments, but they debate continuously. They constantly discuss ideas and alternative approaches for accomplishing their task.

Nor do hot group members usually pay very much attention to their own or other people's feelings. They focus on their task, not on their relationships with one another. Thus, compared to most teams, task forces, and such, hot groups reverse the usual stages of group development. Organization development experts and related specialists usually recommend that new groups first build trusting interpersonal relationships and only later concern themselves with their group's task. Hot groups do it in reverse. They first coalesce around their task, then work back to their interpersonal relationships.

Hot groups often belittle OD workshops and human relations seminars, chiding them and calling them derisive names like "charm schools." They seldom—collectively—want to "waste time" on psychological and social matters. Individually, they may feel differently, but wearing their hot group hats they're likely to treat HR and OD people rather badly, as bureaucratic distractions from their central focus. Those who present such workshops sometimes counter that rejection by describing hot groups' attitudes as "defensive." That response itself, however, seems a bit defensive.

This is not to suggest that interpersonal relationships are irrelevant. Hot groups eventually cool down. That's when the quality of the group's underlying interpersonal relationships can make or break the remainder of the group's life. The issue is *when*, not whether, interpersonal relationships become important.

• *Individual members of hot groups are likely to be good team players, but most hot groups are not.*

The members of a hot group may or may not be good team players, but the hot group as a group is almost never ready to salute and do whatever the organization asks. They want to do their own thing. That laser-like focus on their own task may cause a hot group to appear arrogant, selfish, inaccessible, even neurotic. Their single-mindedness, which is so vital to their success, often makes for less than happy relationships between hot groups and their parent organizations.

• *Hot groups are not cults.*

Earlier we quoted John Sculley describing the Macintosh group as "cult-like," but hot groups are anything but. In cults, each person's individualism disintegrates, replaced by unbroken uniformity. In hot groups, individualism does not melt away. Far from it! Hot groups are likely to examine their task from more angles than there are members. They tend to hold widely diverging opinions, are outspoken in expressing them, and question, constantly, the assumptions of their fellows, their leaders, and all the world's experts.[1] They do not forsake their individualism to gain the approval of the group, nor is "groupthink" likely to be a serious threat.[2] To the outsider, their unity of purpose may give hot groups a cult-like appearance, but their behavior hardly fits the conformity that characterizes cults.

• *Hot groups are not another Japanese import.*

As we have noted, Japanese manufacturing successes in the 1980s stimulated much Western interest in small work teams, but not, however, in hot groups. Most Japanese work groups would hardly qualify as hot groups. Indeed, the large organizations of Japan probably did more to suppress hot groups than those of any other major industrial culture. Japanese work groups often involve very long-term relationships, with consensus slowly and carefully cultivated over many years. Independent, short-lived, freewheeling hot groups are about as far from traditional Japanese norms of conformity, clear-cut status differences, and self-subordination as hot dogs are from sushi. Most current interest in hot groups was born in the bright sunshine of Silicon Valley, not in the shadow of Mt. Fuji.

• *Hot groups are seldom their parents' favorite child.*

Hot groups are at their best doing short bursts of challenging, innovative work, just the kind of work that has become so vital for modern organizations. Hot groups' ways of thinking and working are great for designing new products, responding to crises, and trying to change the world. Yet, their parent organizations are apt to complain vociferously about them. They seldom complain about the *kinds* of work hot groups do. It's the ways they do it that cause the trouble, the noise level, the self-certainty, the disregard for bureaucratic niceties. Hot groups often bend explicit rules and violate implicit norms. Some organizations, wedded to their rulebooks, just can't abide such "undisciplined" behavior. Nevertheless, despite their wide-open styles, hot groups' effectiveness at doing high-intensity jobs has become so valuable that even tightly ordered organizations are beginning to feel the need to accommodate them.

The Wondrous Thinking Styles of Hot Groups

Those are some of the things that hot groups are *not*. Let's turn now to what they *are*, considering, first, how they think, and then, in the next chapter, how they work. These are among their rather unusual approaches to problem finding and problem solving.

- **Hot groups know how to think like children—and that's good!**

Unconstrained by the usual bureaucratic limitations, hot groups can be quite childlike. They can think associatively, intuitively, and creatively, as well as logically and analytically. They are not nearly as limited as cool groups by the hobgoblin of consistency. Like children, they tend to rewrite the rules as the game evolves.[3] They can change their minds and their direction without feeling compelled to provide rationalizations for their actions. They can use their intuition to circumvent what others might have experienced as "blocks." They don't feel compelled to contrive elaborate arguments to "prove" they are right.[4] That's one reason hot groups have such fun, even while they work very hard. It is also one reason they so often perplex and infuriate their parent organizations.

For a hot group to think intuitively and creatively does not require that each individual member must be an unusually intuitive or creative thinker. In contrast to so many committee settings, where a repressive cloud is cast over the expression of unusual ideas, the climate of the hot group releases creativity, even from people who previously have seldom displayed much of it. The urgency and openness of the hot group contagiously free the brain cells.

Outsiders may feel that some of the imaginative ideas dreamed up by hot groups are more preposterous than creative. Every once in a while, those observers turn out to be right. Hot groups do push the limits. They take risks, and risk entails some probability of failure. Still, many of their crackpot ideas lead to quite fantastic breakthroughs.

• *Hot groups occasionally get silly.*

Hot groups do something else children often do: They get silly. They may suddenly decide to take an afternoon off for a picnic. They may play some light-hearted game on company time. They may decide to redecorate their work space in weird, wild ways. Every now and then, they may break into uncontrolled laughter. They may put together a spontaneous party when they need to come down off a high, or when they have worked extremely hard for an especially long time, or when they have made a breakthrough or hit a wall. They are prone to short bouts of ridiculous behavior like the functional foolishness Professor James March described in a classic 1971 article.[5]

This foolishness is indeed functional and serves at least three purposes:

1. That escape into off-the-wall fun and games is thinking time. To think creatively, we need to shed unconscious inhibitions, to abandon, temporarily, the rules of rationality. Temporary playfulness among adults clears the air, so they can begin to see the world in new ways. It disinhibits.

2. Playfulness performs a second, related function as well, a communication function. It is a way of moving the group toward deeper, easier, and more uncensored communicating among members.

3. Occasional foolishness helps in a third, more obvious way. It's a relief valve, reducing tensions imposed by the pressures of intense, consuming work.

It's worth noting that while hot group members may not spend much time together outside the group, they are very likely to socialize intensely inside it. That kind of socializing, however, is almost the opposite of what we usually see on Friday afternoons at the local bar. This is not the TGIF partying that provides a little temporary release after yet another week of ennui. Hot groups' parties do provide temporary refreshment, but that's neither their primary nor their sole function.

- *Hot groups can be diverse in almost all things—except standards of thinking.*

Hot group members share something more than a passion for their common task. Yet it's hard to specify exactly what that something is. It is certainly not mutual affection. Nor is it some special personality trait. "Personality," depending on which definition you choose, is about attributes like self-confidence, shyness, volatility, extroversion, and lots more. Such traits can diverge widely among members of hot groups. Nor is IQ-type intelligence the common factor, although roughly comparable levels of that kind of intelligence will help almost any group. It is not a matter of equivalent educational or occupational backgrounds either. Those, too, can vary greatly. A recent report of Kevin Dunbar's research at McGill University even indicates that "distributed reasoning" in which "several scientists put their heads together to solve a problem" may be a near-necessary condition for many scientific breakthroughs.

> The most important discoveries Dunbar witnessed arose when several participants built on each others' analogies and interpretations. . . . This advantage, however, appeared only when members of the group had varying areas of expertise; when members of the lab all had similar backgrounds, progress was no faster than by individual scientists working alone.[6]

That diversity is necessary, but so is some common ground. Beyond a shared commitment to the task, that common ground appears to be something we can only call *standards of thinking.* Hot group members share implicit standards about what constitute appropriate rules of thought. Different hot groups may hold to quite diverse standards, but each group seems to subscribe to its own implicitly clear norm. So it would be very unlikely, except in acute crises, that three physical scientists and three creationists would ever become a hot group, even if all six were extroverted personalities and all measured very high on a standard intelligence test. The ways they think about the world's problems diverge too much.

We offer the following personal example:

When one of our sons was in high school, he belonged to a small, informal group of friends that periodically heated up as they worked together on all sorts of projects. They shared a unique thinking standard. They were all pretty smart kids, but that certainly wasn't what held them together. Nor was it their personalities, which ranged from overbearing and assertive to shy and withdrawn. What held them together was something like *intellectual taste*. That may sound pompous, but it wasn't. They just had no trouble agreeing on which great undertakings merited pursuit and which did not; which places and events were worth going to and which were not. They would put forward many alternatives, but once the pile of options was on the table, they easily reached consensus about the ones deserving top priority. That diverse little group hung together for almost two years, generating and regenerating heat with one imaginative (some of us parents preferred the word "insane") project after another, working on them feverishly, excitedly, and happily.

On one memorable occasion we returned home to find our kitchen the scene of chaos. The group was baking a cake to present to Jessica Mitford, the now deceased author of *The American Way of Death*, who was coming to visit their school. This, however, would be no ordinary cake. Its thick forest green frosting was crowned with a tiny headstone. Buried deep inside was a minuscule casket containing a minute figure decked out in white tie and tails. This concoction they delightedly, and quite formally, presented to Ms. Mitford after her talk. The group insisted she cut into it so the members could watch her find the hidden surprise, while they stood by, beaming with pride.

That group finally graduated, split up, and went their separate ways. Our now forty-plus-year-old son, having read a draft of one of our papers, called not long ago to remind us about that really hot group. With enthusiasm reminiscent of his high school days (and typical of veterans of past hot groups), he began recalling for us and for himself, at length and in detail, some of the "phenomenal" things his old bunch had done. People don't forget their hot group experiences!

• *Members of hot groups exercise their whole brains, actively and continuously.*

Hot groups pump out ideas and possibilities at an astonishing rate. They really *think*, often in ways and with results that even members themselves would not have believed possible. That's another reason people remember their hot groups. They are among those rare times in our lives when we surpass our mental personal bests.

When an individual thinks, others can't hear it. When a hot group thinks, it can be heard loudly and clearly. A hot group's thinking almost always includes noisy, passionate, and often boisterous debates, similar, perhaps, to the chaotic but functional process that takes place in our individual heads when we confront any important problem.

Hot groups debate constantly, but they seldom argue. They are almost always problem-focused, targeting questions central to their task. Hot group members are not given to hiding their opinions about task-relevant issues. Because their procedures are informal and democratic, and because they are turned on by one another's ideas, multiple, simultaneous, seemingly amorphous discussions are more the rule than the exception. Hot groups' internal debates, we reemphasize, are rarely ad hominem attacks or personal arguments. Issues of power, control, and pecking order are largely irrelevant when groups are in heat. To paraphrase Andrew Carnegie, "[Their] hearts—not their egos—are in the work."

• *Hot groups hardly ever suffer from "groupthink."*

Hot groups' total commitment to their tasks looks like just the condition that could lead both to burnout[7] and groupthink.[8] Because hot group members are at least temporary workaholics, burnout can certainly become a serious problem, one we consider in more detail later. That, however, is much less the case with groupthink. "Groupthink," as Irving Janis[9] described it, is the propensity of a group to reach consensus and make decisions too superficially and too quickly. That happens largely because members do not wish to endanger the group's sense of cohesion by questioning commonly held, though often unspoken, assumptions.

Hot groups are not at all likely to succumb to such quick, easy, social decision processes. They are tough-minded and realistic, not only with one another but with outsiders as well. Hot groups are too dynamic, too open, too full of challenge and creativity for the ice of unquestioning conformity to solidify.

• *The hot group may go off in a different direction from the designated one.*

One might expect any organization to be delighted with employees who willingly, even eagerly, put in extra, unpaid overtime. The trouble comes when that extra effort branches off the beaten track. Hot groups' open and imaginative ways of thinking may lead them to modify their purpose as they go, sharply changing direction to explore interesting new alternatives. The organization, however, may view those branchings as diversions, much more delaying than interesting. Once a hot group begins to sniff out a new trail, it's difficult to pull it back to the main scent.

Still, let's not forget that hot groups don't make U-turns arbitrarily. What looks like a deviation to an outsider may, in fact, be an important new insight or the hot group's belated recognition that the solution actually lies down a different path. Sometimes, changing direction leads to something even better than the target the group originally had in its sights.

Eric Pollard, a former executive with the Rain Bird Sprinkler Manufacturing Corporation, provided us with a wonderful example of a hot group that changed the direction of a project, almost from its very outset.

> The project was called the Inventory Management Plan. It was . . . a buying program that gave incentives to Rain Bird's distributors to commit to purchasing product in the fall . . . for shipment in the early part of the [next] year and through the summer. . . . [The irrigation business] is a very seasonal business, . . . in most parts of the country, and really around the world, selling starts on February 1 . . . and it stops on August 15 or September 1. . . . Our organization was

chronically on back order, as were most of our competitors. So the solution to the problem was to go out and try to cajole the distributors into purchasing product, . . . essentially building inventory; we were shifting the inventory responsibility to the distributor.

When I was given responsibility for the program, we were doing it two shipments a year. It was a very complicated discounting structure, and it was all done on spreadsheets, a manual system that migrated to the PC. The distributor would fill out an order form, and he was never really quite sure what price he was going to pay until the order had been entered [at headquarters] in Glendora, and then we would call him back and say, "Congratulations! You got a 12% discount.". . . Few distributors participated . . . because they were not getting that sort of instant feedback. . . .

That problem landed in my lap as a program manager, and I started playing around with how to make it work. . . . [I] got together with a friend of mine who was working as a consultant for our IS group and said, "What if we . . . computerize this?" And [we] created a database product that essentially walked people through the process of entering these orders and giving them feedback.

We started developing this off line. *We were kind of in a back room in one of the office buildings, and we borrowed a couple of PCs and started hammering on this thing. This project started as a brand new unauthorized innovation. . . . We were supposed to deliver a different program. We were supposed to deliver the manual program again* [Our italics]. My manager . . . originally defined the task. From my perspective, [the task] changed immediately. From his perspective, it did not change right away. It changed a couple of months down the road.

I started working on this in May, kind of saying, "Well, you know there is a better way of doing this," because the previous year I had worked the manual system, and it was a major pain in the butt. . . . Everybody hated it, and it was not that effective in terms of generating sales. . . . So I figured, "Well if I am going to expend all this energy, at least I want to make my life easier.". . . That was one of the reasons why we computerized it. . . . I said, "There has to be a better way to do this" just to lower my own blood pressure. . . . So to a certain degree, it was self-serving to implement this, but we ended up with a product that was far superior to anything that we had conceived of previous to that point.

When we asked Pollard how he felt about the outcome, he responded, with a big grin.

I was very satisfied. I was extremely pleased, particularly when there was a heavy level of resistance in the organization that we converted . . . sort of one layer at a time. The first person that got converted was . . . my manager. He said, "Okay, you have $10,000 to go spend on this.". . . Well, after I had spent about $5,000, we were well on the way to implementation. . . . He kind of came in and said, "What are we doing about this?" I said, "Well, let me show you." I showed him what we were thinking of, and he was like, "I have never seen this before. I don't know what it is, but I trust you to do it right."

Often the parent organization is reluctant to give credit to a hot group that has come up with something different from what was written on their order sheet, even when it is unambiguously successful. Despite the resounding success of the computerized inventory management project, Pollard and his group were not seen as heroes. As Pollard described it,

It always just pissed me off that it took them so long to acknowledge the fact that we were right. Even to the point that when we were finished, the only acknowledgment we got was a memo from the Vice President, . . . the Chief Financial Officer, telling us to make sure that we didn't overspend the budget on the development costs. And we had generated over $40 million in orders that first season! The division at that point was about a $65 million division, so we just delivered two-thirds of their sales in one shot. And that was the acknowledgment that we received for this little process. . . . My manager, [however], was ecstatic. He was very pleased because we managed to accomplish . . . a year's work in a very concentrated period of time.

So give your hot groups a little *lebensraum* to try new tacks. Besides, if you don't give them some space, they'll probably—one way or another—make some for themselves.

• *Hot groups like their own physical space.*

Hot groups generally prefer to isolate themselves physically, too. They like their own separate physical space. They do that so they can think undisturbed, much like writers or artists, and also because isolation usually increases their sense of "specialness." Parent organizations don't necessarily mind having their hot groups hide themselves away. That way they may not cause much trouble for everyone else.

From the outside looking in, hot groups' tunnel vision and self-isolation easily translate into mulish perversity and dangerous risk-taking. That's one reason why both entrepreneurs and hot groups were so unwelcome in the notoriously risk-averse large organizations of the past. Yet, paradoxically, it was often just such hot individuals and hot groups who founded those organizations a generation or two ago.

Secrecy and isolation, of course, are often absolutely necessary to success, as the Manhattan Project demonstrated. Ironically, at the outset and for some time thereafter, even the young physicists whom Robert Oppenheimer recruited to that hot group were themselves kept in the dark about the purpose of their research.

Hot groups' tendency to self-isolation can also cause disruptions and resentments in other parts of the larger system. Richard Neustadt and Graham Allison comment on just those effects in discussing the isolation of President Kennedy's ExComm.

> One can already see in these two weeks [of the missile crisis] frustration rising at official levels. . . . Two weeks were quite enough to build up great concern about being left out of things. At the same time, action officers were finding no department heads to take their issues to.[10]

As a consequence, the ExComm, unlike many hot groups, did not end its own life. President Kennedy decided to disband it, in large part because the absence of members from their regular posts was causing severe disruptions of normal governmental operations.

Although the isolation of hot groups is sometimes mutually desired, it can create negative side effects. Both group and organization will eventually pay a high price if they don't stay in touch with one another, at least enough to prepare the larger organization for the arrival of the hot group's output.

One last point: Hot groups in the past wanted togetherness and physical separation from outsiders. In the informational world, that is often the case. Indeed, physical separateness may shift to psychological separateness. Moreover virtual hot groups, whose members are interconnected only via technology, will doubtless become more and more numerous.

In Summary

Hot groups are not loving, touchy-feely gatherings. Nor do they resemble cults or well-mannered, conformist Japanese work groups. They are hard-working entities, urgent and full of debate. They are too busy to be much concerned about one another's feelings. They are also too busy to worry about their parent organizations' feelings. They therefore are likely to be viewed from the outside as rather unruly and unwilling to be good "team players." Still, they compensate for much of their off-the-wall behavior by thinking fast and imaginatively. In some ways, they think like children. In all ways, they think full time. They really use their heads.

Although hot groups tolerate and even encourage diversity of ideas and approaches, they also require fundamental uniformity on one basic rule: They all must share similar "standards of thought," beliefs, whether implicit or explicit, about what constitutes right-headedness and what constitutes wrongheadedness. Beyond that rule, anything goes.

In Chapter 4, we turn from hot groups' unusual thinking styles to some of their even more unusual working styles.

4

How Hot Groups Work:
Fast, Focused, and Wide Open

In Chapter 2, we described two of the most prominent characteristics of hot groups: a deep dedication to their tasks and an equally deep faith that their work is meaningful and consequential. From those two attributes alone, it is easy to see why many organizations find it hard to love them. Their single-mindedness can make them look self-centered and uncooperative, and their fervent commitment to their cause can easily be misread as pigheadedness. There is much more to hot group working styles, however, than those two features. We now offer a more complete set of working behaviors that typically accompany the hot group state of mind. Some should look familiar to all organization dwellers. A few may seem weird or even absurd, perhaps because they are so uncommon in traditional organizations. Several of them, clearly, carry large costs along with their benefits.

• *In hot groups, people's feelings about one another don't much matter.*

In most other small groups—committees, day-to-day work groups, social clubs—interpersonal relationships loom large. Friendships, status issues, personal likes and dislikes, all play a huge part in those groups' ability to function effectively. "I don't really trust Susan. She's always pushing her own agenda." "Henry never says what he really means. He just wants to look good." "Mary is always sucking up to the boss." "Joe just sits there and frowns like he thinks we're all fools." "Sam always wants to run the show." All those feelings and many, many more build psychological obstacles to effective work in most small groups.

As we suggested earlier, however, those kinds of feelings play only a minor role in hot groups. Or rather, they *appear* to play a minor role because they do not lead the parade—they follow it. Those interpersonal issues are typically submerged beneath the all-engulfing pull of the task. In hot groups, it is not mutual loyalty and trust that generate effective performance. Neither is it friendship, nor understanding of one another's idiosyncrasies. Hot groups work the other way around. It is their task, not one another, that hot groups love, along with the *process* of working on that task together. When each person is being pulled by the magnetic power of the task, mutual trust can follow, albeit ineffably. Mutual understanding, loyalty, and friendship often occur in hot groups, but when they do, they are a result, not a cause, of commitment to their task.

We recently read about the development of such feelings in a rather off-center hot group, a Japanese *bosozoku* motorcycle gang. These gangs get together periodically to make illegal "runs"—high-speed drives through city streets by anywhere from ten to one-hundred young men and women. One participant described the experience this way:

> We are not in complete harmony at the start. But if the run begins going well, all of us, all of us feel for others. How can I say this?. . . When our minds become one, I understand something. . . . All of a sudden I realize, "Oh, we're one." . . . When we realize that, we become one flesh. . . . It's really super.[1]

We also liked Charles Handy's description of an incident that occurred while he was speaking to an English group. He was comparing a team of Englishmen to a rowing crew, describing them as "eight men going backward as fast as they can without talking to each other, steered by the one person who can't row!"

I thought it quite witty at the time, but I was corrected . . . by one of the participants, who had once been an Olympic oarsman. "How do you think we could go backward so fast without communicating, steered by this little fellow in the stern, if we didn't know each other very well, didn't have total confidence to do our jobs and a shared commitment—almost a passion—for the same goal? It is the perfect formula for a team."[2]

In most hot groups, something more or less like that seems to happen. Members develop a sense of community—common unity—around their joint activity. Sometimes that sense of oneness may cause members to socialize outside work, but most often they do very little of that. Occasionally some members become close friends, but usually that doesn't happen either. Once again, the task more than anything else is the wellspring from which hot groups' mutual trust and unity emerge.

As hot groups progress, an emotional spillover usually occurs. Members become infatuated with everything associated with the task. Like people in love, they may make great sacrifices of their own resources and their outside relationships, initially for their cherished task and eventually for their cherished group. In the excitement of it all, the failings of their comrades, if not totally unseen, are mostly ignored or treated as acceptable eccentricities—unless they affect the work. Later, as the task nears completion, the warts may become more noticeable, either to be tolerated or perhaps eventually to cause enough irritation to fracture the group.

Often, in organizations, people selected to work on yet another committee feel as though they've been shanghaied—carried off to a gulag and abandoned there with a bunch of competitive strangers, all sentenced to another term of do-nothing frustration. Hot group members never feel that way. They actively want to become involved in their group's work. That's one reason why hot groups seldom seek help for their psychological stresses, even though it has become commonplace for many non-hot groups to call in outside facilitators to help them sort out their interpersonal problems. Hot groups' initial commitment to the task makes their performance much less vulnerable to the interpersonal distractions that plague so many other groups.

The whole profession of organizational development has evolved over the last half-century precisely to help groups deal with such problems.[3] It actually grew out of earlier experimentation with sensitivity groups in which there is often no external task, only the quite introspective task of analyzing the group's internal relationships. It is thus hard to imagine two more polar types of human groups. Members of sensitivity groups think constantly about their own feelings and about everybody else's. Hot groups think constantly about their tasks and how to solve them.

This is not to argue that the hot group highway is a short route to nirvana. The tendency of hot groups to pay scant attention to their own internal dynamics has both positive and negative effects. Most hot groups could profit from more self-understanding. An ongoing hot group is lucky if some members have pretty good antennae to help them sense their colleagues' feelings. Sometimes, unfortunately, hot groups' narrow focus on the task *über alles* blocks those interpersonally oriented members from expressing their concerns.

On the other hand, it can be extremely counterproductive for a group working full-bore on a consuming task to shut down temporarily to deal with interpersonal strains. For a hot group that lives for an extended period, however, ignoring such interpersonal strains can be dangerously foolish. Hot groups, after all, are not necessarily composed of mentally superhealthy, stable individuals. Like other groups, they include their share of self-centered egotists, withdrawn introverts, slippery manipulators, and chest-thumping power-seekers. Still, in the compelling atmosphere of a working hot group, it is not wise to stop the speeding train for a weekend of psychotherapy.

We speak from sad experience:

A group of us once presented a management seminar for a set of information scientists at a large company's think tank. The group worked at a site intentionally distant from company headquarters, in a rather idyllic setting. The participants included about fifteen very bright researchers, all intensely involved in a set of esoteric projects. They listened to us fairly passively during the afternoon session. At dinner, they drank a lot of wine and beer. After dinner, they began to interrupt our presentations, at first with rather sharp questions, then, increasingly, with derisive comments. It became obvious, even to us, that they felt that all this stuff was utterly irrelevant. We sages huddled briefly during a break and then made the intelligent decision. We said, "Thank you" and bade the group good-bye, departing considerably earlier than scheduled. Then we headed for a nearby bar to lick our wounds and tell one another how blind those guys were.

In hindsight, we think we were the blind ones—they were right. Our timing was way off. If we had exercised due diligence, we probably shouldn't have accepted the assignment in the first place. They didn't need us then. They were in the midst of doing what they wanted to do, and we were simply in their way. Later, the situation within that think-tank group might have been different. Interpersonal issues, which were unquestionably there, might no longer have been obscured by their ardor for the task. Those second-order problems would probably have moved closer to the front burner. Then, perhaps, we might have been able to make a contribution.

In hot groups, the task's the thing, and it should stay that way. Beguiling a hot group away from its task to examine all those intriguing psychological issues can lead to disaster. If, however, *they* choose to detour for that purpose, it is not a good idea to deny them that right.

• *Hot group members need diverse but compatible "achieving styles."*[4]

The most effective hot groups we have ever seen are composed of individuals whose "achieving styles"—their characteristic ways of getting things done—are very diverse yet compatible. In most groups, if some members are very competitive and others very collaborative, trouble is sure to follow. The two kinds of people are likely to grate on one another. In hot groups, however, the more styles the better, for two reasons: First, because all that diversity means that someone in the group is likely to have just the right style to deal with the issue currently at hand, and, second, because the overarching centrality of the task keeps everyone focused on the work, not on one another.

It is appropriate here to elaborate a bit on the concept of achieving styles, those learned, habitual behaviors individuals call on when they want to get something done. We shall sketch only a short description of nine types of such styles. We hope that they will give the reader a general idea of how and why diversity among members' styles is important in a hot group—and why hot groups can exploit such diversity better than many other groups. The nine achieving styles are divided into three general categories made up of three styles each: *direct, instrumental,* and *relational* achieving styles.

People who prefer *direct* styles attack their assignments directly, head-on, without using intermediaries. They are particularly focused on their own tasks. These are the three subsets of direct styles:

1. *Intrinsic* direct. People who prefer the *intrinsic* direct style simply enjoy taking on a new task and doing that task very well. They just like solving the puzzle, doing the job, making it happen. *Intrinsics* measure their accomplishments against their own internal standards of excellence. They don't worry about how well others have done. They don't care about winning, just about doing the best they can do—doing better than they have ever done.

2. *Competitive* direct. Users of the competitive direct style like to be number one, to outdo others. *Competitives*, in contrast to *intrinsics*, use an external rather than an internal standard of excellence. Like Vince Lombardi, they want to win, to do better than anyone else.

3. *Power* direct. The third direct style, *power* direct, focuses on taking control. *Power* people like to organize situations, resources, and, of course, other people. *Power* users are good at coordinating complex, rapidly changing events.

People who operate in the second category, the *instrumental* styles, prefer to use themselves and everyone and everything around them as instruments to help them get their tasks done. They are tuned into groups and systems, and they are very savvy about matters political. The three *instrumental* styles are:

1. *Personal* instrumental. *Personal* instrumentals use all they've got, every aspect of their personal repertoires (i.e., charm, wit, family background, intelligence, education, physical attractiveness, etc.), to draw others into their work. *Personal* instrumental types attract helpers by making themselves and their purposes very attractive to whatever helpers they need.

2. *Social* instrumental. Users of the *social* instrumental style establish and nourish networks of friends, associates, and even friends of associates to provide help on their task. They know just whom to call to help them find this special widget or that key specialist.

3. *Entrusting* instrumental. *Entrusting* people tend to entrust their tasks to others, giving those others plenty of room to do the job in any legal and ethical way those others see fit. Entrusting users emphatically do *not* micro-manage.

The third and final set of achieving styles, the *relational* set, comprises behaviors that contribute actively or passively to *other* people's or group tasks. These are three rather familiar styles:

1. *Collaborative* relational. Those using this style prefer to work in groups. They willingly take their full share of responsibility for the grunt work. They also expect their fair portion of the rewards for the group's success and the punishments for its failure.

2. *Contributory* relational. Users of this style don't need public attention or acclaim. In fact, they're happy to work as second bananas, behind the scenes, contributing to the successes of others, writing the speeches for others to deliver.

3. *Vicarious* relational. *Vicarious* achievers take their enjoyment and pride from the achievements of others. They

take real pleasure in others' success. Not surprisingly, they make great facilitators and mentors.

Over the last two and a half decades, we and many colleagues have measured the achieving styles profiles of more than 35,000 individuals in several countries, ranging from senior executives to Taiwanese homemakers. Most, we have found, rely heavily on two or three styles, using them in all situations, even when those styles are not the most appropriate for the task at hand. It is the rare—and usually quite successful—individual who can comfortably use all or most of those nine styles as the situation warrants. The same, we believe, is true of groups. Having access to a full range of styles permits a group to cope with a wide variety of problems—*if the members can live with one another's styles.* That is where hot groups have the advantage. Hot group members are likely to welcome and utilize one another's weird and wonderful styles as long as the task demands it.

A high dose of the *intrinsic* style, for example, is particularly important to ensure commitment to doing a tough job right. The *competitive* style can be very useful, too, but only if it is directed outside, not inside, the hot group. Having one or two people around who share the *power* direct style is key to keeping some focus in the group, making sure that things stay on course and don't get too chaotic. The *personal* and *social* instrumental styles are very useful for inspiring the group, recruiting new people into it, identifying others to help temporarily, and keeping in contact with the rest of the world. *Entrusting* behavior allows group members to hand off tasks to one another with complete confidence. Most people in hot groups have a reasonable degree of *collaborative* behavior. That's where the excitement that flows from synergy comes into play. The *contributory* style prompts members to assist one another without turf envy. *Vicarious* behavior provides social glue to hot groups, holding them together through periods of stress and strain, and offering advice and support to those in need during ordinary times.

Here's a brief case in which multiple styles really helped a hot group:

> One of us was directing a quite hot research group consisting of three graduate students: two young women and one young man. They

called themselves "EC3," the East Coast Threesome. Their achieving styles were essentially different, but each had some overlap with at least one other group member. Mary Ellen was very high in the *social* and *personal* instrumental and all three relational styles. She was forever reaching out to find still other people who could move the task along. John was very high on the *intrinsic, power,* and *collaborative* styles. Whenever the group began to wander too far from its core task, he would gently and humorously bring them back on track, reminding them of their assignments and the schedule they needed to keep. Claire was quite *intrinsic,* but also *contributory.* She quietly kept the group together, not only doing her own part of the research, but soothing the wear and tear that inevitably result from the intensity of hot group activity.

The EC3 worked as an effective and hot little group while all three members were in graduate school completing their related theses and dissertations. During that time, in addition to their individual work, the EC3 began to do joint research. Over the next few years, they published several articles together. Then, gradually, they went more and more about their own individual lives. They still stay in touch, though, mostly socially, but occasionally Mary Ellen and John still work together, sometimes on consulting assignments or other tasks.

Once again, however, a caveat: The same diversity of styles that can work wonders in a hot group can quickly generate enough conflict and enmity to kill off a cold committee or task force. For hot groups, the task's the thing!

• Hot groups don't try to live forever.

Most hot groups can't stay very hot for very long. They are, by nature, almost always "temporary organizations," and that is exactly what many of their parent organizations are also becoming.[5]

Remember all the heat on college campuses in the late 1960s and early 1970s? Countless little self-support groups and protest groups along with "open universities" sprouted during that period. They also quickly died away after college administrators discovered a very powerful tactic for dealing with them: Just wait them out. Those quite cold administrations remained stable over much longer periods than the hot, but transient, little groups of protesters. Now, of course, many large organizations can no longer count on their own long-term stability, so that tactic has become less reliable. Moreover, in today's world, it would be a mistake to treat the impermanence of hot groups solely as a weakness. Their transitory nature is an important strength in our ever more impermanent organizational world. As we have noted, they fit nicely into a milieu of swirling change.

Hot groups' "get-in, do-it, get-out" style carries another distinct advantage. One of the major bad habits of many other "temporary" groups is their propensity to cling to life, even after their work is done. Often, they burrow into the organization's structure, building permanent dens for themselves and thereby further bureaucratizing their already bureaucratized parents.

The Federal Government provides many examples of organizational units that thrash about or hide out, desperately clinging to life long after their missions have been completed, torpedoed, or abandoned.

> The National Institute of Education (NIE) offers a case in point.[6] It began as a hot group whose mission was to infuse then mediocre educational research, sponsored largely by the U.S. Office of Education, with cutting-edge methods and insights from the social and behavioral sciences. Young turks, recruited largely from academia, worked tirelessly to launch new research and experimental programs that would dramatically improve America's schools. Led by a bright but politically inexperienced young researcher, Tom Glennon, the new entity soon found itself ensnared in the bear-traps of political egos, conflicting federal agencies, and a crowd of other stakeholders. The more established groups saw their sinecures slipping away as this new agency drew the limelight. Over the next two decades, the embattled NIE searched rather desperately for a clear, feasible mission and new political patrons. Failing to find those, and beset by political turbulence, the agency was ultimately reabsorbed into the newly elevated Department of Education. And there it sits, atrophied, only minimally effective, but still alive.

A hot group rarely presents such a history. When its task is completed, that's the end of it.

Of course, there are significant downsides to the transient aspect of hot groups. To have small groups starting and ending here and there, all over the system, will require a resilience and flexibility not commonly found in large organizations. There will be practical issues, like how to relocate hot group members into other roles when their groups end. If hot groups develop frequently—forming, doing their work, and then dissolving—it will put new pressures (albeit, appropriately) on the human resources staff and other managers.

• *Hot groups work informally and democratically.*

Hot groups pay little attention to symbols of rank and authority. Communication flows freely, up, down, and across those groups. Members treat one another with casual respect, focusing on colleagues' contributions to the task at hand rather than on title or status. The behavior of leaders, too, is egalitarian vis-à-vis the rest of the group. This does not mean that all decisions are made by majority rule, but that all members' voices are heard and taken seriously. Such wide-open interaction is highly functional, especially when speed and imagination are vital.

Those uninhibited, often confrontational styles, however, present a problem for traditional institutions, both public and private. Nor do organizations usually cotton to groups that bypass proper channels—and they have reasons. It isn't just that big organizations are dinosaurs, rigid and immutably set in their ways. As organizations grow, some amount of formalization has to happen—not nearly as much as usually entangles most large institutions, but some bureaucracy nonetheless. The dilemma arises because organizations need discipline, hierarchy, predictability, and orderly procedures to get their work done, while hot groups need freedom and disorder to get *their* work done. That's a difficult dilemma, but not an insoluble one. As we shall see in later chapters, some large organizations have managed to work it out pretty well.

There remains, however, another dilemma, this one between the demands of hot groups and those of individuals. As organizations design themselves more around groups and less around individuals—which is what many are doing now—can they focus more on the group as a key unit? Can they still leave room for freedom and diversity among the individuals within those groups? Bart Giamatti, former president of Yale and later the commissioner of baseball, had it right when he wrote, with eloquence and elegance, about the sport he loved so much. He thought of baseball as the quintessential American game because it provides space and opportunity for both the group and the individual:

> Baseball fits America so well because it embodies the interplay of individual and group that we so love, and because it expresses our longing for the rule of law while licensing our resentment of law givers.
>
> Baseball, the opportunist's game, puts a tremendous premium on the individual. . . . If the game flows from the constantly reiterated primitive confrontation of an individual with the world, represented by another solitary individual, nothing that ensues, except a home run . . . fails to involve the team. A strikeout involves the catcher, and anything else brings the community . . . into play. And while the premium on individual effort is never lost, the communal choreography of the team eventually takes over. . . . The subsequent interactions among all the players on the field expand in incalculable ways. When in the thrall of these communal aspects, hitting, stealing a base, and individual initiative give way to collective playmaking, acts of sacrifice or cooperation. . . . Whether on offense or defense, the virtuoso is subsumed into the ensemble. The anarchic ways of solo operation are subdued by a free institution.[7]

In a later chapter, we shall return to this very difficult issue of the fit among the three key players: individuals, hot groups, and organizations.

• Hot groups take pretty good care of their own mental health.

Despite the pressure-cooker conditions under which they work, hot groups generally do a very good job of taking care of themselves. They seem to have their own self-adjusting thermostats for keeping emotional problems under control. Ordinarily, they find ways to level things out and cool things down. Individual members may suffer from one psychological problem or another, but the hot group as a unit is likely to keep itself functioning.

Group members may not be terribly sensitive to the deeper nature of one another's feelings, but they're highly alert to anything that may impair their work, and that includes one another's psychological well-being. When Mary begins to falter, Joe steps in to spell her and perhaps to supply enough emotional chicken soup to get her back to work.

Hot groups even help take care of one another's physical health. So real chicken soup, albeit sometimes the canned variety, may be served up when a member is under the weather, battling the flu, or simply exhausted. More often than not, another hot group member steps in to cover the patient's duties.

• *Hot groups work very long hours, but they don't perceive it as work.*

For many hot groups, their exhilarating task is a source of joy, not a sentence to hard labor. Members of hot groups often forget to go home at closing time. Sometimes they bring cots to work so they can grab a few winks between 3 A.M. and dawn. Hot group behavior is often hyper, concentrated, and focused, much like the movie caricature of the mad scientist rushing about in the crammed laboratory, on the verge of both the great discovery and the imminent breakdown. Political campaign workers, frantically trying to get their candidate elected, often work this way. They just can't stop; they work around the clock. And when it's over, they wonder how they did it. Those very qualities are caught in Chris Hegedus and D. A. Pennebaker's film, *The War Room*, which documents the all-consuming atmosphere that surrounded the first Clinton/Gore presidential campaign.[8] In the film, George Stephanopoulos, after working continuously for two days and nights, returns to his desk to watch the final countdown to the election. Talking to a friend on the telephone, Stephanopoulos confesses the strain of his round-the-clock schedule: "I got up this morning. As I was driving to work, I started to cry. I couldn't keep it. I can't cope right now."

Exhilaration, nonetheless, perfuses exhaustion. That was certainly true when paleontologist Dr. Paul Sereno, of the University of Chicago, led a 1993 expedition to the Republic of Niger in search of dinosaur bones. Despite a host of difficulties and dangers, the excavators—mostly undergraduates without much experience—discovered a previously unknown dinosaur species. After a long, grueling day in the heat of the desert, a day that had begun at dawn, one member of this little hot group exclaim with awe and excitement: "We've exposed . . .10 or 11 bones, mostly articulated. It doesn't get much better than that! We spent all day finding bones!"[9]

A bit later in this chapter, we describe a study by Roberts and King about a hot group of educational policy entrepreneurs who successfully changed the Minnesota school system. They displayed that same kind of an all-out work ethic:

> Many [observers] declared [the policy entrepreneurs] to be effective because they outworked everyone else, putting in as much as eighty hours a week. One entrepreneur's dedication was so renowned . . . that an observer described him as a "policy junkie" who never stopped working because "it's his cause."[10]

Such resolution and its inseparable companion, obliviousness to normal routines, are still another reason why hot groups have a hard time in many large organizations.

• *Hot group members work for the group, even when they're away from it.*

In "normal" committees, teams, and task forces, participants may try hard to avoid extra duties. Not so with members of hot groups. They tend to volunteer for extra work, even to make additional work for themselves. Their motivation is intrinsic.

Even when they're away from the group, members are likely to work long hours on the group's task. They then frequently carry the fruits of their solo efforts back to the group, presenting it as a kind of gift, an intellectual offering. "I was thinking about that problem in bed last night, and I had an idea. So I got up and tried a few things on my PC, and here's what I got. What do you guys think?" Such special donations are often early indicators that a group is really heating up.

• *Hot groups create self-defining symbols.*

Hot groups often make up unique mottoes, logos, even special words and phrases, that have meaning for just them. They may implement such insignia via the usual flags, T-shirts, hats, or more imaginative markers of their identity. If group members are older or more senior in rank, they may prefer something appropriately more conservative, like neckties or coffee mugs. For the Macintosh group, it was the skull and crossbones flag, with an apple in its eye. One very lively cancer support group we encountered preferred somewhat grimmer humor: They wore T-shirts emblazoned "Don't mess with us. We've got cancer!"

Of course, many cold groups use symbols, too, usually in the vain hope that they will cause group heat. Every high school sports team makes up a dramatic, usually aggressive name for itself— "Panthers," "Raiders," or "Buccaneers"—and wears sweatshirts to match. Such symbols, however, do not cause group heat. If those teams do heat up, it will not be attributable to their exotic names. It will be in response to the clean, clear challenge of their task.

• *Members of hot groups know they're hot, and they like to strut their stuff.*

When a group is hot, members feel that they are special. They're on a high. Like the aerospace executive we quoted in Chapter 1, they believe they are "out there ahead of the whole world." That kind of hubris obviously carries both benefits and costs. It pumps the adrenaline of energy and imagination. It generates a readiness—because the group thinks so highly of itself—to take on challenges that others may see as too risky to touch. Some of the time, of course, those more risk-averse people turn out to be right. Risk-takers are bound to lose a few.

This self-confidence, however, also has its downsides. It is usually read by outside observers as arrogance, and it can generate significant resentment.

• *Individual performance appraisals disrupt the work of hot groups.*

If there is any single managerial practice that virtually everybody uses and nobody loves, it is performance appraisal. Those annual evaluation rituals regularly send whole organizations into divisive argument and complaint. In hot groups, performance appraisals can wreak extraordinary havoc.

In 1957, Douglas McGregor published a classic piece entitled "An Uneasy Look at Performance Appraisals."[11] In it, he enumerated many of the problems caused by such systems even then. In 1996, the *Wall Street Journal* published a front-page, lead story headlined, "It's Time to Evaluate Your Work, and All Involved are Groaning."[12] That article outlines almost exactly the same set of problems McGregor was concerned about in 1957. In the *Journal* piece, Timothy Schellhardt writes:

> The year end rite has begun anew for millions of employees and managers. But in almost every major survey, most employees who get job evaluations and most supervisors who give them rate the process a resounding failure. A 1995 survey indicates that 44% of 218 companies with evaluation systems have changed theirs in the previous two years and that another 29% expected to do so.

Plus ça change, plus c'est la même chose. Despite frequent revisions, reconceptualizations, and redesigns,[13] performance appraisals remain a pain in the organizational anatomy. The appraisal process kept personnel managers hopping back then, and it does the same for HR managers today. Every few years, when the decibel level of the protests becomes deafening, the HR department brings in another consulting firm to revise the system. They then introduce the latest appraisal form, with its revised rating scales and newest supervisory training procedures, claiming (and hoping) that this model will cure all those ailments. It never does.

It has always struck us as curious that few executive development programs, whether at universities or within companies, formally evaluate the performance of their individual participants. Yet, we do just that to people back in the organization. We lay more on our people than just the grades we give college students. We tell them what their "superiors" believe are their adequacies and inadequacies, their good qualities and bad. We infantilize forty year olds. Then, as surely as the winter snows follow the autumn leaves, the complaining and politicking begin. Step into the local coffee shop just after this year's appraisals have come out. Anger and frustration will be palpable. "It was so unfair." "He just plays favorites." "I did everything they told me to do last year, and I still got a lousy evaluation." "Just be a yes man. That's all you need to do to get a good evaluation around here." The protests are many, frequent, and loud, yet all those involved continue to sweat them out, year after year, decade after decade.

For hot groups, individual appraisals cause even more than the usual pain. They introduce a competitive counterforce that tends to split apart the group. It is difficult for a group to act *e pluribus unum* when each *unum* must also try to be *numero uno*.

Appraising the group as a whole offers a partial way out of many of those "normal" problems, but not all. It's much easier, for example, to determine how well a whole project got done than to evaluate, from above, the contribution each member made. Besides, managers at levels above any group seldom know nearly as much as group members themselves about who contributed the most and who goofed off.

Performance appraisals are usually linked to bonuses and raises. For hot groups, that signals more trouble. Like the rest of us, hot group members are not immune to the attraction of money. They care about what money can buy and as a quantitative index of accomplishment. Still, when a group is hot, money, like most other organization-sponsored incentives, is not high on their priority list. The excitement of the task sidelines all such issues. Nevertheless, members of hot groups can become quite exercised about financial rewards, *if those rewards are allocated differentially, by "outsiders," to individual members*. The question then shifts from "How much did I get?" to "Did I get my fair share?" It's not the money. It's that *déjà vu* performance evaluation problem all over again, the problem of distributive justice, symbolized, this time, by pieces of silver.

We shall say more in later chapters about some kinds of incentives that help, rather than hinder, the growth of hot groups.

• *Individual incentive schemes don't help either.*

Like performance evaluations, individual incentive schemes usually work poorly. Treating each person's performance as if it were an isolated activity is to deny the interdependence of all facets of the modern organization. Indeed, as groups become more and more central to organizational life, the problems generated by individual incentive plans will get much worse. Like individual performance appraisals, they split group molecules back into their individual atoms, thereby straining the delicate web of cooperation essential to group success.

Any executive reader can surely supply many examples of the problems likely to arise when companies try to single out individual "stars" for special financial rewards. Witness, as just one instance, a *Fortune* magazine story describing the "hand-to-hand combat" that resulted from an effort to institute a bonus system at Lantech, a Louisville manufacturing company:

> At one point, each of the company's five divisions was given a bonus determined by how much profit it made. An individual worker's share of the bonus could amount to as much as 10% of his or her regular pay. But the divisions are so interdependent, it was difficult to sort out which one was entitled to what profits. "That led to so much secrecy, politicking, and sucking noise that you wouldn't believe it," says CEO Jim Lancaster.[14]

In the Lantech case, a battle erupted among divisions, but that sort of divisiveness is even more commonplace when incentives are applied to individuals. Hot groups may need help in handling difficult members, but they do not need outsiders to tell them which of the children deserve an extra dessert and which ones should be sent to bed hungry.

When it comes to managing hot groups, at least two morals emerge:

1. Keep potentially divisive money incentives in the background, not on center stage—at least until the end of the game.

2. To help maintain the integrity of a group, try, when reward or punishment is necessary, to apply it to the whole group, not individual members. Leave internal sharing and discipline to the group itself.

- *Many hot groups make real enemies and often create imaginary ones.*

It should come as no surprise that hot groups sometimes view themselves as embattled enclaves, their backs to the wall, besieged by barbarian hordes of number crunchers. When the relative isolation of hot groups is added to everything else, we have ideal conditions for generating that kind of Alamo-like self-portrait. That's not just paranoia. It's also functional for a group to see itself that way. External enemies increase internal cohesion. "Those SOBs think we can't do it. Let's show 'em we can!" Outside enemies also minimize nascent conflicts within the group. When the enemy is scaling our walls, who's going to complain because old Charley missed his turn making coffee?

Hot groups can be extremely creative in devising clever ways of evading those real or imagined attacks, ways of circumventing organizational rules and cutting the bureaucratic ties that, they believe, bind them. They find ingenious ways to outgame "those bean counters" who want to "nickel and dime us to death." In doing so, hot groups often baffle and bewilder their organizations in much the same ways that teenagers baffle and bewilder their parents. Teenagers, parents complain, won't get off the phone. They stay out too late. They argue about the simplest requests. Besides, they just won't listen to reason. Hot groups, some executives complain, do analogous things. They set their own hours. They ignore company rules. They insist on doing things their own way. Besides, those groups aren't even likely to feel any guilt. They don't consider such behavior wrong—quite the reverse. Because they're sure that their cause is just, they can easily defend it, simply by characterizing disliked regulations as bureaucratic boulders blocking the highway to success.

To an unbiased observer, many hot groups' complaints may seem both reasonable and understandable. Long-time veterans of the bureaucratic life too often develop a beaten-down, that's-just-the-way-it-is tolerance for nonsensical regulations. Large organizations might do well, therefore, to take their hot groups' protests seriously. Those lively, task-obsessed groups may be pinpointing just the spots at which a dozing organization needs a loud wake-up call.

Previously, we quoted briefly from a book by Roberts and King[15] about a volunteer group of educational entrepreneurs. That book offers a fine example of both the costs and benefits of such "enemy-generating" behavior, along with reactions by those "enemies." The hot little group of policy reformers described in the book, after an extended and intense effort, successfully changed major educational policy in Minnesota's public school system. Typically, though, in the course of their work,

> The policy entrepreneurs . . . came under attack for their interpersonal style. Observers maintained that the entrepreneurs always thought they were right and refused to listen to other points of view. They were said to want change for the sake of change and options for the sake of options, without respect for the experience and knowledge of professionals. Some educators viewed them as arrogant and patronizing, referring to them as single issue zealots who were rigid and unwilling to compromise. . . . Some participants . . . saw them not as independent thinkers but as parrots of an accepted party line who acted and sounded as if they were on a mission or crusade. . . . A member of the Governor's executive team added that the lawmakers were fed up with the recognition and credit going to the policy entrepreneurs, saying a "powder keg" situation had developed between the two groups. (pp. 131–32)

Further, some legislators attacked the policy entrepreneurs with yet another familiar device, the jungle predator's tactic of going after the most vulnerable member of the herd:

> One policy entrepreneur . . . was criticized for being too much of a radical, having "a fuzzy-haired Einstein look." . . . His ideas were good . . . but his PR was bad. (p. 132)

It is quite understandable that outside observers often regard hot groups as irritants. Who wouldn't get mad at groups that (a) are unshakably convinced of the greatness of their cause, (b) define certain innocent others as bad guys, (c) prefer to work in semi-isolation, (d) are unswervingly certain that what they are doing deserves the highest priority, and (e) ignore or dodge rules that others must obey?

That enemy-enacting process usually cycles both ways, from hot group to the chosen "enemy" and then back again, often spiraling downward into unbridled hostility. Although some hot groups initially set up enemies to intensify their own task-focus, that tactic can easily do just the reverse. As others retaliate, the hot group must divert resources from its central task to fight useless, irrelevant wars. One of the few good things that can be said about such attacks and counterattacks is that they are highly stimulating for all concerned. In that sense, they energize the organization, but they also drain it. Leaders of hot groups had better know how and when to set limits on their groups' propensity to thumb their noses at other groups.

• *Hot groups tend to work obsessively, often secretively.*

Hot groups, we repeat, focus obsessively on their task. They think and talk about their work everywhere and all the time. Other prosaic day-to-day functions are likely to be pointedly ignored or viewed as wasteful distractions. Not surprisingly, hot groups also tend to "forget" weekly progress and expense reports. That unswerving focus on task causes nightmares for administrators who must keep the numbers straight. It can also trigger migraines for colleagues outside the group who need information stored only in the heads of these temporarily inaccessible group members.

Hot groups also have a propensity to be secretive. Love of their task can make them quite possessive and clandestine. They talk a lot, but only to those likely to be knowledgeable about their task, and only occasionally do they breach security. In fact, they sometimes become so secretive they won't openly acknowledge exactly what they are doing, even to their own bosses, for fear they will be ordered to stop.

Two other episodes at Rain Bird Sprinkler provide good—and to many readers surely familiar—examples of small group initiatives taken *sub rosa*, without prior approval. Eric Pollard described these situations to us:

> The golf rotor product line was declining at a pretty precipitous rate, about 20% a year; so we had this big chunk of sales that was just declining faster than we were able to replace it. [But] we had these four other products that were growing . . . at 50% to 60% per year, all relatively new low volume products. So, we were dealing with the

introduction stumbles that go along with new products, and we had this host of older products, about eight or ten older product lines, that were . . . declining very precipitously.

So, when I took over the line, I was looking for an opportunity to make a quick impact on our revenue. When I came in, I had the strategic plan, and we had the budget to match the plan. These [engineers] were guys who had a way of doing things. There was nothing in the plan that would let them do anything regarding new product development, so they did just what was in the plan. So, one of the things that I did to . . . get their enthusiasm going was to sit around with them and say, "If we had control of the budget, what would we do?" And we would just kind of shoot some ideas out, like "I would make a valve that would do this." Or "I would make a nozzle that does that." "I would make a case that doesn't break."

I said, *"Why don't we work on those things? As long as we get the strategic plan stuff done, we can do all these other things kind of in the background. No one really needs to know about it."* *We funded it out of the plant's operating budget. I was using marketing money to do the authorized product development and using plant maintenance money, the actual money that was supposed to be spent on building the tools and various other things, to fund this research and development.* [Italics ours]

A second, related example:

We had been talking to the folks in our international group who were looking for a small de-featured product. Traditionally, a golf rotor would have a built-in valve so it could be individually controlled from . . . a remote site. . . . They wanted a product for the European market that had excellent performance characteristics, but did not want any of the pressure regulation or internal valves or anything on it that added cost to the product.

I . . . went back to some of our engineering guys, . . . and I said, "What is the possibility of making a product that will kind of look like this?" describing what I thought the market wanted. Actually three of the four engineers were working on different elements of the program. We got together, and we built a prototype—by the next day I had a prototype of the product. It was sort of nonfunctional, but I mean it showed where we were headed. . . . In eight weeks, we had working functional prototypes.

So, we had these parts that we were assembling. We built the case from half of an existing mold and half of a new mold that we built to do that. We had a rubber cover that we had to design and attach to the case, which was something that we had not done before. *Basically, the project never got approved until we were already essentially in pilot run. We were producing functional products to the finished goods product specification by the time that we had the budget approved.* [Italics ours]

We did a large pilot run of about 30,000 units and sold them all. So we paid for the entire development cost which was around $100,000 . . . out of the initial production run, and everything else after that was gravy. We sold half a million dollars of product in the first month.

• *Sometimes their penchant for secrecy and creating enemies may cause a hot group to cross the line.*

Those Rain Bird cases resulted in happy outcomes, but the propensity of hot groups for self-isolation doesn't always end up that way. Self-isolation and secrecy are fraught with danger for both group and organization. When few people outside the group know anything about what a hot group is up to, watch out. Organizations, as we point out again and again, don't take kindly to surprises. So when the hot group finally and proudly unwraps its surprise package for all to admire, all may not admire it. Remember how, early in President Clinton's first term, Hillary Rodham Clinton and Ira Magaziner's group, charged with redesigning the American health care system, ran aground on those shoals of secrecy? They infuriated many other stakeholders who had been left out of the charmed circle.

On rare occasions, hot groups' self-isolating behavior can even lead to illegal and unethical excesses. That seems to have been the case, a few years ago, at the fertility clinic on the Irvine campus of the University of California. The group's zeal to increase their pregnancy "hit rate" led them to take eggs from one patient and implant them in another, without either woman's knowledge or consent.

Remember, as well, the junk bond scandal at what used to be Drexel Burnham Lambert? There, too, secrecy and isolation—carried out in Los Angeles, 3000 miles from its New York parent office—prevented more objective outsiders from applying the brakes to Michael Milken's hot group of junk bond traders. Their secretive machinations ultimately brought down the entire company.[16]

We recently read about another case in which a hot group, managing a new newspaper (part of a large chain), set out deliberately to destroy its locally owned competitor.[17] The enthusiastic new group, dubbed "the Dobermans," devised extremely creative ways of scaring advertisers away from its competitor, misrepresenting the competitor's actions, and otherwise behaving in ways that moved well beyond ethical, if not legal, bounds. Similarly, during political campaigns, small hot groups of dedicated supporters of one candidate—convinced of their own righteousness—can think up myriads of dirty tricks to skewer their opponents. Sometimes, the dirty trick means simply giving the press legitimate information it would not otherwise have gotten. That is what happened when Bill Clinton's '92 campaign staff alerted the media to the fact that President Bush's reelection committee had its campaign flyers produced in Brazil, a procedure disallowed when federal funding is involved. At other times, as we have seen all too often in recent American politics, dirty tricks cross the line, distorting an opponent's record, or feeding the media false information about a candidate's personal life, or bugging an opponent's headquarters.

Such grossly unethical behavior, however, is very infrequent in organizational hot groups, probably less so than in many other organizational units. Nevertheless, due diligence is always in order, and hot group leaders had better make sure their groups do not become so committed to their cause that they ignore ethical boundaries.

• *When hot groups end, they end.*

As a hot group approaches its impending dissolution, its characteristically focused state of mind begins to disintegrate. Task-based feelings of excitement and camaraderie give way to feelings of sadness and loss. One woman in that hot group excavating dinosaur bones caught the sense of loss when she described how she felt on the last day of the dig:

> When we were leaving In'Gall [in Niger], I remember kind of searching around for something to hold on to, because all of a sudden we were leaving, and it felt like we had just gotten started.[18]

Yet, when a hot group ends after successfully completing its task, the sense of loss is mixed with an enormous sense of accomplishment and pride. We hear it in the words of a male member of that same Sahara hot group:

> Coming home was triumphant, really. There was a tremendous feeling that we had accomplished what people said we couldn't have accomplished. And we did it! We've got the proof right here in the truck! Right behind us! That's a great feeling. Knowing that you've done, absolutely the best you could have done and you came out with something, something that's going to last, something that is really important.[19]

The dissolution of a hot group is almost always a bittersweet event. Even when the group ends in glory, individual concerns may begin to surface, concerns like "Where do I go from here?" "Will I be welcomed back into my former unit?" and "Do I want to go back?"

Companies may find it difficult to repatriate veterans of hot groups, to rehabilitate them back into the routines of the cool, everyday world. Like soldiers fresh from combat, employees fresh from the vitality of a hot group sometimes need patient support and counsel. Some members may feel altogether exhausted. Some, now addicted to the high that hot groups produce, may even depart the organization in search of lively action elsewhere. On occasion, a few members will remain bonded, teaming up on successor projects, like some pairs from the original Macintosh design team.

Although hot groups end, their memories linger on. In fact, that is precisely what the leaders of some hot groups intend. One member of Paul Sereno's excavators' hot group explained:

> Paul once said that he wanted to make this the greatest trip of everybody's life. . . . And I think that it has been. There's nothing like this. I mean the whole idea of the trip itself is exceptional. To experience it is like nothing else.[20]

Decades later, despite (or perhaps because of) their frenetic intensity, hot group memories will still be recalled warmly and minutely. Thus, when five key members of the early 1980s Macintosh team got together again in 1994, on the occasion of their dream machine's tenth birthday, the *Washington Post* reported:

> Today, they are among the best known, most influential names in the computer industry. But a decade ago they were toiling in a nondescript building known as Brandley 3, finishing work on an innovative new computer . . . the Apple Macintosh. . . . The members of the Mac team say they learned to strive for perfection, to work as a team . . . to learn from their mistakes. In one instance, they recall, they even taught themselves how to do something more experienced engineers had viewed as nearly impossible. . . . The members of the Mac team say they remembered the three years at Brandley 3, subsisting on pizza and soda, as a defining time in their lives and careers.[21]

In Summary

Big, stolid organizations try to live orderly, stable, unemotional lives. Little, agile hot groups live volatile, temporary, impassioned ones. In these chapters, we have tried to spell out some hot group ways of thinking and working. We have highlighted the contrast with the styles that large organizations have long expected and demanded. Yet the fast-changing new organizational world seems to us to require a pragmatic marriage between those two sharply disparate entities. As organizations confront today's frenetic environment, they will need many of the characteristics of hot groups—speed, flexibility, creative thought, and innovative action. On the other side, many hot groups will not be able to go it alone. They will require the massive resources of large organizations to permit them to do their things.

Of course, such marriages will have their problems. Some hot group characteristics, like their tendency to work alone, their impermanence, and their inclination to create enemies, carry pluses but also significant minuses for the organization. Nor can we expect large organizations to make perfect sweethearts for hot groups. They will try to overcontrol hot groups. They will want those groups to fill out the proper forms, dress properly, and keep somewhat regular working hours. Moreover, the front office may well view the hot group's brainchild, like the now famous graphical user interface at Xerox, as either outlandishly expensive or idiotic. Yet, the synergies that can follow from such a Mutt and Jeff marriage are so enormous, so awesome, that they easily eclipse the difficulties.

The rest of this book examines how little hot groups and big cold organizations can try to find happiness together. Whether they do will depend a great deal on their leaders. The next three chapters focus on the leaders of hot groups and also, though less directly, on the leaders of modern organizations.

II

WHO LEADS HOT GROUPS?
AND WHO SEEDS NEW ONES?

5

Leaders of Hot Groups I: Three Kinds of Leadership

In this first in a triad of chapters about the leadership of hot groups, the spotlight falls on three kinds of unusual individuals. Each can properly be called a hot group leader, but each acts out a different aspect of leadership. What kinds of people play each role? What motivates them? How do they operate? What types of situations bring them to the forefront?

Leader Who?

Although these chapters examine the leaders of hot groups, the fact is that many hot groups don't have any. Lots of spontaneous hot groups live their entire lives without ever having had any acknowledged leader. Members simply work on their task, not even thinking about the issue of leadership. They are too busy seeking their grail. In such groups, different members are likely to do various kinds of specialized work to help keep the group going. Someone may take on administrative duties, setting meeting schedules and circulating agendas. Others may approach an internal or external "angel" for seed money. Others may play social roles, calling time outs and arranging social events. This is where a broad repertoire of achieving styles, spread throughout the group, comes into play. Are those "leadership" jobs? Does it matter? In such groups, the reply to the question, "Who is your leader?" may be answered with a blank stare: "What leader? Stop distracting us with meaningless questions!"

Here's an example from that hot group of educational entrepreneurs we talked about in Chapter 4. This is how they saw the leadership situation in their own group:

> Group members regarded leadership as shared, although they did defer to Quie, if he were present, out of respect for his past experience. . . . The position of chair tended to rotate depending on who called the meeting, who set the agenda, who was present. As one member put it, "We are all leaders. . . . No one dominates, there is sharing and respect for ideas." . . . Said another, "If you were to ask me who was the leader in the group, I'm not sure I could answer that question."[1]

Other observers of highly productive groups have noted the same dispersion of leadership. Thus Katzenbach and Smith, in *The Wisdom of Teams*, point out that "high performance teams [close to our concept of hot groups] also share leadership within the team more than other teams."[2] On the other hand, many—probably most—hot groups do have special people who play particular leadership roles. They are the ones we focus on in this and the next two chapters.

Entrepreneurial Individualists Jump Start Hot Groups

Consider this curious, perhaps Freudian, paradox: Although the founders of most large and successful organizations were themselves free-spirited, individualistic entrepreneurs, the organizations they built typically can't abide people like those who whelped them. Though the founder's revered portrait beams down from the boardroom wall, his (seldom "hers" in those days) organizational grandchildren are likely to offer a cold reception to any ornery characters who think and act like their intrepid forebears. That last sentence, however, constitutes an example of what psychologists call an "attribution error." Those grandchildren probably aren't to blame for the organization's disapproval of people like grandpa. More likely, it's the other way round. It's the massive organization—the one the founder chose to build and the one in which the grandkids grew up—that is both too imprisoning and also too fragile to house vigorous people like those who built it. And "fragile" is probably the right word. For although steel and stone organizations look anything but fragile, even a modest amount of internal diversity can give many of them the shakes.

Nevertheless, the seeds of all hot groups are sown by individuals and mostly by individualistic individuals like some—not all—of those founders. They are members of the same subset of the general population who initiate most things: People who love challenging tasks; people who are explorers and searchers; people who don't know—and don't think much about—their own limitations.

In the past, when such entrepreneurial individualists turned up in large, established organizations, they were likely to be treated as irritating outliers, not part of the mainstream. Some were ambivalently admired as "entrepreneurs." More frequently, though, they were punished as chronic troublemakers or pushed off into peripheral jobs. That's why many of them quit to start their own businesses. Even today, despite the apparent popularity of "intrapreneurs,"[3] it is hard to find many of them inside the cores of large bureaucracies. Most have long since either departed in search of more welcoming environs or else they have been shipped off to organizational Siberias.

Although rare in most large, traditional organizations, entrepreneurial individualists are still quite common in several other organizational settings. They're plentiful in high-tech companies, in the arts, and even in academia. They are also still likely to be welcomed in small and small-in-spirit organizations, where imagination, speed, and innovation are highly prized. Silicon Valley continues to swarm with them and with the hot groups they help to generate. It's getting harder, however, to find them in some fields where they used to grow profusely, like corporate R&D units, largely because marketing considerations increasingly dictate research agendas. One also used to find such individualists among independent, outspoken college presidents, but that oasis has pretty much dried up.

Again, we hasten to add, it's the situation that has driven the change, more than the people. So there is a call arising for the return of "strong leaders" to universities. Thus, Robert Rosenzweig, president emeritus of the Association of American Universities, recently commented, "It would be hard to find a CEO who is weaker than a university president."[4] He then went on to call for university leaders strong enough to deal with their difficult faculties. It is not clear to us why he did not also call for university leaders strong enough to deal with their boards and their large donors. Or, better yet, why not leaders strong and agile enough to bring these diverse groups together to work on their mutual interest—the university's well-being? But more later about such "connective" leaders.

Entrepreneurial individualists can also be found in a host of other settings. They start new businesses, produce films and theatricals, form new political parties, organize athletic teams, and initiate every imaginable sort of community activity. The good news is that the fast-changing world is causing many leading-edge corporations to begin laying out the welcome mat for such entrepreneurial individualists. In some organizations, that process is painful, much like the misery felt by all-white, all-male clubs that find it distressingly difficult to admit blacks, Jews, Catholics, or women.

Hot Group Leaders Belong to a Special Set of Entrepreneurial Individualists: The Connective Set[5]

Not all entrepreneurial individualists propagate hot groups. Indeed, a large proportion are terrible cultivators of such groups. Although their enthusiasm and dedication can usually inspire others to join up, perhaps even to form one initial hot group, such entrepreneurial soloists don't have the patience, nor do they feel the need, to adapt their goals and visions to accommodate others. What they want most is a chance to do their own thing and get others to help them do it. First and foremost, however, it must remain *their* own thing.

Only a special subset of strong entrepreneurial individualists has both a driving interest in growing hot groups and the ability to make them happen. That subset we call *connective leaders*.[6] They are the seeders, feeders, and weeders of hot groups. These connective leaders perceive and enhance the connections among very diverse people and groups, thereby earning their name. They are also people who call upon a very broad array of achieving styles to meet any situation. These connective leaders are worth a closer look. Like most other entrepreneurial individualists, connective leaders are seldom driven by the need for power or glory. They are motivated much more by intrinsic forces, by their need to understand, explore, and build. They just plain like to make things happen, particularly things that have never happened before. Although they vary from one another and in the kinds of leadership roles they play, they share a compelling drive to push beyond existing boundaries.

They also tend to be thinkers. They need not be great thinkers, or philosophers, theorists, or theologians, but they are people who like to use their heads, who like ideas, and like to solve puzzles. Nor are they averse to philosophy, theory, or theology.

What most differentiates connectives from many other entrepreneurial types is their readiness to do things with others. They don't have to do it all themselves. Doing it with others is their way of life. They see and value the connections among unlikely people and unlikely ideas. Diversity of almost any kind doesn't disturb them. They thrive on it. In fact, they have the skills to bring together very different groups. They can identify oases of mutuality even among the fiercest antagonists.

Because hot group leaders are connective, they often don't look—from the outside—like stereotypical leaders. You'll seldom find them riding on great white stallions far ahead of the adoring masses. It's not that they are low key or self-effacing. It's just that in hot groups everybody is influential and active, so the group's leader, if there is one, doesn't stand out sharply from the crowd. Moreover, connective leaders willingly move aside to let others ride in front. They use their wide range of achieving styles to attract, inspire, and entrust others, to facilitate and contribute to the goal.

Many company rulebooks require that every organizational unit must be ruled by a single, specified, enduring leader. Organizations usually back up those designated leaders by adding extra gold stars of authority to their uniforms. No such requirement can be found in hot groups. In our information age, the big stick of authority is rapidly shrinking to toothpick size. Some hot group leaders may wear lots of gold stars, but that's not what makes them good hot group leaders. It's their drive, dedication, their capacity to enthuse, and, most of all, their connective sensibilities that make other members of hot groups want to work with them.

Connective leaders are not lone rangers. They are men and women with two seemingly contradictory characteristics: They are team players, yet they have strong egos. Their ego strength allows them to feel quite comfortable working with others. Connective leaders are willing, even eager, to share plans, goals, and glory, and to incorporate multiple approaches and multiple ideas into their thinking. But while they like working with others, they don't like massive bureaucracies. They prefer small groups and direct, face-to-face relationships.

Three Kinds of Connective Leaders: Conductors, Patrons, and Keepers of the Flame

Connective leaders can further be divided into at least three subsets:

1. One set we call *conductors*—as in orchestra, not railroad, conductors. They are the hands-on, here-and-now leaders of hot groups.

2. A second set are *patrons* of hot groups. They are leaders once removed. They are larger scale growers, supporting and championing the development of many hot groups, though they seldom participate actively in the groups they help to form. They are the unobtrusive needles that stitch hot groups to their parent organizations.

3. The third set we call *keepers of the flame*. They are leaders who carry on from one task to the next. They build the connective bridges that allow ideas and projects to move from one stage to another. They maintain the connections, through thick and thin, from task to task and from group to group.

Leaders of Hot Groups 1: Conductors

Conductors are working leaders of hot groups. When conductors encounter a challenging idea, they immediately set about putting together a group. Conductors are often, but not always, rather outgoing, charismatic personalities who find it easy to persuade and inspire others. Some are quieter and quite undramatic, yet also capable of evoking great music from the orchestra. Their competence, integrity, and deep knowledge are enough to attract and stimulate others.

In general, conductors are at their best in face-to-face settings, where their dedicated styles inspire the initial motivation needed to solidify their groups. Often, conductors turn up as the inspirational leaders of small, innovative companies. More rarely, they can be found leading small, semi-autonomous, and usually temporary units within major companies. The conductors who do manage to prosper in large companies are likely to be highly visible. Their voices, though not always welcomed, are always heard. They become foci of much talk and gossip, most of which may be less than flattering. Everybody knows their names.

Conductor/leaders need not be the only leaders in the groups they initiate, though they usually set the high standards that draw the best from their members. In this hot group, today's follower may become tomorrow's leader, as one part of the task, requiring one set of skills, is supplanted by another. In that group, leadership may be widely distributed, with almost everyone playing, at one point or another, both leader and supporter roles, as their achieving styles dictate. The formal leader, at any given moment, is not set apart from the group. He or she is simply the first among equals. Such variation and dispersion of leadership are not surprising. It is what we should expect, given the flexible, dynamic structures of hot groups.

Leaders of Hot Groups 2: Patrons

Patrons are to groups what mentors are to individuals. In fact, mentors are often also patrons. Patrons are connective leaders who play indirect leadership roles. They encourage and sustain hot groups but do not themselves participate on a day-to-day basis.

They catalyze the formation of hot groups as well as protect, support, and nourish them. In large organizations, patrons are particularly valuable. They are horticulturists, sowing the seeds, tilling the soil, and warding off pests and predators. Although a pathfinding, charismatic conductor may spark and lead a single group, a patron is more likely to nourish a whole field of flowering hot groups, a field that continuously reseeds itself.

Patrons are frequently respected senior members of organizations, people who have earned enough brownie points to feel secure in their positions. They tend to act unobtrusively, sometimes almost invisibly, as second, rather than first-order leaders. They behave more like coaches than star players. In large organizations, many people don't even know their names—but those who do respect and appreciate them.

Examples of patrons are familiar to us all: the high school teacher who inspired groups of students to seek out and take on difficult and exciting challenges. Or that soft spoken, upper-level executive who somehow mentored most of the company's current crop of top executives. In organizations, patrons are the people you or I would approach with a great new idea when we need the support, resources, and wisdom to help us get it off the ground. Many patrons become something like impresarios, championing and sponsoring large numbers of hot groups.

We once worked with Science Applications International (SAIC), a California company that is now quite large. Its founder is just such an impresario. Dr. Robert Beyster built his organization by searching the nation, and later the world, for struggling but promising little hot groups of scientists. Leaving them wherever he found them, he invited them to join the company. "Joining" simply meant that he provided each group with enough of a financial umbrella to let it carry on with its beloved tasks until it bore both scientific and financial fruit.

A few years after he began, we counted twenty-three such groups in SAIC, in as many different locations. As consultants, we gravely advised Dr. Beyster that he just couldn't go on in that helter-skelter way. He'd better get all those scattered bits and pieces organized and controlled. Fortunately—and characteristically—he ignored us. The company, a company not so much of individuals as of groups, now has upwards of 400 such units, far more widely scattered. Despite our initial doomsday forecasts, SAIC continues to prosper. Its sales in 1997 were over $3.2 billion. The company recently acquired a very large unit of another company—one with a much more traditional structure—for almost $1 billion. What the acquisition will mean for the open, federalist form that has characterized SAIC remains to be seen.

Why, one might ask, should patrons want to be patrons? What's in it for them? Why should savvy veterans stick their necks out to back long-shot hot groups? Patrons' motivations are varied and complex. Often, they do it for the best of all reasons, just because they believe that a particular project is really worth doing. Sometimes they are more strategically motivated, believing that many small lively units are just what their organizations need. Much of the time, like coaches who were once players, they are themselves ex-members of hot groups. Hence, they appreciate both the worthiness and the difficulties of such groups. Sometimes, they believe in the originators of the idea and want to support them. Some patrons are entrepreneurial refugees from stolid, immutable bureaucracies, ex-slaves who want to make sure the people of their current organizations never suffer the same fate. And of course some patrons are driven by "self-interest, rightly understood."[7] By backing a promising hot group, a patron may be trying to earn his or her own brownie points. "If that group comes through with a major win, I'll be a hero."

Here's one example of a patron's rationale for backing hot groups.

> Each day, the director of a major research lab meets for breakfast with a different one of his many first-line supervisors. He listens to their problems, helps them when they need help, and urges them onward. He knows he is bypassing two layers of intermediate managers, and he knows they don't like it at all. His motivation: He wants to make sure his first-line teams—the teams who "do the real work around here"—will never have to fight their way up through multiple layers of the bureaucracy to get the support they need.

That particular patron doesn't work backstage. He's right up front. He figures his middle managers will just have to live with their boss's idiosyncrasy.

Conductors and patrons very often work together, the conductor out there doing it and the patron in the protective backup role, providing resources and protection from predators. In Warren Bennis's *Organizing Genius*, which includes several fascinating studies of highly creative groups, he points out the same phenomenon. "Many Great Groups have a dual administration. They have a visionary leader, [read 'conductor'], and they have someone who protects them from the outside world, 'the suits' [read 'patrons']."[8]

Leaders of Hot Groups 3: Keepers of the Flame

Keepers of the flame (KOFs) are those men and women who stick stubbornly to the task, staying with it, pushing it ahead, all the way through to its full implementation. They are a special breed of connective leaders whose continuing commitment provides organizations with the connective tissue they need. Keepers of the flame are vital because, in the real world, "completed" tasks are almost never completed. Work on an initial task invariably generates new, related tasks, which, in turn, open up still others. When one hot group ends, KOFs are the ones who push the follow-ons that spring from the original task.

Examples of KOFs, like examples of hot groups, are all around us. Here is one from family life that we hope will feel familiar to many readers:

> Think back, if you will, to some brisk Thanksgiving Thursday afternoon not so long ago. Remember how, before the whole family sat down to dinner, three or four children and maybe a couple of adults, too, would go to work on a huge jigsaw puzzle? They would sit and stand and move noisily around the bridge table, shrieking gleefully every time another piece was inserted, squabbling now and then, but always deeply involved in their important endeavor. Someone might more or less take charge for a time, but what really drove the process was the magnetism of the task itself. The puzzle was all the motivating challenge anyone needed—for a while.
>
> In our family, working on those puzzles was usually a lively and rather messy process. "Workers" would join in and then, when they felt like it, they would opt out. A pair of grandchildren might be crawling underfoot in search of a piece that had fallen on the floor. Two participants might suddenly decide they'd prefer to feed the

squirrels, so they abandon the group. Another is summoned to duties in the kitchen, so he departs, too—for a while. Uncle Harry and Aunt Polly and their children arrive late, as always. They join the puzzle crew. And out of the chaos, the puzzle-picture—a pastoral winter landscape—begins to take shape.

When dinner is finally ready, everybody quits and heads for the turkey—everybody, that is, except Emily. She is the keeper of the flame. She stays behind, continuing to work on the puzzle, stopping reluctantly only when Mother insists—for the third time—that she come to the table RIGHT NOW! Even so, as soon as she can manage to excuse herself, Emily heads back to the puzzle, sticking with it as more fickle souls continue to arrive and depart. She calls others back to work. She recruits new arrivals. She hangs in there until the last piece has been fitted into place.

Keepers of the flame, like Emily, are the ones who stay with the task. They are also the ones, though this example doesn't show it, who stay with successor tasks, from stage to stage, through time and trouble. KOFs carry on, finishing the unfinished, attracting others to work on the interesting new problems spawned by the old ones. Unlike patrons, they participate actively in each group, but also unlike conductors, they don't necessarily lead the groups they spawn. Their most vital role is connective. They are the thread that is drawn from the first through the second and on to multiple related groups.

What Kinds of Hot Group Leaders in What Kinds of Situations?

Hot groups are not all alike. Conductors of hot groups are not all alike either, nor are patrons or KOFs. Their personalities and styles vary with the situations in which their hot groups arise. Consider, for example, these three quite different kinds of hot group situations and the most probable characteristics of their leaders.

Dissident, Protesting Hot Groups and the Kinds of People Likely to Lead Them

Those few hot groups that somehow find a way to sprout and grow in bureaucratic organizations are likely to be viewed as disruptive, potential threats to organizational law and order. Those groups then usually reciprocate by fulfilling that prophecy. They try to battle their way into a tenuous existence. Usually they fail. The organization stomps on them before they get much chance to develop. Sometimes, however, despite the organization's best efforts, such hot groups succeed. Indeed, sometimes, like some trade unions and minority groups, they gather strength and eventually work out an accommodation with their host organizations. Later, for example, we shall describe how, early in World War II, General Claire Chennault's dissident little group of Flying Tigers had to struggle until it finally won a respectable place in the U.S. Army Air Corps.

Such upstart groups usually rally behind a single, acknowledged leader. Excited by an idea that others disdain or, more likely, turned off by what they see happening around them, a small daring set of people joins together. The members around a central, persuasive, usually charismatic individual. In such embattled groups, those central figures are likely to be the toughest fighters, the most outspoken, most committed, most articulate, and most persistent members of their groups. They are the Gorbachevs and the Gingriches, the leaders of revolutions. Unmistakably identifiable because they stand visibly out in front of the rest, they are also likely to be among the first to be shot down.

Hot Groups Born in Crises: Who Is Likely to Lead Them?

Crises provide a very different kind of seedbed for hot groups. A crisis is just the kind of all-consuming task that hot groups love. What is more likely to grab everyone's undivided attention than the sudden winds and darkening clouds of an approaching disaster? Again, as with dissident groups, individual leaders almost always take initial command in crisis situations. That happens for at least two reasons: First, when a crisis occurs in an already highly structured organization, pre-established rules and expectations dictate who should lead. The lieutenant leads the platoon, and should she fall, the sergeant takes command, and then the corporal, and so on. Second, in the anxious atmosphere accompanying a crisis, most of us, whether in organizations or not, usually turn for reassurance to those in positions of authority or expertise. If there's a fire, we expect the firefighters (who also expect) to take a leadership role. If there's an illness, is there a doctor in the house?

Authority and expertise, however, are not always where crisis leaders come from, nor should they be. Max Weber taught us long ago that charismatic leaders are "born of distress," in times when the standard old solutions won't work.[9] In the absence of a formal system, those who initially lead in a crisis are likely to be the most self-assured, most assertive members, but those individuals do not necessarily remain leaders throughout the critical period. In crises, while leaders show up very quickly, they are judged almost as swiftly, and, if found wanting, are replaced. At the beginning of World War II, Prime Minister Neville Chamberlain was soon replaced by Winston Churchill. In many cases, unfortunately, such leaders are not replaced quickly enough.

The criteria for leadership change in crises, as do the bureaucratic constraints that normally delay action,[10] but those criteria and constraints often change too late. The crisis overwhelms us because our leader, though inappropriate, doesn't step down (or get pushed out). Unfortunately, many chief executives, generals, and presidents, from Captain Queeg of the *USS Caine*[11] to Saddam Hussein of Iraq, hang on too long. Moreover, some leaders who were indeed effective during a crisis continue even when the crisis is over, only to be stripped of their heroic stature when they try to lead in calmer, colder times. Winston Churchill, after his intrepid leadership during World War II, met just that fate in the postwar period.

Leaders of Hot Groups in Supportive Environments

In organizations that actively try to breed hot groups, the leadership process usually works something like this: One or more entrepreneurial people, somewhere in the organization, become turned on to a great idea. Maybe Helen has just returned from a seminar, excited about a new approach to an old problem. Maybe Mark has just made an accidental discovery of a potentially important new drug. Maybe Sam wakes up one night inspired by a dream about a new set of flavors for the company's ice cream. Maybe Louise becomes so irritated by some frustrating procedures that she vows to streamline the whole system. Whatever their intent, those people do enough front-end work to make a persuasive pitch to the people higher up, the ones who control the needed resources. If they are given a green light, they then go hunting. They hunt for space, equipment, and, most of all, for people. Typically they search for people one or two ranks down the organizational ladder from themselves, special people who are already deeply interested in the core idea. Conductors implicitly and reasonably consider themselves the boss of this new group. They had the idea, and they got the money. They are the entrepreneurs. Of course, as in the Rain Bird case, some conductors know how to jump start a hot group even in much less supportive circumstances.

The chances are pretty good, in a supportive surrounding, however, that such newly forming groups will heat up. Three important requirements have been met: First, they have one or more potential conductors who feel deeply committed to a task; second, they now have a reasonably open playing field; that is, they have received an initial go signal from those with organizational clout; and third, they have rounded up some relevant, turned-on people to join their crew.

We don't know how much time or freedom the new group will be given. If their champions were smart, however, they inserted a generous deadline into their arrangements with the folks upstairs.

Some Characteristics Needed by All Hot Group Leaders

Whatever their origin, some common denominators are shared by all hot groups. Here are some of those commonalties and the characteristics leaders need to deal with them:

- *Hot groups tend to use cut-and-try strategies, so leaders have to be comfortable with ambiguity and near-chaos.*

Typically, as we shall see in Chapter 8, hot groups go about their work by first trying one tack, then another, until they find one that seems to move them a few steps ahead. They then iterate the process, beginning at that new point. From the outside looking in, that approach may look disorderly and nonlogical. We mention that "muddling through"[12] approach here to emphasize that hot group leaders need to be highly tolerant of ambiguity. They have to feel comfortable with relatively unplanned, spontaneous styles of working. Conductors and patrons of hot groups get into trouble if they insist on laying out carefully crafted, step-by-step blueprints for their groups.

Hot groups are quite unorderly—or so it seems—in other ways, too. They may engage in loud debates, with several people talking at once. Confrontational disputes are common. A group may suddenly want to take an afternoon off. So leaders, especially conductors, have to be secure enough to deal gently with such jumbled behavior. Leaders with a strong need to tidy things up are not likely to keep a hot group hot very long.

• *Many hot groups are politically naïve, so their leaders have to be politically savvy.*

Every group is a piece of the active, buzzing, crowded new world, a world that will necessarily intrude on the group's privacy, nattering at it, making demands on it. Nor is all that just a one-way street. Not only must the world pester the hot group, the group must also pester the outside world. Much as they might want to get away from it all, hot groups, just like the rest of us, need the help of others. This interdependency can cause serious problems for group leaders. Many hot group members, absorbed in their task, don't much want to get involved with the down and dirty realities of organizational life. They don't want to raise money, or put on shows for the boss, or try to charm administrators. Issues of power and politics are not their thing. Their attitudes about such matters can be quite defensive. When people feel politically naïve and inept, they may take a holier-than-thou stance, pompously asserting something like, "We didn't come here to waste time with those lightweights. We have important things to do!"

Whether its source is arrogance, ignorance, or fear, such political naïveté is a common failing of hot groups, one that leaves them vulnerable in the predatory organizational world. Their self-confidence can mask their political ineptitude, even from themselves. The real predators out there—not the ones they set up to increase their own pulse rates—can trip them up before they know what's hit them.

The leaders of hot groups, therefore, whether conductors, patrons, or keepers of the flame, need to understand the workings of the larger systems in which their groups are embedded and the points of connection between those systems and their groups. Someone—either the group's conductor or patron—has to have the know-how to gain the backing of the right people in the right power positions. Someone must be able to negotiate skillfully for time, money, space, equipment, and people. Someone must be capable of fending off higher level executives who step in—as they often do—to make premature, perhaps ill-informed decisions that can do serious harm to the group. Hot groups need protection from other groups, too, those organizational units whose real or imagined territories they may be invading. Hot group leaders who have strong personal and social instrumental achieving styles typically have the system savvy for such tasks.

Most such problems, most of the time, should and will be piled onto the shoulders of group leaders. Those leaders need to know whom and how to persuade, cajole, or fight. They need to understand when to hold out and when to give in, how to negotiate and with whom. They need to establish the right alliances and the right friendships. In a word, using the broadest range of achieving styles, they have to be able to operate comfortably and ethically inside the circles of organizational power and politics.

Patrons are likely to be good on that political front. Most are veterans of past organizational wars. They've been around. They are not as consumed as conductors with their hot group's search for its pot of gold. They can work more subtly, lobbying behind the scenes rather than on center stage. Not caught up in the nitty-gritty, they can link hot groups to their parent organization and other relevant outsiders. Patrons are, therefore, in a good position to champion their hot groups' interests, protecting them from would-be despoilers. Conversely, they are also in a good position to cool down overheated groups, persuading them to back off from potentially suicidal acts of bravado.

Conductors, too, must be politically sensitive. They aren't usually as knowledgeable or experienced as patrons, but they had better not be innocents and, fortunately, most are not. There seems to be a natural selection process that goes on with conductors of hot groups. The ones who get chosen (or volunteer) are seldom political innocents. Many carry—often proudly—the scars of past bureaucratic battles. If they are astute enough to succeed in putting a hot group together, they are also likely to have at least a modicum of savvy about political and social networks. At worst, they are fast learners. In any event, they had better make it a point to develop what one of us has elsewhere[13] called the art of "denatured Machiavellianism."

"Denatured Machiavellianism" involves *ethical* political skill. Successful connective leaders, particularly patrons, are usually adept at it. They understand and use the "system" and everyone and everything in and around it for the good of the group—not to enhance their own personal power. Like most other hot group members, conductors have their noses to the ground, intent on sniffing out the path to their grail. So they are apt to be quite insensitive to issues of organizational politics.

Whoever assumes it, the political role must be played and played well if a hot group is to survive inside a large organization. Human organizations, after all, are more than just economic and social institutions. They are also political systems.[14] Every organization has its core stakeholders, relevant constituencies, factions, and self-interested politicians. The leaders of hot groups had better be capable of dealing with all of them.

In these times, those interdependencies among very diverse groups extend well beyond any organization's boundaries. The conductors and patrons of hot groups, like all modern leaders, must look outward, too. Leadership for the third millennium will require a vision that extends, in both time and space, far beyond the local scene. It will also require more connectivity than authority, more capacity to develop alliances than to defeat enemies, and more skill in identifying common interests than insoluble differences.[15]

• *Hot groups' leaders need to be sensitive to their groups' interpersonal problems, even if members don't pay much attention to them.*

Conductors may not be as well schooled as patrons on matters of power and politics, but that isn't their primary job. Their primary job is with their particular group and its particular task, with getting that task done and getting it done right. They are seldom trained in general management. More likely, they are expert in some specialized area related to the task and are personally committed to the task. Yet, although conductors and patrons need not be professional counseling psychologists, they had better not ignore the psychological aspects of their jobs. Though hot groups' intense focus on task overrides interpersonal problems, it does not solve them. So whether or not other group members are sensitive to time bombs ticking within or between individuals, wise conductors are always scanning and listening for them.

Leaders? Some Hot Groups Just Grow Without Them

At the beginning of this chapter, we asserted that many hot groups have no identifiable single leader. We want to reemphasize that point here, with examples:

- In California, several design engineers in an aerospace company believe they are on to an important idea. They want to develop it, but need technical support. They talk it up with a few buddies. A potential hot group begins to sprout.

- Over lunch one day, in Cambridge, Massachusetts, three young faculty members in three separate departments of a university discover that they share an interest in related aspects of a challenging problem. The group begins to build up heat.

- In an Asian city, four friends, all primary school teachers, feel dissatisfied with the educational bureaucracy. They decide to open an entirely new kind of private school. The heat rises. Wow! Let's just do it!

In such self-generated groups, leadership may be neither clear nor relevant. The traditional distinction between leader and follower simply doesn't apply.

Why Even Worry About Leaders and Leadership?

If leadership is such a slippery, messy concept, and if many hot—and cold—groups manage to operate without leaders, why do so many sensible people worry about it? Perhaps because, deep in our psyches, we are ambivalent about leaders. We want them and often need them, yet we fear them. We want omnipotent leaders to help us maintain the illusion that they will protect us from the existential dangers of life and from our pervasive fear of death.[16]

As we mature, however, we learn that it ain't necessarily so; that our leaders, too, are endowed with clay feet. Yet, our dread is usually more than sufficient to counter our rationality. We want the reassurance that someone is protecting us from whatever lurks in the scary shadows. We also don't mind having someone around to take the blame for the inevitable fallout that always accompanies complex decisions. So we set up leaders and invest them with godlike attributes, even as we also resent the obedience bills we have to pay.

Mature human beings will probably always need groups, but must they also always need leaders? Not always, perhaps, but surely very often. And although most leaders can't save us from our mortality, many can surely help us to reach for the stars.

In Summary

Some hot groups don't have any clear leaders, but most do. Those leaders are of three kinds. Hands-on, working leaders we call "conductors." They lead the band. Hands-off, but supportive "patron" leaders help with resources and political backup. They are usually powerful senior figures. The third set, "keepers of the flame," are group members who carry on when the hot group's task is completed, coalescing new hot groups to make sure that follow-on tasks get done.

Hot groups are so focused on task that they are often naïve about issues of power and politics. Most hot groups need all three kinds of leaders to help them gather needed resources and survive the hazards of the organizational jungle. The next chapter, therefore, continues to focus on leaders, but in a more how-to-do-it way. It considers some of the practical and specific steps conductors and patrons can take to lead and maintain hot groups inside large organizations.

6

Leaders of Hot Groups II: Some Options for the Leader of a New Group

Leading a hot group is more like leading a rough-and-tumble political campaign than working at a steady government job. It's much more like leading a military squad in a tough combat situation than managing an ongoing operating unit of a large company. Hot groups, that is, are hot. They are here, and they are now, vitally, intensely, actively involved in pursuing their task. So, to lead them, a leader must think more like a campaign manager than a civil servant, more like an infantry officer than an accountant. Treat your group as what it is: a small enclave of dedicated human beings in a hurry to do an important job. Don't view it as a system, or a set of job descriptions, or a hierarchy of authority.

Some of those distinctions are made clear in a study comparing military and civilian leadership in Israel.[1] The author, Micha Popper, illustrates the points by quoting the distinctly different comments made by a business executive and a battalion commander. The executive describes his job this way:

> In my work I know exactly where we all stand, where everything belongs. We have specific job descriptions, certain ways to dress every day, we have names and titles, . . . we have clear identities. I am

a vice president. Three hundred and fifty people who report to me all have a certain rank on the ladder. . . . Nothing is blurred by friendship or emotion. (p. 19)

That executive feels much clearer and more well ordered about his organization than most of the executives we know, but his description sets the contrast for this comment by an Israeli battalion commander:

The battalion cannot be defined as just a place of work. It is a way of life, a shared tradition. . . . the battalion is a home that will be hard to leave. (p. 20)

A hot group, because its life is usually short, may not be quite like a battalion, but the personal commitment and the sense of community are there. In certain respects, the hot group leader's job is even more difficult than the battalion commander's. Although we usually stereotype the military as all order and discipline, emotional solidarity in a military unit is quite consistent with military culture and tradition. Senior officers want their battalions to feel a sense of cohesion and pride. In many business organizations, however, a hot group's sense of unity may stand in sharp contrast and sometimes in direct opposition to the larger culture of its bureaucratic parent. Could a hot group, for example, possibly feel welcome in the organization described by that Israeli executive?

For our present purposes, let's not assume either extreme: neither an organization that despises hot groups, nor one that loves them. Let's assume a reasonably flexible organization, moderately tolerant of small semi-autonomous task groups. Given such an environment, we now ask the reader to do a little role playing. Whatever your real occupational role, please, temporarily, don the hat of a middle manager right in the middle of that middle-of-the-road organization. You are starting a new project and forming a new group. Pick any group you wish: an engineering team working on a new product, an *ad hoc* crisis management team coping with the aftermath of a disastrous tornado, a small group in a financial institution preparing for a major sales presentation, or a group of secondary school teachers designing a new curriculum. You are a would-be conductor of that group, and you want it to develop a hot group state of mind. Now, what can you, conductor, do to irrigate, fertilize, and prepare the soil so that your group is likely to heat up, become deeply committed to its task and highly effective in doing it?

We offer a baker's dozen of suggestions. Some are new, others have been mentioned earlier.

• *Think and act "people first," not "task first."*

To develop a hot group, a leader needs a theory. Not an elaborate theory, not even an explicit, conscious theory, but a theory nonetheless. There is nothing, an astute observer once pointed out, as practical as a good theory. Consider these two sharply contrasting theories:

1. Task-first theory. A bad bet for developing a hot group.

Hot groups are task obsessed. Yet, counterintuitive as it seems, if potential hot group leaders begin building their groups by thinking task first, they will very likely fail. Task-first theory works from the task backward. It begins by analyzing and decomposing the projected task. If you think task first, you will probably work in this order: (a) Analyze the task. Break it down into subparts. (b) Lay out a structure of jobs appropriate for the various parts. (c) Find the right people to perform each job and assign them appropriately.

If you think that way, your chances of developing a hot group will be slim. You may end up with a good task force, and it may even be successful. The various parts may mesh nicely, or they may not. The people may also mesh well and even become a highly cohesive group, or they may not. But envisioned in that rational/analytic way, there is only a low probability that such a gathering of individual specialists will become a hot group.

2. People-first theory. A much better bet for starting a hot group.

Alternatively, you can begin by thinking *people first*. People-first theory works from people forward, rather than task backward. It begins by asking "Who and where are the people I need to help me on this undertaking?" You, not your boss or the HR department, will begin actively searching among a broad set of candidates potentially relevant for your task. You will keep on searching until you find a few knowledgeable people who become excited about this adventure and who, in turn, send the word out over their personal networks to help recruit other colleagues. You may have to do much of this quietly, for security reasons, but it can be done.

Your search must be active, not passive. Beginning with only a general sense of the number and variety of people you want, go forth to proselytize and excite the relevant people. Make them eager to join. Push forward from there. Now you can use the nuclear group to help analyze the task and choose tentative initial steps. Gather ideas. Try this, and try that, building as you go. If you approach your task in that participative, people-first way, the chances of developing a hot group are much better.

The analytic reader may well argue that the people-first approach may attract the most motivated people, but it won't identify the best specialists in each relevant part of the task. That could indeed be true, although one would hope that the best candidates would want to get a crack at this task, too. Even, however, if your new group ends up staffed by excellent people, but still lacks some needed skills, fear not. Life is full of tradeoffs, and this may just be a very good one. Don't forget that hot groups are dynamic. They can learn, and they can change. Indeed, we would venture this observation: Better a set of good generalists passionately committed to the task than a collection of good specialists whose interest in the task is low or whose egos are so large that they eclipse the task.

Suppose, for instance, that a young hot group, working on a tough problem, hits a glitch and finds that it doesn't have enough knowledge or skill to handle it. What happens? One of two things: (a) The group goes and gets the help it needs. Members seek out specialists or consultants, or they recruit new members who *do* have the needed knowledge or skill. Or (b) the group's members simply learn to do it themselves. Indeed, hot groups are often the first to learn how to do things that no one else has ever done.

A small example of such self-learning appeared in a news story in the *Straits Times* of Singapore:

> Mr. Lim Ching San, managing director of Octogram [a Singaporean design firm] can breathe more easily now that his product is a hit. . . .

But in the early days, Mr. Lim wondered if he would "lose his shirt" on the venture.

"This business is not for the fainthearted," he said. When he came up with the idea two years ago, CD-ROMs were new technology.... Mr. Lim and a team of nine created MAC-graphics. *All had to teach themselves how to make a CD-ROM.* [Our italics] Sleeping on the office bed to meet deadlines happened often, he said.[2]

A general rule:

> To help develop a hot, task-obsessed group, think about people before you begin laying out a flow chart. Bring on the people. Getting the task done is not your solo job. It's the whole group's job.

• *Part of leadership is a dramatic art, so use your whole self, your persona.*

Some of what most of us call "leadership" is a form of acting. That doesn't mean that leadership is, as one thoughtful writer called it, all "humbuggery and manipulation."[3] It means that leaders, on occasion, have to dramatize themselves.

To be a good actor, one must use one's self—all aspects of one's self—as an instrument of influence and persuasion. That, too, is part of being a connective leader. In achieving styles terms, it means using the *personal instrumental* style. If a newly formed, people-first group begins to heat up, you can be reasonably sure that its leader or someone has been doing a lot of that, using his or her individual self to spark the group, set high standards, inspire dedication and enthusiasm among its members. Hot group leaders are not just hollow shells. Often, an articulate group leader, starting off with cool, even skeptical people, can still heat them up by dramatically articulating the group's possibilities.

Charismatic, inspirational "evangelists" are generally frowned on by both the business and academic communities, except perhaps in sales. Such extroverted behavior—like Donald Trump's or Ted Turner's—is likely to be seen as somewhat unprofessional or even a bit uncouth, by the conservative, white-shoe establishment. So like any good actor, a conductor will calibrate his or her performances to the audience, not pushing too far and too fast beyond local norms and values. A soft word or a smile may show passion enough in one setting, while another may require the leader to emote vigorously and shout loudly.

We need to distinguish here between Machiavellian manipulation and what we earlier called denatured Machiavellianism. When leaders try to manipulate their groups solely in their own interests, that behavior is neither ethical, nor will it work in a hot group. Trying to stimulate passion for a trivial task won't fly very long, nor will inauthentic preaching about ennoblement.

On the other hand, using one's self in "denatured" Machiavellian ways can be both appropriate and functional. That use of self means more than just the expression of one's personality. It means being aware of whatever attributes happen to attach to you and using them as tools. It might mean, in some situations, using the status or social class of your family for fund raising. It might mean using your close relationships to famous or powerful people to gain protection for your group. Perhaps you happen to be well-liked throughout the organization, or you are a highly respected member of a relevant profession. You can use those aspects of yourself to help recruit and gain the autonomy and resources your group needs. Perhaps your long, unbroken record of successes can be used to generate confidence among group members. With such a winning leader, members can feel, "Our group may really be able to do the impossible."

We meritocratic Americans tend to feel uncomfortable employing such methods, viewing them as self-serving and pushy. The British, of course, probably believe we Yanks are self-serving and pushy enough already—in comparison to them. In many other cultures, however,—in Asia and southern Europe—such behavior is the daily stuff of which influence is made. This new era of interconnectedness is the time for us to rethink our attitudes and hone our instrumental skills, not for self-aggrandizement, but for the larger good.

We offer this general suggestion for would-be conductors:

> To get a hot group started, use everything you've got, not just your intellect.

• *Great work is not enough! You also have to sell it.*

Of the organizational hot groups we know who are not in marketing most don't like to sell their products. Aside from those in marketing, many hot groups just don't like the idea of selling anything.
A few are willing to, but most see marketing and selling as peripheral to their main purpose and mostly unpalatable. They just want to
create something new and brilliant, sure that its appeal will be self-
evident, drawing buyers like ants to honey. Just solving that huge
problem should be enough to earn them a tickertape parade
through the executive suite.

Many hot group members simply take their pleasure intrinsically,
in knowing for themselves that they have done something worthwhile. We've reached the summit of Everest, or we've found the
lost treasure, or we've rescued the family whose house floated away
in the flood. What more can you want from us?

In the organizational world, however, the right answer is not
likely to be the whole answer. The rest has to do with getting other
parts of the organization and the world to believe, accept, and use
your group's earth-shaking breakthrough. Failing that, your great
output could—as so many have—quickly sink deep into the sea of
the forgotten and foregone.

Intentionally or not, hot group members too often ignore and
even scorn those "ancillary" parts of the task. "We aren't salesmen.
We've done something great. Now it's up to you guys." That attitude,
unfortunately, can so infuriate relevant others that the net effect is to
shrink support for the hot group's truly beautiful new baby. Which
brings us back to you, Ms. or Mr. hot group conductor. Two of your
unenviable jobs are (1) to restrain your group's assertive, but often
politically guileless, members, lest they irreparably damage the whole
group's relationship with other units of the organization; and (2) to
build, actively, the most positive relations you can with other relevant
groups inside and outside your institution.

Hot groups, especially technical hot groups, can be incredibly
blind and stubborn about this relational issue. Many have been imbued so long with the true analytic religion that they will even abandon their beloved task before they soil their sinless souls with such
stuff as organizational networking. We still remember an old acade-

mic friend who, after years of hard work, had just come up with some fascinating and potentially very useful research findings. When we asked if he had thought about how his research might be applied, he reacted as though we had insulted him. "I don't do that sort of thing! I do research!" he replied and stomped out of the room.

Group leaders in real-world organizations have to shepherd such principled—perhaps overly principled—people, to encourage and reward their contributions to the task, protect them from evil, but also prevent them from doing major harm to the group's cause. So, as a conductor of a hot group, you would do well to seek counsel from a wise patron about how to make yourself a card-carrying member of your organization's old boys' and girls' networks. It is you leaders,—conductors, patrons, and keepers of the flame—who must form the alliances, build the relationships, and make the connections that will cause your group's output to be implemented. Your group may be able to handle the technical and professional networks, but when it comes to application and implementation, it is most often you who must carry the ball.

We have another general suggestion:

> You are the main link between your group and your organization, so (a) understand and appreciate the strengths and weaknesses of each and (b) guard that link well. Make sure that neither side weakens it. Otherwise, your group's good work may just rust away into oblivion.

• *Identify a new worthy task or find ways to make an existing task more worthy.*

In this context, "worthy" can have at least three meanings:

1. A worthy task can mean an *intellectually* difficult task, a challenge, a puzzle, a conundrum.

2. A worthy task can mean an *implementationally* difficult task, one that requires arduous, Herculean feats, actions that test the group's physical and/or psychological mettle.

3. A worthy task can mean a *morally* appropriate task, one that is worth doing because it has positive social value.

Of course, a task may be worthy in all three senses. In each case, the sense of worthiness emanates, at least partially, from the task itself. The task creates a powerful magnetic field, drawing even reluctant observers into its orbit. Moreover, when a task initially looks boring and unchallenging, but is connected to some larger, more significant task, even the menial can become worthy. Remember Rudyard Kipling's "Gunga Din,"[4] about the Indian servant distributing water to the troops in the midst of battle? A wounded British colonial welcomes the blessed drink with these words:

> Though I've belted you and flayed you,
> By the livin' Gawd that made you,
> You're a better man than I am, Gunga Din!

Spending long hours in a downpour filling sandbags may not look very "worthy" unless those bags are being filled to hold back the flood waters that threaten to engulf your town. Welding steel plates all day may not be a turn-on either, unless those plates are being welded onto the hull of a desperately needed destroyer in wartime. Even the dullest task, when part of a larger cause, can help your group to heat up pretty rapidly.

Ultimately, though, worthiness lies in the eye of the beholder. Here, as in so many situations, the perceived world is the only relevant world. If the task itself does not have enough power to attract people, can you increase its attraction by tacking on your own enthusiasm and excitement? Or by connecting it to something bigger and more challenging? Almost all managers can. Few do.

If you, yourself, are generally uncomfortable about showing great passion and excitement, you may—inadvertently—be communicating disapproval, disinterest, uncertainty, or cynicism, any of which can quickly cool down your group. So introspect a little. Ask yourself (or your friends or significant other) whether you, perhaps unconsciously, shy away from showing any outward signs of deep commitment. If you do, work on it. Otherwise, you may be neutralizing much of your task's intrinsic pull and your group's all-out dedication.

We leave it to you to decide for yourself when it feels morally acceptable to use your own behavior to impassion others, a power that your leadership role has enhanced and lent to you. Be aware, too, that such power has limits. You may be able to convince a child, as Woody Allen says his parents did, that although he couldn't have a dog, an ant, with a thread as its leash, was a worthy substitute. We suggest, however, that you do not try something as far out as that on a lively, already warming group. The best way for a leader to convince a group that a task is worthy is to identify one that every potential group member—especially you—truly feels is intrinsically worth doing.

Two rules of thumb:

1. If a task turns you on, it is likely to turn on others. If it doesn't excite you, don't expect it to excite your people.

2. If a task does turn you on, say so, loudly and clearly!

• *When possible, keep your group in an underdog position.*

When a respected figure or group higher up in the organization deprecates your group's efforts, the group is likely to become angry and upset, causing it to cool down. When an important *outside* competitor does exactly the same thing—ignores or ridicules what your group is trying to do—the effects are likely to be precisely the opposite. Their "insult" will be read as a challenge, strengthening the group's resolve and sharply raising even a cold group's temperature. When our competitor is favored to win, most of us feel an extra bounce from that competitive stimulation. Let the other team feel they're smarter and bigger and better than we are. That will really energize us. When, on the other hand, a group believes its competitor is stupid and weak, even a charismatic coach may have trouble raising the team's temperature. It's hard to charge up a team of great big rugby players preparing for a game against Lilliputians.

This cultural preference for the underdog role makes things difficult for very large organizations. When you're the biggest kid on the block, it's hard to locate larger, stronger competitors. There is a way out, however. Most of us identify more strongly with our small work group than with our large organization. So, although your little group may live under a big organizational tent, you can still exploit the competitive tool. The battle then becomes more evenly matched; not all of General Electric against a small competitor, but our little group—albeit within GE—against those (relatively) big guys. If your bosses understand that, they, in turn, may be more tolerant of your hot group's autonomous, stand-alone style.

Another suggestion:

> If there's a strong competitor out there, you can increase your group's heat by keeping the competitor's threatening shadow close and clear. Just don't try to make the threat seem so great that it shifts your group's focus from its core task to fighting off the competitor. Make it a race, not a war.

• *Hot groups need deadlines and other route markers.*

To stay hot, groups need markers to signal progress along the path toward their distant goal. If your baseball team has no way of knowing how many games it has won or lost, its coach will have a tough time keeping the team focused on winning the pennant.

In hot groups, those indicators of progress come in two varieties: *Hard* markers—clear indicators of visible movement toward the goal—and *soft* markers—in the forms of approval and optimism from valued leaders and colleagues. Both kinds will be needed at intermittent points along a hot group's path.

Hard markers are unambiguous indices of progress. "When we finish X, we'll have done 40 percent of what we need to do." If you can find hard markers—real ones, not fakes—they are great mechanisms for recharging your group's batteries. They signal positive movement that means we're making good progress or insufficient movement that means we need to work even harder.

In most hot group situations, however, hard markers are scarce. The novel, trailblazing tasks typically undertaken by hot groups don't often provide clear benchmarks. There are no road signs in the wilderness.

• *Deadlines: real and phony.*

Deadlines become interesting here because they can serve as hard markers—but, again, only if they're real. Leader, beware of setting phony deadlines! Too often "deadlines" turn out to be meaningless, with no factual basis beyond somebody's arbitrary decision. Group members will quickly discover the ersatz quality of such elastic deadlines and will stop taking them seriously.

In fact, fake deadlines can quickly cost you much of your credibility. Even if they don't emanate from you, but from people upstairs, your group will treat them as another silly administrative ploy, one that further reduces their already limited faith in the organization's integrity.

Hard deadlines, based on situational realities, are quite a different matter. Hard deadlines are not usually controllable by group leaders or anyone else. "Those Soviet missiles are right now on freighters steaming toward Cuba. They will arrive there in two days." That's a real deadline, and one to which the United States, fortunately, was quite capable of responding. Unfortunately, things aren't always that real or that clear:

> One of us once worked on the staff of the President of the United States. In that setting, deadlines filled the air like confetti. Hot groups and hot individuals continually worked to near exhaustion. Again and again, personal appointments had to be canceled to meet "absolutely vital" deadlines.
>
> We remember phoning a dinner hostess late on a Friday afternoon to apologize because an emergency assignment had just landed on our group's desk, a report that absolutely, positively had to be on the President's desk by Monday morning. Every moment of the weekend would be needed to get the job done.
>
> In the early hours of that Monday morning, right on time, our group, which had worked almost without sleep since Friday, set the document on the Chief of Staff's desk. Exhausted, yet exhilarated, we waited expectantly to hear that the President had either approved it, rejected it, or wanted some changes.
>
> We waited, and then we waited some more. Not until Thursday— three days later—did the President even see our report. That deadline, it turned out, had been a casual creation of the Chief of Staff's office. Of course, the next time such a tight deadline was announced, the group was decidedly wary and more than a little skeptical.

• *Keep real deadlines realistic!*

One more warning about hard markers: When deadlines or any other hard markers are perceived to be hopelessly beyond the possibility of achievement, they will either be laughed off, or they will simply depress the group's morale. At the other extreme, if deadlines are trivially easy to beat, their motivational power will also be trivial. To raise a hot group's pulse, deadlines must hit inside a narrow range. They must be tighter than what the group thinks it can beat, but not so tight as to seem utterly hopeless.

There are steps which you, as leader of a group, can sometimes take to make sure your real deadlines fall into that effective range. You may, for example, be able to control the size of your group. Then, a deadline that is too easy for a team of ten may become challengingly difficult for a group of, say, six. On the other hand, a deadline beyond possibility for a group of four might be a difficult but feasible challenge for a group of seven. When confronted with a nearly impossible deadline, perhaps you can subcontract out portions of the task or acquire, temporarily, equipment and other resources that will make attacking it feasible.

For hot groups, soft markers are often more important and more available than hard ones. Soft markers are simply voices of encouragement and support from persons whose competence, integrity, expertise, and good sense are trusted by the group. Those voices may come from patrons outside the group, from you, the group's conductor/leader, or from other group members. "OK. We're moving ahead. So, that tack didn't work. No big deal. Let's try a different angle." "Look at this bit from today's *Financial Times*. It means there's actually a bigger market waiting for our stuff out there than even we had thought!"

Some general advice:

> Use soft markers, even when hard ones are scarce, but don't let yourself or your group be seduced by false deadlines or unreal hard markers.

- *Open up access routes from your group to the rest of the world and from it.*

In earlier chapters, we talked repeatedly about hot groups' preference for isolation. That does not mean that members don't ever want to speak to anyone outside their own group. They will probably want to communicate with all sorts of people, in all sorts of places, but only with people and in places of their own choosing. When they do talk, they will want to focus almost solely on matters directly related to the completion of their task.

Most hot group members are not likely to care much about free trips to conferences in New Orleans—unless those conferences look very task related. When a hot group member goes to a meeting or to visit another organization, it is almost always in a targeted way, in search of ideas and information that can contribute to the group's task. Of course, if a Hawaiian junket is offered *after* the hot group has completed its work, when some R&R may be very much in order, it is likely to be willingly accepted.

Hot groups behave much like "cosmopolitan" individuals.[5] Although members are not likely to want to read every piece of paper in their field or attend every meeting, they will always be searching, very selectively, across a broad spectrum that extends to areas well outside the boundaries of their specialties. Hot groups are constantly on the alert, their antennae ever-sensitive to any hint of something relevant, no matter how remote its locale.

In rare cases, hot groups can become security risks. Despite their tendency to secrecy, they like to talk about their work with people who understand it and may be able to help them. Unfortunately, a few members may not sense when they are talking too much.

As a general rule:

> Give your group members the time and opportunity to search anywhere for information and ideas that may help them complete their task. Don't try to make decisions for them about what they need, and don't try to seduce them with offers of fancy junkets. Do, however, try to make sure they don't give away the store.

• *Develop a sense of community.*

The task itself is the strongest glue that binds hot groups together. Social glues, however, can certainly add extra strength. A sense of membership and community, blended with the cohesive power of a vital task, will add significantly to any group's productivity.

For a hot group, most of that sense of mutual trust and community will derive from the centrality of the task. When members feel they are doing something important and worthwhile, they soon begin to build feelings of fellowship. Those feelings can be enhanced in many ways. They can grow from shared ethnicity, nationality, or gender, like being African American or Ukrainian or female. They can issue from other important shared beliefs and attitudes, like being electrical engineers, or Harvard MBAs, or born-again Christians. They can arise from simply being isolated on a "cultural island," like living in an American enclave in, say, Saudi Arabia; or from feeling put upon by outside aggressors, like being an executive in a company confronting an unexpected and hostile takeover attempt. And they certainly occur over a wide range of other crises. Any of those scenarios and many more can act as powerful builders of your group's sense of community.

That community feeling can be developed even in groups composed of widely diverse individuals. Some of it can come from members' personal achieving styles, those characteristic problem-solving strategies that we described in Chapter 4. When some individuals, for example, simply enjoy working collaboratively and like to make contributions to their colleagues' achievements, they help to build the group into a community.

Your own style, as a working leader, can be another huge factor. It behooves you and all members to support one another, buoy up those who falter, and encourage breaks for rest and relaxation. As we pointed out in Chapter 4, hot groups usually handle such issues quite well, without special help, and their timing is frequently quite exquisite. So, while you need to audit the state of human relationships in your group, scanning continuously for nascent cracks and slippages, you must also be careful not to overplan and overprogram the social aspects of your group's life.

Suggestion:

Once underway, let the group build its own sense of community. Don't force it, but help it. A little immodest pride, an attitude that says, "We're special," certainly won't hurt. The creation of unique rituals or regalia, ranging from Sunday afternoon picnics to tailor-made mouse pads, can help to build a useful sense of "we-ness."

- **Do your best to provide your group with generous breathing time.**

Hot groups languish under micromanagement. They become irritable and peckish when people keep looking over their shoulders. They don't want to have to "prove" that what they are just beginning to understand will become cost effective within six months.

You, as leader, may find it psychologically difficult to remain hands-off your group, but it will be even harder to keep other people's hands off of it. Some executives have such strong needs for control that they simply can't stop interfering. Others may be afraid to risk giving control to their "subordinates." Still others, quite properly, simply want to stay in close touch with what goes on in their organizations.

Keeping hands-off has also become bureaucratically difficult, particularly in these lean, yet interconnected, times. Controllers and administrators must guard the safe and make sure that everyone in the organization abides by a thousand and one externally imposed regulations. Mistakes, failures, or misdemeanors by any unit can cause major repercussions all over the organization and beyond.

Nevertheless, it behooves you, as a hot group leader, to keep a finger in the dike, to hold yourself back and resist the tide of extraneous pressures. As leader, you need to provide your group with a reasonable chance to get underway before detailed inspections are imposed and payout is demanded.

Another suggestion:

> To help a hot group heat up and stay hot, give it as much freedom as you possibly can, from you and from day-to-day organizational pressures.

- **Don't try to keep your group running at full throttle all the time.**

Hot groups don't work at a feverish pace continuously, nor should they. Just as they range from very small to moderately large and exist anywhere from a few hours to a few years, hot groups also keep changing their degrees of heat, from tepid to scalding. They can come close to boiling over on Tuesday and slide down to lukewarm on Wednesday. Henrietta comes in one morning with a great new idea, and the group heats up into lively discussion and debate. Later, the idea turns out to be full of holes, so the group cools down, perhaps even slipping into mild depression.

Occasionally, newly anointed group leaders, themselves excited and impatient, use all their charismatic persuasiveness to keep their groups working at peak level. That's like overfertilizing a nicely flourishing plant. The plant will grow and flower profusely for a while, only to collapse and die a short time later.

That doesn't mean that hot groups can't stay hot longer than one might believe possible. Given a really exciting, difficult task, a sensitive and stimulating leader, and, perhaps, a big, bad competitor, small hot groups can work at a very high pitch for astonishing lengths of time. Here's an example from a partially paraphrased account of a report from MIT's *Technology Review.*[6]

In 1956, the United States was trying to develop its first spy satellite surveillance system. The project, shrouded in secrecy and code named "CORONA," had only recently been declassified.

Walter Levison, the project manager, and Frank Madden, his chief engineer, along with teams all over the nation, had been working on the enormously complicated problem for a very long time. They encountered so many intractable difficulties that at one point they were on the verge of tossing in the towel. With support and encouragement from Edwin Land (of Polaroid fame), then head of an intelligence advisory group, they decided to give it one last push. Faced with a do-or-die deadline of just three months, they would try to launch the first U.S. spy satellite.

In those next months Levison and Madden would often sleep in the milk factory in Needham, Massachusetts, that, under the innocuous sign of the optical firm, Itek, concealed the secret project. "During that period we hardly ever left the laboratory," Madden recalls. "People were working round the clock." Neither man could ever explain to his family why he spent so many nights and weekends away. . . . Levison could scarcely dream that just nine months later, on the fourteenth attempt, a satellite would finally pierce the Iron Curtain.

[*An aside:* Notice, once again, the tendency of this account to focus on individuals rather than whole groups. Although several groups made vital contributions to this work, the writer chooses to emphasize the roles of just two individuals.]

That kind of extended period of high heat is fairly rare. Most hot groups only stay very hot for shorter periods. After that, they either overheat, burn out and break up, or drop back to a more tolerable temperature.

Moreover, many tasks don't require a group to maintain a feverish pace over a long period. A basketball team needs to bring its temperature way up just before a big game, but afterwards it can cool considerably. The team may maintain moderate heat throughout the season, only rising to fever pitch on game days. That, incidentally, is not just the coach's doing. Most teams will raise their own adrenaline levels at the right times.

In general, the "natural law" governing the temperature cycles of hot groups goes something like this:

1. After a brief warm-up period, small hot groups, working on short-term projects, will operate at very high temperatures, from start to finish.

2. Larger hot groups, working on longer term projects, will run at moderately high base temperatures, with occasional bursts up to the near boiling point. They will intersperse these with periodic breaks to cool off. As they approach the finish line, of course, they may give it a final, climactic burst.

Once again, don't try to keep your group running at full throttle, and don't attempt to bring it down from a high before it's ready to do so on its own. So here is yet another rule of thumb for leading a hot group:

Read it more. Lead it less!

• *Keep an eye open for incipient burnout.*

Burnout can happen even when work is fun. Clearly, the high intensity of hot groups, their long hours, and hectic pace can wear down their members. Nevertheless, members of hot groups are much less vulnerable to burnout than many other organizational employees. There are, we believe, at least three important reasons for that.

While hot group members certainly don't love every aspect of their work, their task is still their passion. And, as the American philosopher Mae West is reputed to have said, too much of a good thing can be simply wonderful. Any of us, doing something we actively want to do, may feel exhausted at day's end, but it is not the weariness of mindless routine. It is exhaustion laced with the exhilaration of challenging work well done.

When we are deeply involved in our work, anything that keeps us away from it is unwelcome. That's the way hot group members feel about their own fatigue. Physical exhaustion becomes a frustrating barrier blocking them from their goal, like a canceled flight that prevents us from meeting a waiting lover. When our work is our love, it is only reluctantly that we set it aside, and then only long enough to revivify ourselves so we can race back, refreshed, to our beloved.

Surely, somewhere out there, there must be limits to our human capacity to work day and night, even when we want desperately to do so. Those limits, however, are singularly elastic. When the conditions are right, they can stretch beyond our imagining. Like the Central American highlands community whose people purportedly routinely run twenty or thirty miles just for fun, hot group members can stretch themselves far beyond "normal" limits, and they can do so for extended periods. After the fact, of course, they may wonder how they did it and whether they ever could—or would— do it again.

Hot groups carry another anti-burnout medication, one not available to individuals working alone. Members have one another. They are not always empathic to one another's feelings, but they are quite aware that they're all running fast and panting hard. When they notice a colleague gasping for breath, they step in to help. "Take a break." "Cool it for a day or two. We'll cover for you." Such a show of support from one's fellows is a powerful regenerator of the human spirit.

Hot groups, as we suggested in Chapter 4, have other quite marvelous ways of caring for themselves. When the tension level has crossed some imperceptible threshold, a built-in self-regulating system sets off a silent alarm. It's time to slow down, take a couple of hours off, have a beer. Such automatic, self-administered prophylaxis, applied informally and irregularly, prevents many burnouts. More than that, those brief digressions into play and foolishness are freeing times, when even a hot group's unusual thinking rules can be suspended, permitting previously withheld ideas to bubble up out of the deeper recesses of their minds. The Japanese save those periods of foolishness until after hours, via group dinners and drinking parties. Hot groups prefer to do more of it on company time.

Yet, even their self-adjusting controls will not always be enough to keep your hot group in good shape. So, it behooves you to watch for any buildup of tension and to open appropriate relief valves when the pressure gets too high. That may require some astute sensing, careful listening for subtle signals indicating that a private one-on-one talk is in order, or a picnic, or, at the extreme, that it is time to ease someone out of the group. In some acute crisis situations, those medications may not be available. Then, debilitating burnout can become a real and present danger.

Here's an example of a near miss, a case in which the tensions of overwork almost, but not quite, destroyed a valiant hot group:

> A very effective hot group of nurses worked in the burn unit of a large, urban hospital. Every member of the small team was dedicated, skilled, and compassionate. Together, they invented ever-better ways of reducing the suffering of their severely burned patients. They were a proud team, acknowledged everywhere as the best burn unit in the entire region.
>
> Suddenly, in the course of just a couple of days, an extremely large number of new patients was admitted. Many were badly hurt and in tormenting pain. At about the same time, a new, selfless, and dedicated young physician also came on board. In his effort to help, and out of extraordinary concern for the plight of his patients, he drove himself and the whole unit relentlessly, day after frantic day. As the overworked nurses tried to cope with their massive load, with the misery of their patients, and with the twenty-four-hour pressure from their new physician/leader, the stress level climbed dangerously high.
>
> Finally, as they approached the precipice of breakdown, the group came to its own rescue. They got together, in the few moments when they could find the time, to hold several short, highly emotional, on-

the-spot meetings. There, they first vented their fury and frustration. Among themselves, they thoroughly excoriated the hospital administrators and that new physician while providing one another with sympathy, support, and understanding.

Then, after that emotional catharsis, they turned back to the task at hand, designing better ways to handle both the workload and that too-dedicated young doctor. They carried on. No absenteeism, no long term recriminations, no burnouts.

Most hot groups, if left alone, find ways of dealing with the bulk of their severe stresses and strains. Still,

> You, the conductor, should be keeping an eye on every person in the group for signs of excessive stress. If you detect even minor trouble, don't hesitate to step in with a one-on-one talk or some other appropriate action. The worst thing you can do, either through inadvertence or anxiety, is nothing at all. We shall offer more suggestions about burnout in Chapter 11.

• *Expect periods of doubt, drought, depression, and dissension.*

You can be sure, over the life of any hot group, that there will be ups, downs, and crises. Hot groups are no more immune to the winds of uncertainty than any other individuals, groups, or institutions. Customers will cancel contracts. Competitors will beat your group's bid on a proposal. Grant funds will evaporate. People will become irritated with one another. Critical members of the group will leave unexpectedly. There will be periods when your group will hit a wall and retreat into a dark dungeon of despair. Hot groups, however, are enormously resilient. It is true that, on rare occasions, such destructive events do have lethal effects. A group will simply give up and splinter, leaving members with a lasting aftertaste of cynicism and rancor. More often, however, just when a group seems ready to fall apart—as with those burn unit nurses—it will snap itself back, becoming more solid than ever before.

We have seen it happen again and again. A group sweats over its task and seems to get nowhere. Strife begins to develop among members. The central point is lost, as some subgroups worry obsessively about one peripheral detail or another. Personal anxiety and disaffection arise. "This is too revolutionary. If we try it and it fails, they could fire us. I have kids to support." "Look, we've been going around in circles for hours and hours, and we haven't gotten anywhere. To hell with it. I have to catch a plane."

Here's another real-life example.

A committee of seven upper-level executives from diverse parts of a large insurance company is trying to lay out a presentation to the Board. A real deadline confronts them. They must make their pitch tomorrow at 9 A.M.

This morning, they were full of enthusiasm. They were onto something great, convinced that they had just the right plan, one that would bring the archaic culture of their organization into the twenty-first century. All the proposal needed was a little editing and polishing.

Now, however, on the eve of the big day, they are in trouble. They have been working for almost eleven hours straight, trying to complete their presentation. Time and again, they have had it almost right, until somebody pointed out a loophole or raised an objection. "Hey! Hold it! We never agreed on that." "But that paragraph contradicts what we said earlier!" As the hours pass, fatigue begins to take its toll. Squabbles erupt. By 5:30, frustration and anger are surfacing. A few people refuse to sign on to the most recent draft.

Finally, at about 7 o'clock, four of the seven members simply announce that they are leaving. They have very long commutes. "It's hopeless," they argue. "We haven't gotten anywhere. Let's just go in there tomorrow and play it by ear, or else let's just tell them that we need another month." Before they depart, they agree to come in a half hour early the next morning to talk about how best to acknowledge to the Board that they just couldn't get it together.

The four go home, but the other three hang on. They order in sandwiches and continue to struggle. Close to midnight, they think they've finally gotten it right. They reassure one another. Feeling better by the minute, they phone the others, awakening them at their homes to ask that they come in an hour, rather than a half hour, early. Then the three finally head for home.

At 7 in the morning, the three stalwarts are back at work. At about 7:15, the others arrive, downcast and wary. The three, now full of enthusiasm, show the new arrivals what they have done. Initially, the others are suspicious and doubtful. Then, extraordinarily rapidly, their enthusiasm rises. They see the point. They suggest a modification here and a different wording there. By 8:55, on the elevator up to the boardroom, they are once again a solid, enthusiastic team. All seven stand resolutely behind their output. They make their presentation, articulately and persuasively.

That kind of bounceback doesn't always happen, but it happens to hot groups surprisingly and puzzlingly often. Why? We're not sure. We think a period of fractionation may provide a chance for individual members to vent the doubts they have been silently harboring, particularly their concerns about the possible negative consequences of the group's daring actions. Once those pressures have been ventilated by a mini-revolt, by kicking and complaining, the group can come together again and get on with its work. Hot groups, we have found, just hate to fail. They will go many extra miles to avoid failure.

In our example, another strange thing happened, and in hot groups this, too, occurs frequently. Only three of the seven members did the critical, last-minute work, yet the other four were able to take up the project wholeheartedly, accepting what the three had done and even embracing the others' work as though it were their own. Instead of picking at their colleagues' decisions, the same people who had been full of objections yesterday become fully supportive today. How can that happen? The key, we believe, is trust. When members of a group trust one another's motives, their competence, and concern for the task, the work of any becomes the work of all. Group dynamicists know that. It's one reason they try to build interpersonal trust from the very start. In hot groups, the same principle applies. It's just that hot groups build their trust from the task backward, instead of from relationships forward.

Solidity does not imply uniformity. Even after a hot group has re-solidified, all members know very well who made which contributions. They know who stayed up until midnight to rescue the project, and they appreciate and willingly give credit to those individuals. The Board, however, may never get that news. They may never learn about the internal ups and downs of the group. That's one reason why top-down individual performance appraisals so often miss the mark. Looking at individual group members downward, from above, is like looking at reflections in one of those distorting circus mirrors. Things aren't what they seem.

What's the group leader's job during such down periods? The leadership of a hot group is, we have suggested, something of a dramatic art. Leaders must, on occasion, effectively manage the meaning of distressing situations. They must be very good actors. They must radiate confidence even when they're scared and maintain the appearance of calm even when turmoil rages within. A group's capacity to function is closely correlated with the confidence its leaders and colleagues communicate to one another, particularly in times of trouble. Just as parents of a seriously ill child must communicate believable reassurance, though they are beset with terror, you, as conductor, must keep your group's chin up, even in moments of great adversity.

A suggestion to conductor/leaders:

Don't sound abandon ship just because your group is listing heavily. The vessel can usually come back on even keel, and you can help to bring it back. Be patient. Be supportive. Be optimistic. Give the natural dynamics of the group a chance to operate. The Chinese have a saying: "Don't worry if the boat is drifting down the river sideways. When it gets to the other bank, it will right itself."

• *Like it or not, you have to manage meaning.*

Ineffective management of meaning can spell disaster for a hot group. This is especially likely when hard markers point one way and soft ones, set by leaders or other members, point another. Consider how fragile the morale of individuals, groups, or even whole societies can be. At what point during a crisis do we shift from calm confidence to panic? After panic has taken hold, can serene confidence ever work its magic again? As we encounter disappointments and glitches in our work, what determines whether we give in to despair? What does it take to overcome those reversals and carry on to a successful conclusion?

The realities of the situation almost always play the single most important role here, but not the only one. Still, the meaning attributed to the situation by respected leaders plays another far from trivial role. Sometimes, indeed, the meaning ascribed to a reality may be even more critical than the reality itself. When, for example, is a "crisis" really a crisis, instead of just a "problem"? When is a disaster nothing more than a "disturbance"? Or, conversely, when is a disturbance reconfigurable into a "disaster"? And when, in the midst of defeat, can we proudly proclaim victory? And make it stick?

Conductors must manage meaning and deal with all the complex moral issues that accompany that process. In today's jargon, conductors of hot groups often have to be "spin doctors." You, as conductor, have the power to make a dull task look at least somewhat exciting and an exciting one look quite dull. Every practicing executive, every teacher, and every parent knows that an otherwise mundane task can be converted to greater worthiness in any number of ways, among them:

- By demonstrating its link to other desired and important events.

- By turning it into a race or a game.

- By acting as a model of the desired behavior. By hands-on, intense personal involvement in the work, thereby infecting the group with your own psychic energy and enthusiasm.

- By demonstrating the importance placed on the task by valued others, like the CEO or Uncle Mike.

- By selecting a task that is somewhat—but not too far—beyond the group's reach.

For additional help on managing meaning, consult your nearest politician's PR people. Since the days when publicist Edward Bernays converted John D. Rockefeller's image from a callous robber baron to a sweet old man handing out dimes to kids, that profession has honed its skills. Whether we approve of them or not, they're good at what they do.

You might also seek counsel from your local high school athletic coach. Coaches, too, know a lot about managing meaning. Most are quite skilled at converting dejection into determination during just the few short time-outs scattered throughout a big game.

Remember:

Spin is not always sin. Use it—in measured doses.

In Summary

The heart of a hot group is its task. Consequently, conductors of would-be hot groups had better make sure that their task has "soul." The best test is the leader's own feeling about that task. Is it something really worth doing? If we could do it, would it make all of us feel we had done something important, that we had made a contribution, no matter how small, to the betterment of the world? Beyond that, find qualified people who are excited by the idea. Give them lots of room, provide the best markers of progress you can find, protect them, help them up when they are down, and get the rest of the organization to appreciate them. Then, give them the space they need to get the job done.

In the next chapter, we turn our attention from conductor/leaders of single groups to patron/leaders who spawn and support many hot groups.

7

Leaders of Hot Groups III: Leaders Who Seed Many Crops of Hot Groups

You have, for purposes of this chapter, just been promoted to the prestigious and responsible job of vice president in charge of a large, semi-autonomous division of your company. In your broad domain, you're the almost-but-not-quite-absolute ruler. You would like your new shop to move swiftly, developing new products and services and generally moving out ahead of the competition. To this end, you need to breed multiple crops of small, spirited hot groups. You want colonies of such groups to be an ongoing characteristic of your organization's culture. To help move in that direction, which levers should you pull? Which walls ought you to bulldoze? What will be the rules of the game? How should you recruit, reward, and evaluate your people? What kinds of people do you want?

One good way to get a fix on such issues is to pull out the standard HR checklist—the one usually applied to individuals—and try it with hot groups. You may want to begin with questions such as these:

- What kinds of people are we now recruiting? Are they good candidates for hot groups? Are we out looking for innovative, entrepreneurial types? Or do we go after more passive, obedient, "nice" folks? Are we searching for sharp, logical, analytic minds? Should we also be seeking out imaginative, associative, inventive minds?

- How does your new domain orient and train new people? Do training programs teach newcomers the rules and the terrible consequences of failing to abide by them? Or do they encourage creativity and initiative? Are we teaching our people to work alone and for themselves? Or to work together? Does our division really support what we tell our recruits we want? Or is it smoke and steam?

- What kind of incentive systems are we using? Do we reward independence and imagination? Do we, in truth, encourage teamwork, or is ours an individualistic star system? Do we tend to fragment groups by rewarding only individual performance, even to the point of stimulating political competitions? What about our performance appraisals? Done from above? Only on individuals? Do those appraisals steer our people toward doing productive work or beating the system? Or, worse still, toward beating one another?

- Look back over the last five years. Have we provided an environment that has encouraged the formation of small groups? Have we backed up those that got started? Given them resources? Time?

- Over those last five years, what, in fact, has happened to those individuals and groups who have taken significant risks? How about the ones who have taken risks and failed? Siberia? Or applause for good tries?

In this chapter, we want to concentrate on the answers to such questions. We want to outline several kinds of actions that an organizational leader, like you, can take to seed and cultivate many hot groups and keep them going and growing.

- *If you want more hot groups, communicate your relevant beliefs and attitudes, loudly and clearly.*

Let's begin with something so obvious that it's often overlooked. If you want to encourage the formation of lively little task groups, just say so! Say it simply, clearly, and often, and make sure you mean every word. One of the best and simplest ways to influence others to do what you want them to do is simply to tell them what you want them to do and ask them, please, to do it. Then back up your requests with active support. If what you are asking does not grossly violate your people's fundamental ethics and values, things will begin to move in your direction.

Thus, if you want more small, task-oriented groups, don't keep that news to yourself. Don't make the usually incorrect presumption that everybody already knows what you want. Unless you have some very good reasons to keep quiet—and occasionally there may be some—express yourself. That you don't speak doesn't mean you aren't heard. Seniors in organizations are heard, even when they say nothing. As you have long since discovered, your smallest actions, even your silences, will be magnified and their "meanings" interpreted and usually distorted. Attitudes you don't hold and beliefs you don't espouse will be attributed to you. It is critical, therefore, that you send clear messages, again and again and again.

Words speak much louder than unexpressed opinions, but actions, of course, speak even louder than words. Actions that you take to demonstrate your support for newly sprouting, potentially hot groups will add consistency and believability to your words. Such actions might include establishing a seed money bank to fund proposals from such groups, or encouraging informal cross-unit and cross-level meetings, or urging intermediate-level managers to act as patrons of innovative group projects.

Tell your people what you believe in and where you want to go. Then tell them again. Ask them to help you move the organization in those directions, and then help them find the tools they need to do what you have requested.

- *Identify and support potential hot group conductors.*

In every organization, no matter how rigid and conformist, a few individualists usually manage to survive. Those persons, frequently viewed as "difficult" by people farther up the hierarchy, are often admired and respected by their peers. They are highly regarded for their independence and their apparent ability to overcome bureaucratic constraints. They are also, very often, valued for their creative, off-the-beaten-track ideas. They may also be esteemed for their stubborn commitment to what they believe and their determination to push their ideas through to fruition. Those individualists are almost always easy to find. They stand out clearly against the dull gray background of most organizational life. Some of those are potential conductors of hot groups. Everybody down in the bowels of the organization knows who they are. Everybody also knows who, among that small set, are potential leaders and who are simply chronic malcontents. Locate the leaders, help them, and let the whole organization know that you value them.

Do the same with potential hot group members. Look for people who think creatively and work energetically; people who initiate things even when they aren't asked; people who explore and experiment; who become intrinsically interested in what they are doing. They, too, are easy to spot. Frequently they are to be found among the younger, newer people who have not yet been "trained" and tamed.

Advice:

Make sure all the talk about how we value creativity and innovation is really implemented, from recruitment practice all the way through to paychecks and other rewards.

• *Recruit wild ducks.*

Remember the story we told about Thomas Watson's interest in recruiting some "untamable" wild ducks into IBM? Such wild ducks are absolutely necessary if hot groups are to grow in any profusion. If your organization happens to be quite rule-bound, most of your wild ducks have probably already flown the coop. You may, therefore, have to search outside to recruit the next generation of such potential hot group leaders. Once again, where hot groups are wanted, recruiting the right people becomes a core requirement.

Some readers may recall a case study published in the September-October 1992 issue of the *Harvard Business Review*. It was called "The Complex Case of Management Education"[1] and it described one company's unhappy experiences with newly recruited MBAs. The case includes a memo from the corporate VP for Human Resources to the CEO. The memo recommends that the company stop recruiting MBAs and, instead, hire people with lesser degrees and more experience.

The VP offers data to demonstrate that MBA hiring has simply not paid off. Initial salaries for MBAs are too high, he argues, and their turnover rate is intolerable. He complains that "the MBA 'kids' want to move up too fast, they don't understand politics and people, and they aren't able to function as part of a team until their third year. But by then they're out looking for other jobs." (p. 18) Earlier in the same memo, he asserted, "My biggest concern, though, is how much we have to retrain the MBAs we hire. We've gone from 41 hours of training a year in 1981 to 241 hours in 1991. . . . None of them knows anything about good management techniques when we hire them." (p. 17)

Isn't that HR VP really urging the company to avoid wild ducks? Is his position an appropriate one in our speedy new world? No matter what your stereotype of MBAs, do you stop hiring bright young men and women because they want to move too fast? Would we really prefer those who are content to move slowly? Indeed, in today's environment, shouldn't we be worrying much more about the people in our companies who don't want to move fast?

Take that case one step further. If we go on hiring those expensive and difficult MBAs, shall we continue to invest large amounts of money and effort to "train" them? What happens, one wonders, during those 241 hours of "training"? How much of it is really spent sanding and polishing those recruits in the hope that they will emerge from the training shop looking just like everyone else in the company? The HR VP and the CEO, too, might take a moment to ask themselves why so many of those youngsters, carefully pre-screened and educated by graduate schools of business, decide to leave their organization after only a short stay. Perhaps some have gone elsewhere, driven by egotistical ambition. How many have left because this company hasn't given them the space, encouragement, or opportunities to do exciting work? Indeed, some of them—by no means all—might well have been the wild ducks who could lay the eggs from which hot group ducklings could hatch, ultimately to enliven, refresh, and add flexibility to the whole company. Therefore:

> Check out the mavericks in your organization. Do you have some? Are they being treated well? Do you need more?

● ***Help your groups bring the right people in, get the wrong people out, and cope with unexpected departures.***

Never underestimate the effects of new arrivals and old departures on existing hot groups. Although comings and goings of members are inevitable in any group, those entries and exits pose special difficulties for hot groups.

The reasons for departures can vary from rejection, to illness, to greener pastures; the reasons for new arrivals can range from simply filling vacancies to needs for special new skills. Whatever the cause, both can be extremely disruptive, but for quite different reasons.

●   *Bringing the right people in: They'd rather do it themselves.*

How are newcomers to be selected, oriented and taught the real ropes? In hot groups, those questions become just a bit more complicated than usual. In many organizations, recruitment is turned over to specialized recruiters who search the world for just the right people to fill pre-specified job descriptions. In hot groups, recruiting doesn't work that way—or rather, it shouldn't. It is generally a bad idea for outsiders, such as HR specialists or division managers, to select new members for those groups. Even though recruiting means temporary deviation from their task, most hot groups would rather do it themselves, using their informal and usually extensive private networks. Moreover, even if they'd rather have someone else do it, they ought to do it themselves.

Hot groups usually prefer to recruit in much the same way that corporate boards seek out senior executives. Hot group members know their special fields, and they know how to locate other relevant people, both in and out of the company. If they feel Susan Jones, who works down the street at XYZ Corp., might make a real contribution, they prefer to go after that specific individual and to do it quietly, via personal contacts.

Large organizations don't much like having their people casually crossing organizational borders, especially without visas. That causes all sorts of troubles, from violations of job-posting rules to concerns about security. The advantages of such personal searches, however, are many. By selecting people whom group members know firsthand, they sharply reduce the chances of failure and sharply increase the chances of quickly integrating the newcomers into the group. The recruiters also now have a stake in making sure their cadets succeed.

- *Getting the wrong people out: Hot groups are quite capable of playing hardball with difficult members.*

Every once in a while, a hot group, like any other group, will decide that one of its members isn't doing the job, or that a person is actively blocking progress or in some other way has become a drag on the group's effectiveness. Then the group may intentionally eject that member. That doesn't mean they dispatch the victim with either a stiletto or a chain saw. Hot groups may not be especially sensitive to peoples' feelings, but neither are they intentionally cruel. Yet, when they feel it necessary, they can quite effectively marginalize or amputate negative contributors.

Of course, in some situations, it isn't that easy for a hot (or cold) group to get rid of a difficult or unproductive member. That person may be quite unremovable, perhaps because he or she is a member of the owner's family or has been inserted into the group by powers higher up in the organization. It takes, as we shall see in Chapter 11, a committed group and a wise leader to cope with that sort of problem, to work around that troublesome member and yet maintain a tolerably positive relationship.

- *Leader beware. Think thrice before rejecting a "deviant" member of a hot group.*

A hot group—even more than other groups—should rarely have to eject one of its members. Hot groups, after all, thrive on divergence. Of course, there can be many different reasons for going after someone who causes difficulty—some good reasons, many not so good.

> Is that member irremediably lazy or incompetent? That's a fairly good reason for removing someone.

Does that member meet the "standards of thinking" shared by the rest? That, too, may be adequate justification.

Is that person not fully committed to the task? Or does she only appear to be uncommitted because she knows she is unloved by the group?

Are that person's ideas unusual, off the beaten track? That's not a good reason. If a hot group rejects someone for unusual thinking, the group has probably already lost its heat.

The complex relationships that build up between groups and their individual members have been studied backwards and forwards by social psychologists for several decades.[2] Their research has turned up some clear patterns of behavior on both sides of the group versus individual issue. Although difficult individuals can cause serious problems for groups, difficult groups also cause serious problems for individuals. When, for example, groups are faced with a single member who insists on holding to position A when all other members hold to position B, the group may view that individual as "difficult." At the same time, when an individual cannot convince the group to see the light that he or she has seen, then, for that individual, the group becomes the "difficult" party.

One interesting observation that has come out of that research is that groups of all kinds handle their deviant members in about the same way. Typically, up to four stages are involved in the process. We say "up to" four because the deviant member usually comes around or leaves before Stages 3 and 4 become necessary.

The first step, Stage 1, doesn't look like the group is pressuring the deviant. It appears—intentionally—like rational discussion among reasonable human beings. "Joe, why don't you explain why you feel that your position A is a better answer to our problem than our position B. Then we'll explain why we prefer B. We're all sensible people. Surely we can work things out." That may not look like pressure, but the targeted member will quickly understand what it really means. It means that after we have all talked it over, you, Joe, the minority of one, are expected to come around to our position.

If Joe doesn't grab this chance to join up gracefully, if he instead continues to hold out, the group slips into Stage 2, wherein the pressure increases, but in a subtle way. The group abandons rationality in favor of emotional seduction. "Look Joe, we know our position seems different from yours, but if you examine both of them carefully, they really turn out to be quite similar. So, for the sake of the group's solidarity and the success of our project, try to see it our way. Let's put on a united front when we have to face the skeptics upstairs." Given the accompaniment of much purring and stroking, Joe may then decide to go along with position B—or he may not. Suppose Joe replies, "That's a bunch of BS. Our two positions are not similar. They're poles apart. What's right is right, and I'm right!" At that point, the group makes a sharp turn to Stage 3, direct attack. "Dammit, Joe, you've made those same kind of damn fool arguments for weeks now. Knock it off! It's time you stopped this nonsense. We've got work to do. We've all agreed on position B, and you damn well better, too."

If that direct attack doesn't work—and it may not, because abject surrender at that point is too humiliating—the group moves on to Stage 4. The reader can surely guess the nature of Stage 4: Amputation—which is probably an appropriate word because it means that the group simply cuts off one of its own members, one of its own limbs. This is the group's most extreme form of punishment: banishment, isolation, solitary confinement.

Until now, Joe has been at center stage. At this point, the group turns away from him. All the attention he had received, albeit much of it unwanted, abruptly disappears. When he speaks, nobody listens, as though he isn't even there. The group may even literally turn their backs to the deviant member, cutting him off physically as well as psychologically. From Joe's perspective, it's a cruel game the group is playing. They're punishing him unjustly, simply because he's a free and independent thinker. "All they want is yes men," he may complain. "They're so set in their ways that they won't even listen to a different idea." And so on.

Note, however, that putting on the pressure carries high costs for the group as well as for Joe. Groups don't like to waste time in useless argument, and they don't like to cut off a part of themselves. Now, they must limp along, probably beset by guilt, diminished in size as well as in spirit.

Fortunately, wide-open, task-obsessed hot groups are only infrequently caught up in this conformity/deviation problem. Still, it can certainly happen to a hot group, and when it does, it requires careful and sensitive handling by group leaders.

Some suggestions:

1. To the degree possible, encourage your groups to do their own recruiting. That will reduce the likelihood of unwanted members.

2. When a valued member departs, be aware of the enormous shock effects felt by the group. Offer counsel, reassurance, and any other support possible.

3. When a group chooses to get rid of someone, stay clear and let it happen. Then, provide support for both victim and group.

4. When a member is imposed on the group from outside, but is lazy, incompetent, or operates from entirely different rules of thinking, you, as leader, will have to work your charm to keep that person reasonably happy, but distant from the rest of the group.

- *Coping with the loss of a valued member: Hot groups need all the help you can give them.*

Losing a full-fledged member is extremely painful for any group. When an acknowledged leader departs, the loss can even be fatal. Such departures can send a group into depression, much like the death of a sibling. But the unmourned departure of someone the group itself has ejected can have the opposite effect, giving the group a new burst of energy.

We shall examine in greater detail some of the things that can foul up hot groups in Chapter 11, but, for now, we simply want to emphasize that hot groups are fragile, living entities. Members are seldom even aware of how much they depend on one another—until someone leaves. The fear and sadness that accompany a departure may remain unspoken, but they are there, slowing things down, generating doubt and uncertainty.

> We know one very hot group whose conductor died, suddenly and unexpectedly. At first, the group, in shock, mourned the loss. Then, in several very different ways, it struggled to maintain its equilibrium. It struggled internally, just to stay whole and focused. It also tried hard to identify a new informal leader. Finally, the group found two people who shared the role, so the group lived on, though never achieving its earlier verve.
>
> That, however, wasn't the end of its difficulties. Even greater tension developed between the group and its parent institution. The deceased leader, highly respected throughout the organization and the profession, had been the only strong link connecting the group to its large, parent organization. Once he was gone, no one else in the group was able to regain the organization's trust and respect.
>
> Eventually, lacking support, the group languished. Resources dried up. Other members departed. The group eventually disintegrated.

All things considered, the circumstances of separation are almost as critical as the individual who departs. Is the loss due to some fairly benign cause, like retirement? That's difficult, but most groups can cope. Is the departing member leaving because he or she feels the group is incompetent or heading down the wrong track? That may leave permanent scars, especially if the leave-taker has been a respected member of the group. What if the group suspects that the departure has been politically "arranged," that an outside enemy of the group has caused one of their number to be transferred? The effects of that are likely to be explosive. Indeed, as many a clever manipulator knows, one effective way to wound and, perhaps, even kill a hot group is to engineer just such a removal of even one highly valued member.

When the diagnosis is depression due to a key member's departure, what treatments can help? Here are a few suggestions:

1. The first sensible step is early detection. Most departures emit early warning signals. If the group can be forewarned, it can take measures to cope.

2. A second step may be to try a radical organ transplant—immediate insertion of a replacement for the departed member. Suitable replacement organs, however, are usually hard to find.

3. A third possibility, in parallel with the other two, is to provide extra active support from patrons. A valued member's day of departure is a moment when a sensitive conductor, keeper of the flame, or patron needs first to acknowledge and talk through the emotional impact of the loss, and then, as soon as possible, provide some reenergizing, upbeat reassurance.

• ***Competitions among groups can be effective, but very dangerous.***

Competitors make great temporary fuel for small groups. Bigger competitors are almost always better than smaller ones, and outside competitors are almost always better than inside ones.

> • *Competition with groups outside your organization? Use it to your advantage.*

Athletic leagues formalize intergroup competitions among more or less equally skilled teams. Competition is the reason for their existence.

In industrial organizations, something similar happens. Teams from one company compete with other companies' teams for customers and clients. Advertising agencies, in competition with other agencies, present competitive proposals to the same prospects. Underwriting teams compete to win a chunk of a public offering. Architectural design teams compete for design contracts. That kind of outside-our-walls competition is a powerful furnace that can quickly raise the temperature of a small group. Competitions increase internal group cohesiveness, too. One wise social psychologist once asserted that nothing increases a group's internal cohesiveness as much as the threatening presence of another group.

Those outside competitions seldom cause much trouble within the home organization. In fact, they usually help improve relationships between the group and its parent. When our stalwart little team sallies out to compete for the favors of a prized client, the rest of the company becomes its cheering section, urging them on to victory. Those competitions can cause trouble, however, when our team loses, particularly if it loses quite regularly. The sequence of wins and losses that a team encounters can have an enormous effect on how it feels about itself, as well as on how its fans respond.

An unbroken series of losses is likely to be disastrous, generating frustration, dejection, and anger in both the team and its rooters. Previously loyal fans now become critics and needlers. Ad hominem arguments and even internecine warfare may break out within the group, perhaps eventually leading to its demise. A steady diet of wins, however, isn't all good either. It keeps the crowd with the team, but may also cause the team to go soft and dampen internal debate and self-criticism. If we win all the time, why change the lineup? Let's keep doing the same old thing!

A sequence of frequent wins interspersed with a few losses probably constitutes the best of all worlds. The wins keep the cheering section cheering and increase the team's sense of competence and confidence. The losses promote essential self-criticism. Members feel more motivated to analyze the causes of their losses and modify their tactics and strategies accordingly.

As a patron of hot groups, you cannot and, indeed, should not guarantee a group's competitive success. There are, however, ways you can help them, whether they succeed or fail. You may be able to influence the amount of cheering or jeering that goes on, and you can manage the meaning of the group's successes and failures. You can, for example, actively help to celebrate success. Even more important; you can also celebrate "good" failures, rewarding a group's all-out effort and muting the catcalls and baleful looks when the group has stumbled. Thereby, you can help make it clear that you want to encourage innovative risk-taking, even though it necessarily entails occasional failures.

- *Competition with groups inside your organization? Handle with great care!*

Competitions inside the organization are quite a different kettle of fish. Approach this one cautiously! Internal competitions can go either way, energizing all competing groups or causing destructive, morale-eroding warfare. Intentionally encouraging internal competition may, in some special circumstances, serve as a useful short-run tactic for the conductor of a single team. Mostly, however, it's bad news both for the conductor and for the patron trying to develop many such groups.

It is in the nature of groups to distrust other unfamiliar groups. That's a grand generalization but, we believe, a true one. The evidence from anthropology and social psychology supports it. When members of our group first encounter another group, the immediate effect is to solidify our own group identity. We become more "we" than ever, seeing the other group as "they" and holding them at arm's length. From there, it's a very short hop to distrust and hostility. For that reason and many others, competitions and wars are much easier to start than stop. The actual differences between groups need not be great, nor must each group initially feel very solid or cohesive. Competition will exaggerate the differences and glue each group solidly together.

Here's a quick summary of some research that illustrates the power of competitive conflict.

One famous experiment[3] conducted at a summer camp for teenage boys showed how simple it is to start a competitive, near-war between the occupants of two bunkhouses. The youngsters in the two groups were not significantly different from one another and had been randomly assigned to their houses. With a little help from the experimenters, they soon became competitors. The competition quickly became so intense that the two groups even refused to play softball against one another or ride in the same truck when they took trips. That initial part of the study lasted only a few days. Most of the competitiveness and the mutual hostility that followed went on for weeks.

The same experiment then demonstrated how difficult it was, once hostilities had begun, to make peace. That required the rest of the summer. Fortunately, there's a happy ending. Peace began to break out when both groups encountered a "superordinate goal," in this case a crisis involving something that both groups needed more than they needed to hate one another. The camp counselors secretly punched holes in the long pipeline supplying the camp with water from a far-off hilltop water tank. Soon the whole camp was short of a resource that everyone required.

When the two groups went searching through the underbrush for leaks in the pipeline, they didn't worry much about which member of which group discovered it. Whoever was at hand would help to patch it. That process started things going in the other direction, toward cooperation.

So, before you encourage active competition among groups within your organization, consider the potential long-term negative effects. Are the motivational advantages of short-term competitions worth the extended costs of having groups dislike—or even despise—one another, perhaps for years to come?

• *Two Kinds of Competitions: Wars and Races.*

We need to make a distinction here between two varieties of competition: wars and races. In wars, the goal is to destroy the enemy. We can't think of many circumstances under which intraorganizational warfare can produce net positive results. In races, the purpose is not to destroy, but rather to outperform others and also, at least as much, to outperform ourselves, to exceed our personal best. In organizations, races can be productive, if they can be kept safely within that category.

Many hot groups, brash and self-confident, enjoy races. Their confidence also makes other groups irate enough to want to beat them. Thus, the competitive excitement can spread. Everybody puts his or her back into the effort. Given clear rules, meaningful scorecards, and vigilant, honest referees, everyone can move ahead. New hot groups may even spring up in the enthusiasm of the moment. There will be costs, however. If groups feel very competitive with one another, and the stakes are high, they will play hard, but they may also begin to play dirty. That's when tough-minded referees are needed.

Newer, more open organizational architectures usually have less trouble than old ones in integrating the "disruptions" generated by internal races. For such organizations, those races are not disruptions. Unlike their predecessors, the newer designs do not implicitly envision calm, orderly regularity as the best of all possible organizational worlds. They treat turbulence, including internal tensions, as normal conditions of organizational life, as stimulants, adding spirit and effervescence to the entire system. Several writers, like Andy Grove[4] of Intel and Tom Peters,[5] have pointed out the positive effects that can derive from a bit of "paranoia" and "chaos" in organizations.

Even earlier, Professor Cohen and March coined the seemingly oxymoronic phrase "organized anarchies."[6] They used it to describe organizations that showed anarchistic characteristics, but were in fact quite organized. "Organized anarchies" seems a pretty accurate descriptor of the kinds of structures becoming more commonplace these days. That phrase is also an apt descriptor of the organizational cultures likely to feel comfortable with hot groups and vice versa, as well as organizations that are likely to feel comfortable with intraorganizational races.

Clearly, one cost of competitions among groups can be "irrational" duplication of effort and physical resources. Why waste time, money, and people having two groups try to accomplish the same thing, when only one outcome will be used?

One option: Design competitions that do not have two groups doing exactly the same thing. For example, one frequently effective form of internal competition sidesteps some of the costs of duplication as well as many dangers of long-term enmities. The idea follows the old dictum of thesis and antithesis, having one group play a counterimplementing, devil's advocate role for the other. Group A goes to work developing several possible options for solving problem X, while Group B tries to figure out how to neutralize or countermand each of Group A's proposals.[7] Although the situation is competitive and management-instigated, few resources are being duplicated and the sensible larger purpose is obvious to everyone. President Kennedy's ExComm did something close to that during the Cuban missile crisis. At one point, they split into two groups, each developing its own options. Then, each group critiqued the other's proposals.

Some of the duplication of resources and effort inherent in such intraorganizational races may indeed be irrational. Still, the purported advantages of rationality can easily be overplayed, as we once discovered when we were both working in Bulgaria.

A senior Bulgarian executive was lecturing about his nation's then new "self-management" system, presumably a radical departure from the old central planning tradition. The self-management plan was supposed to free individual companies from governmental control, allowing each firm to make its own decisions.

To make sure we understood, we asked the speaker whether that meant, for example, that each company could now make its own purchasing decisions. Our informant shook his head emphatically. "Oh no. That would be irrational," he replied. His interpreter then explained that under the new self-management plan all enterprises in the same industry would still be required to pool and clear purchases through a central government agency.

When we suggested that such centralization hardly seemed like autonomous decision-making by each firm, he reiterated that allowing each company to make its own purchasing decisions would be "irrational." If organizations made their own decisions, how could their industry possibly take advantage of quantity discounts?

"But wouldn't individual managers themselves soon figure out that by pooling purchases they could jointly obtain those economies of scale, without going through a government agency?" No reply. The notion of rational central planning was too deeply embedded.

Before we dismiss that Bulgarian position as typically totalitarian, we might pause to think about our own organizations. Aren't very similar notions—economically rational, but psychologically naïve—also deeply embedded in the value systems that prevail inside some of our own large institutions?

There are, of course, several other varieties of internal group conflict, each with its own special set of costs and benefits. The worst are those that have evolved out of ancient enmities, enmities that began in the dim past, before any living soul can remember. Those have few redeeming qualities. Even when there is little fire still left, the ashes can smolder on and on, forever threatening to flare up again. Think of all the examples we have witnessed, in just the past few decades, of unspeakable violence generated by ancient enmities: Serbs, Croats, and Muslims in what was Yugoslavia; Catholics and Protestants in Northern Ireland; Palestinians and Israelis, as well as Sunni Muslims and Shiite Muslims in the Middle East. Those hatreds are as real for many of those groups today as they were for their unknown ancestors hundreds of years ago. Like those old ethnic, religious, and regional hatreds, the quiet wars between sales and production, or research and marketing, or Divisions X and Y can just go on and on. Sometimes, the matches that lit such wars were "innocent" intergroup competitions.

Those internal wars are not always intentionally and consciously created. Often, they are unintended. Structural and policy decisions can inadvertently drive futile and costly kinds of intergroup conflict. Some forms of internal transfer pricing, for instance, can generate just such long-term animosities.

> At meat packing Company X, the Sausage Division makes and markets pork sausage, while the Fresh Pork Division prepares and distributes fresh pork products. The Fresh Pork Division is also the sole supplier of the Sausage Division's necessary raw material: fresh pork.
>
> The company long ago had decided that it would be irrational to use anything other than its own fresh pork to make its sausages. So, company policy requires the Fresh Pork Division to supply the needed product to the Sausage Division and to do so at a "fair" price. That "fair price," of course, is the hooker. How does one determine a fair price in a closed market? The Fresh Pork people, at certain times, demand a price the Sausage folks think is exorbitant. The Pork people shrug off those complaints. They have options. They can freeze and hold "fresh" pork until the market's right or sell it to the supermarkets as loins and hams and chops whenever the market price is attractive. Why sell it to Sausage now for less than we'll get for it on the open market next week?
>
> That posture infuriates the Sausage Division. The profit margins on branded sausage are much better than the narrow margins on unbranded fresh pork. Yet, they are prisoners of Pork.
>
> The complaints and arguments have gone on for years. "Why should we have to sell pork to Sausage for less than we can get outside?" "Why should we have to buy our raw materials from the Pork Division? Why can't we buy them on the open market? That would put a stop to the Pork Division's price gouging!"
>
> Long ago, Sausage folks began to use unprintable words to describe the Pork Division's people, especially its leaders. Indeed, some of the Sausage loyalists insist that they'd rather starve than eat one of their own company's pork chops. Not surprisingly, the company's sausages seldom grace pork people's breakfast tables.

Who's to blame? In large organizations, a thousand forces can drive groups into such fruitless competitions, even into open warfare. Two or more units want to sell overlapping services to the same important customer. Two or more professional schools, in the same university, want to woo the same wealthy donor, and so does the university's central development office.

In many of those conflict situations, groups will rise to the challenge, becoming very hot, ready to work day and night. But to work on what? Perhaps, our sausage people will be driven to think more creatively. Maybe they can replace pork with tofu. More likely, when they think creatively, it will be about ways to outwit and undermine the porkers.

Once again, getting such groups together and talking things through is the laborious strategy of choice. Knocking heads has been an old favorite, but it seldom does more than drive the competitors into surreptitious guerrilla warfare, a smile on the face and a stiletto in the back.

• *Look to the young.*

The young believe themselves immortal and indestructible. Consequently, young people are likely to be less risk averse and less socialized into the "right" ways than older folks. Their hubris allows them to try things that their seniors "know" are foolish, if not impossible. Some of those foolish and impossible things may well be exactly what the organization desperately needs.

Thirteen hundred years ago, St. Benedict—there were consultants even then—offered this counsel to the abbot/managers of the great monasteries of that period:

> As often as any important business has to be done in the monastery, let the abbot call together the whole community and himself set forth the matter. And, having heard the counsel of the brethren, let him think it over by himself and then do what he shall judge to be most expedient. . . .
>
> Now the reason why we have said that all should be called to council, is that God often reveals what is better to the younger. . . . But if the business to be done in the interests of the monastery be of lesser importance, let him use the advice of the seniors only![8]

• *Once again: Beware of individual bonus plans and performance appraisals.*

Although this chapter examines what leaders can do to promote the continuing growth of hot groups, we should not end it without a warning about two policy areas that frequently stunt their growth: reward systems and their close companions, performance appraisals. To the patron/leader, we recommend:

Deemphasize individual rewards and appraisals, at least during the lives of hot groups. To the extent possible, put such issues on the back burner. To maintain healthy hot groups, reward the whole group, support the whole group, and leave it mostly to the group to reward and appraise its individual members.

In Summary

If, as a patron leader, you want to move your whole organizational culture toward the acceptance and encouragement of hot groups, you may want to consider these suggestions:

1. Communicate your intent, loudly, clearly, and often. Then, demonstrate that you mean it.

2. Identify and, when necessary, recruit potential hot group leaders.

3. Find and support wild ducks; that's where you're likely to find potential leaders.

4. Make it as easy as possible for groups to bring in the people they want and remove the ones they don't want.

5. Encourage some (not all) competitions with outsiders. With insiders, you may want to encourage races, but beware of wars.

6. Check out your reward and appraisal schemes. Make sure they reward total group performance, not just the performance of individual stars.

Our next chapter looks into the ways that hot groups can function as change agents, as stimulants to liven up other parts of the organization and even as instruments with which to revitalize an organization's whole culture.

III

HOW DO HOT GROUPS OPERATE?

8

Hot Groups' Structures and Strategies: How Do We Get There from Here?

Structurally, a hot group looks something like a school of fish, but there's one unusual aspect of this particular school. It's diverse. It's a school of mixed species. Each is different from every other fish in the school, a cod here, a tuna there, a little minnow cruising among them. Nevertheless, the whole entity maintains a clearly discernible form, a form that changes continuously as the school quickly and smoothly alters speed and direction. If one focuses on a single mackerel, that individual may be out in front of the school at one moment and in the rear the next. The most prominent, most noticeable unit, however, is never the individual. It is always the school.

In hot groups, too, the prominent unit is not the individual. It is the group. "We" dominates "I." Individual roles and functions change frequently, swiftly, and subtly, but the group remains intact. This afternoon's first baseman may well be tonight's center fielder. Nobody seems to report to anybody. Or rather it's the other way round. Everybody seems to report to everybody. The structure is fluid, ever-changing, but the hot group remains a single entity. Despite all that fluidity, hot groups still show several relatively enduring structural and strategic characteristics. Let's consider the structural characteristics first, including some that make it easy to see why most large organizations have trouble integrating them.

Structural Characteristic 1: Hot groups are fully interconnected

The structures of hot groups are flat and circular. More properly, one should say they are spherical, three dimensional. They are flat only in the sense that they are egalitarian rather than hierarchical. They are spherical in the sense that there is no clear top or bottom, no up or down. Things move in all directions. Communication channels are open from anyone to everyone. Symbols of rank and authority are put on hold, even by members who carry high rank and much authority in the parent organization. No uniforms here, no gold braid or epaulettes. The index of individual worth is not age, wealth, race, sex, or office size. It is contribution to the task. These open, multichanneled communication networks do not mean that power is distributed equally, or that there are no leaders. It means that while hot groups are working, input to the task is what matters most. That input can come from anyone, anywhere, and go to anyone, anywhere else. It also means that the barking of commands is never heard, but the motley sounds of urging, hustling, persuading, and cussing go on constantly.

Such wide open communication nets, so typical of hot groups, stand in sharp contrast to the defined and delimited communication channels characteristic of formal organizations. Organizational charts in formal organizations not only specify who reports to whom, they also specify who is supposed to communicate with whom. Consequently, those organizations look orderly and systematic, while hot groups appear disorderly and chaotic.

Let's not make the mistake, however, of equating disorder with inefficiency. The advantage of hot groups' fully interconnected networks is that much information can be processed simultaneously by many individuals. In "normal" organizational structures, messages have to climb laboriously up the up-channels, then down the down-channels, leaking energy and validity along the way.

Many of us, even now, are so imbued with the hierarchical paradigm that we almost automatically assume that only tightly disciplined hierarchies can operate efficiently. More permeable structures are too messy, too tumultuous. After all, people can't listen to more than one person at a time. Or can they? Maybe we also have so little faith in our human capacity to handle large quantities of information that we build information-rationing organizations. Then, once we've starved people of the information that is the database of thinking, we complain that our people are using only a minuscule portion of their intellectual potential.

Certainly those jumbled, free-and-easy communication networks have their disadvantages, but they also carry a number of great benefits, especially for organizations trying to make it in today's high-speed, high-tech world. Consider, for example, a well-known series of laboratory experiments on communication networks. Those studies of small, five-person groups were conducted over many years, in many different parts of the world.[1] Everything in the experiments was held constant except the groups' structures. All groups were made up of equivalent people, all were given the same job to do, the same time limits, the same pay, and the same instructions. The only factor that differed was the structure within which the groups worked. Some groups worked in hierarchical structures and others in circular, nonhierarchical arrangements.

Participants were free to do anything they wished that might help them get their job done as quickly as possible, just so long as they worked within their prescribed structures. They were paid a flat rate for participation, without regard for how fast or how well they did the job. Each group performed the task many times so that learning curves could be studied.

Here are two of those structures and what happened in each.

This structure was called a Star:

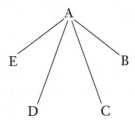

And this one was called a Circle:

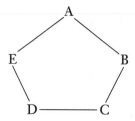

Each line represents a two-way channel of communication. Participants could use only those channels, but they could use them as they saw fit.

The findings: Regardless of whether the groups were composed of engineers, executives, hourly workers, or nurses, and regardless of the country in which the experiment was tried, these consistent results emerged:

1. *Speed*: The Star groups came down the learning curve more quickly than the Circle groups, and, by the end of the experiment, were doing their whole job significantly faster than the Circles. The Circles never came close to the speed of the Star groups.

2. *Quality of output*: Both Stars and Circles made about the same number of errors.

3. *Number of messages sent to one another*: Star groups used no more messages than the minimum needed to get the job done. Hardly a single unnecessary or redundant message flowed over their communication channels. Circle groups sent many extra messages, about 50 percent more than the minimum necessary.

4. *Working systems*: All Star groups, whatever their ethnicity, occupation, or gender, organized themselves in the same way: They set up a two-level hierarchy with B, C, D, and E

"reporting" to A. The four "subordinates" sent their information to A, who then solved the problem and sent that correct answer back out for implementation by the other four. Circles, on the other hand, almost never got fully organized; that is, they seldom did the job in a regular, standardized way. Their way of working varied from one run to the next.

5. *Leadership*: When asked at the end of the experiment, "Did your group have a leader?", almost all Star group members identified A as their leader. Circle groups seldom pinpointed anyone as their leader and often professed that they didn't understand the question because no one had been appointed leader.

6. *Members' ability to specify their jobs*: At the end of the experiment, when Star people were asked to give a detailed description of their jobs, they could do so very precisely. "My job was to do this, then that, then this." Asked the same question, Circle people said things like, "I do what's necessary, what makes sense. Sometimes doing X made sense. Sometimes doing Y was what was needed."

7. *Replaceability*: Star members could quickly and easily be replaced. Their behavior became so regular and well structured that a replacement for B, C, D, and E could be trained in a few minutes. Training A's replacement would take a bit longer. Replacing Circle employees was more difficult. Theirs were more like executive jobs. Instead of precise operational, step-by-step instructions, Circle trainees would have to be instructed more contingently. "Do what needs to be done. Figure it out." Their training would have to take place much more on the job than off.

Thus, by all those criteria of effectiveness—speed, number of communications, regularity, predictability, clear leadership, and clear job definitions—the hierarchical Star was far more effective than the loose, egalitarian Circle.

Should anyone have been surprised by those results? Certainly no one who had ever had a course in planning, organizing, and controlling. The Star is orderly, systematic, well-organized. The Circle is sloppy, irregular, disorderly.

That, though, is not the end of it. If we turn to some other, perhaps more contemporary criteria of effectiveness, things begin to look different. Consider these:

8. *Morale*: The morale of the Star group was very low. Most Star people actively disliked their jobs—everyone, that is, except the person in the A position. The morale of participants in the A spot was high; there people were interested, excited, ready to work overtime. Bs, Cs, Ds, and Es, however, wanted to get their pay and split. They found their jobs dull and boring, even though they knew their team was effective. Circles, in contrast, had high morale. Members were confident they would improve and showed few signs of boredom or frustration.

9. *Creativity and its implementation*: When someone in the Star, other than A, came up with a creative idea—an idea that would, if implemented, speed up the work—the "not-invented-here" syndrome came into play. The idea was usually rejected by A, who saw it as disruptive. "We're doing fine now. Let's not shake things up with some crazy new method." In the Circle, though, the same idea had a much better chance of being accepted and implemented by the whole group.

10. *Flexibility*: When the task was suddenly and unexpectedly changed and made more complicated, the Star groups had a great deal of trouble adjusting. They typically got stuck when confronted with a new, more complex task, making the same mistakes again and again, and adapting only very slowly to the new situation. Occupants of the A position in the Star found themselves overloaded with questions and complaints. Circle groups adapted to the changed conditions much more quickly and more fully.

In summary, this is the way the "effectiveness" of the two structures looked:

	STAR	**CIRCLE**
Speed	Fast	Slow
Quality of output	About the same	
Number of messages	Minimum required	Many unnecessary
Leadership	Clearly A	Usually none
"System"	Regular and orderly	Irregular
Morale	Very low (except A)	Very high
Creative ideas (acceptance of)	Mostly rejected	Mostly accepted
Flexibility (coping with a new task)	Rigid, inflexible	Self-modifying, adaptive

Which structure is better? The answer, of course, has to be, "It depends." If we equate "better" with the familiar standards of speed, orderliness, and predictability, then the Star-type hierarchy wins hands down. From that perspective, the Circle isn't even a "real" organization. It's just a bunch of people sitting around in a ring. It deserves epithets like "sloppy."

If, however, a "better" structure is one that is flexible, creative, and able to adapt quickly to a changed environment, then the Circle becomes a "learning organization," deserving of positive adjectives like "self-adjusting" and "flexible," while the Star now gets the nasty bits. It's "rigid," "inflexible," and "set in its ways."

Moreover, the Star generated disaffected, disinterested participants. Star members, except A, actively disliked the experiment, spent more time doodling, sent more task-irrelevant messages (such as bits of poetry), and left the laboratory sooner than the Circle people.

In the context of hot groups, consider two more points. Why was morale so much higher in the Circle than the Star? It was not because the Circle was a warmer, friendlier environment. Both Star and Circle were quite impersonal. Participants in both structures often didn't even meet one another. The answer, we believe, is that the Circle structure caused people to focus on the common task. Everyone was actively involved in the search for a solution. Once again, as in hot groups, the dynamics worked "backwards," from task to feelings, not from feelings to task. In the Star, almost all the interesting parts of the job—gathering information, making final decisions—belonged to A.

Another point: Notice that it was the structure—not the people—that generated Star members' attitudes. If, after the experiment, a recruiter had asked the experimenter for an evaluation of, say, person C in the Star, the answer might well have been, "Well, C's a bit lazy. He's not very interested. He doodles a lot when he should be working. And he's rather sullen and negative when you talk to him." How about person A? "Oh, she's great! Hard working, full of ideas, offers to work overtime! She's a very promising young woman."

Those conclusions, of course, are another of those attribution errors. As, Bs, Cs, Ds, and Es were all drawn randomly from the same pool of subjects. It's not A who's great and C who's a bum. It's the A position in the structure and the C position that are responsible. If we had taken Mr. C and put him in the A position, he would be the one who looked like a hero. It's not he who's a bum. It's his bum, dull, spirit-killing job.

All things considered, which type of structure is a better fit for our new global metropolis? Surely, it's the Circle model. Less hierarchical, more open, more interconnected structures are the ones likely to generate the innovation and continuous self-modification the new world will demand. Remember, though, whichever alternative we choose, there's still no free lunch. If we prefer Star-like structures, we may have to pay in morale, creativity, and flexibility. If we choose Circle-like designs, we may have to pay in speed, regularity, and orderliness.

Hot groups almost always prefer Circle-like structures. Large organizations have, in the past, almost always preferred Stars. Do they still? We think changing circumstances may be opening their hearts and minds to more circular designs.

Structural Characteristic 2: Hot groups are usually small

Don't expect many huge organizations to behave like hot groups. A few do, at certain periods in their lives, and, in a later section of this chapter, we shall talk more about them. But while it is certainly true that some hot groups can be quite large, just as some can live a rather long time, that is not the norm. Most hot groups are small enough to allow people to work with one another face to face—or at least terminal to terminal. Burgeoning communication technology is already spawning many new forms of groups, including closely knit ones whose members have never even seen one another's faces. Will that technology also enable the growth of much larger hot groups? We don't think so, but we urge the reader not to put much faith in that forecast. Remember that IBM's Thomas Watson predicted, in 1943, that "there is a world market for about five computers."[2]

Currently, groups that get hot usually range in size from three to perhaps thirty. Groups much larger than thirty are rather rare. Size varies with the organizational context as well as with the complexity and time frame of the task. While bigger tasks, coupled with longer time frames, make for larger hot groups, those larger groups are also more frangible.

Hot groups are usually small for many of the same pragmatic reasons that many committees, task forces, and other working groups are small: Intercommunication is much easier when numbers are small. It is hard to get much airtime in a very large group. Arranging for five busy people to meet can be difficult enough. Getting fifty together is often near impossible.

Why Large Hot Groups Are so Rare

Few tasks ever succeed in gaining the single-minded commitment of a huge number of individuals. Most nations and most other large human institutions are, themselves, composed of patchworks of small, often mutually hostile or distrustful groups. Many of those groups are forever trying to break away from their larger warders. The Soviet Union fragments into a constellation of previously independent small nations, which then split into even smaller ethnic and regional groups. So does Yugoslavia, that once tense amalgam of religions, languages, and ethnicities. At this writing, even a poor, small nation, Albania, is on the verge of a split, and Quebec is once more threatening to separate itself from the rest of Canada.

That propensity of smaller groups to split off from larger ones appears to be universal, extending across both space and time.

Readers familiar with corporate life probably don't need examples. Still, the following incident describing a group that was once part of Varian Associates, then an independent firm, and finally a subsidiary of Xerox, seems particularly illustrative of some of the causes of those tensions.

A small group of technologists breaks off from Varian Associates to start its own high-tech business in Northern California's Silicon Valley. Led by a charismatic and energetic philosopher/patron, Renn Zaphiropoulos, the new company, Versatec, is launched successfully. Versatec designs and manufactures state-of-the-art electrostatic printers, and its innovative machines soon dominate the world market. A few years later, Xerox Corporation acquires Versatec, leaving Renn Zaphiropoulos (RZ) in place as its CEO and also naming him a vice president of the parent company. For several years, RZ continues to run Versatec in the way he feels it should be run, without undue interference from Xerox.

Versatec expands and, at one point, decides it needs additional space. RZ asks the same architectural engineering firm—let's call it D and Associates—that designed and built his company's original buildings, to submit a plan and a bid. Versatec's relations with D are long-standing and mutually positive. When Xerox headquarters in Rochester, New York, learns of the proposed new construction, its Corporate Real Estate Division steps in. Company policy requires that in-house staff experts must approve all new construction of Xerox buildings.

A pair of Xerox real estate staff people fly out to San Jose from Rochester. They examine the plans and contractual arrangements for the new building. They suggest several modifications and many changes in the contract. One afternoon, after a multitude of such changes, the CEO of D and Associates, Versatec's long-time contractor, storms into RZ's office and announces that his firm wants out of the project. Those Rochester guys, he says, are nit-picking him to death. They are wasting so much of his people's time that his costs are skyrocketing. It's not worth it. He just doesn't want the job. RZ tries to soothe his hurt feelings, then makes several phone calls to Rochester. Finally, he politely asks the corporate real estate people to go home. Reluctantly, they depart.

We come now to the nub of the story. Some weeks later, RZ receives an invoice—a sizable invoice—from Xerox headquarters, covering charges for the recent services and expenses of corporate real estate staff in connection with planned construction at Versatec. Outraged, RZ lets Rochester know that he is not about to pay that bill, that Rochester ought to be paying Versatec for the trouble those experts caused. He reminds headquarters that he hadn't asked for their "help" in the first place and that their help was anything but helpful.

A long squabble ensues. The President of Xerox eventually intervenes. To smooth the troubled waters, he pays Real Estate's bill from his own budget. The relationship between Versatec and Corporate Real Estate does not soon improve.

A few years later, fiercely independent and protective of Versatec, RZ retires. Later, when asked what had become of his unique, lively, and very human enterprise, he replies: "It's been Xeroxed!"

That example, replicated so many times, in so many ways, in so many companies, is perhaps illustrative of the continual tensions that arise between semi-autonomous units and their parent corporations. Such tensions make the smaller units wish they could get out and the larger ones want to "make those guys realize which company they really work for."

A task with the pulling power to counteract such stresses must be so compelling that it can dwarf—at least temporarily—all those "normal" intergroup tensions. Only then may the whole diverse organization willingly drop whatever it is doing to give its all to a new, a superordinate, task. That's when connective leaders become key forces, welding together diverse constituents who previously had only the slimmest of common concerns.

The last national task we can recall that met those requirements was winning World War II. We had bad enemies then, bad enough so that we could clearly delineate one central task and commit all of us to it. For a while, our whole nation behaved like a hot group. So did many other nations. It was surely Britain's most cohesive, as well as her finest, hour. That task was so clearly life-defining that even highly individualistic leaders like Charles de Gaulle joined forces with his British and American counterparts to address their one common purpose. Of course, that war did not end the underlying differences among all the groups that had joined in that enormous effort. In the United States—and elsewhere—the Marines continued to make up nasty songs about the Army and vice versa.

Nonetheless, they both fought the Japanese and the Germans. Deep, durable differences were just temporarily submerged beneath the enormous common threat. As soon as the external war was over, internal warfare resumed.

That propensity of large groups to fly apart is surely a major reason why kings, presidents, and CEOs always have to juggle two quite separate jobs. One is to move their institution toward its core goals, toward democracy, or efficiency, or profitability. The other is to maintain the delicate unity of their diverse constituencies, to keep their institutions from splintering into a wrangling mass of warring tribes. That second job, even when it is helped along by threatening enemies, is often more difficult than the first. It requires the skill and vision of truly connective leaders.

Structural Characteristic 3: Hot groups seldom last long

In contrast to their parent organizations, which may live for decades, hot groups tend to form, work, and dissolve over much shorter periods. Sometimes they melt into other groups, or evolve into large, cool groups, or just die young. The reasons they don't last very long are simple enough.

First, they are usually organized around tasks rather than functions. When they have completed their tasks, there is little left to hold them together.

Second, hot groups seldom seek longevity. Unlike other living creatures, they don't struggle just to keep themselves intact.[3] And also unlike many other organizational units, hot groups don't try to guarantee their immortality by encircling themselves with impenetrable bureaucratic fortresses.

Third, hot groups' high metabolic rates tend to shorten their lives. After a while, they must slow down until they reach some less fuel-consuming speed.

Fourth, their openness and flexibility are simultaneously the wellsprings of their strength and a source of their frailty. Tighter, more formal structures may be imprisoning, but they are also stabilizing. Their formal rules and roles solidify them, making them less immediately susceptible to the whims of individual personalities and fluctuations in their changing environment. Thus, in World

War II, the French postal service, it is said, thoroughly formalized and routinized, went right on delivering the mail even on the first day the Germans occupied Paris. Of course, a hot group might do something similar, but for quite different reasons. It might be so much preoccupied with its task that it is totally unaware of some great happening going on out there.

When a hot group's job is done, its structural fragility converts into an advantage. It is then in everyone's interest to let the group fold its tent and allow its members to slip unobtrusively into other parts of the organization.

Structural Characteristic 4: Every hot group member does multiple jobs

Participants in organizational hot groups lead a double life. In their ongoing roles as members of a larger organization, they are endowed with formal titles and ranks, along with job descriptions and all the rest. In the hot group portion of their lives, however, those paraphernalia disappear. Rank and title, as we have noted, play minimal parts. One's position and activities within the group may vary sharply from day to day. That doesn't for one moment mean that all members do the same things. Internally, hot groups are apt to be highly differentiated, both in members' special expertise and in the various roles they play. Those differences, however, are not cast in concrete. Large chunks of those roles are informal and changeable, depending much more on situational demands than on rank or position. And, of course, their jobs are documented neither in formal job descriptions nor on organization charts.

Hot groups, as we have repeatedly said, are intensely focused on their tasks. Members, therefore, quickly learn about one another's task-relevant abilities. They become very savvy about who among them knows the most about what and who has the most appropriate skills for doing this or that. Hot group members are quick studies on issues related to their task. If they don't have a needed skill and can't easily get it from someone who has it, they're likely to go out and learn it for themselves. That's part of the "we're good and we can do the impossible" syndrome. Many hot group members who go in as amateurs come out as professionals.

We previously cited the example of such self-learning in a small

Singaporean company and in the early Macintosh group. How many other small hot groups have done the same, eagerly and painfully, learning to do what they did not know how to do, or, better still, what no one had known how to do before? New territory is familiar territory to hot groups. In the unknown is where they live.

Structural Characteristic 5: Hot groups need generous "time spans of discretion"

Time is a structural characteristic. Some organizations give people plenty of time. Others are time-stingy. Some organizations don't bother their people for long periods. Others check up on them frequently. The length of that period between inspections has been called "the time span of discretion."[4] It has sometimes been used as a rough index of an individual's power in an organization. The shorter the time between oversights, the less that person's power. The operator on the line, for instance, is likely to have his or her work inspected very often, even minute by minute, but the new CEO may be allowed a whole year before being checked out by the board.

Successful hot groups are almost always given generous time spans of discretion. To heat up, they need time as well as "space." The group that built the first IBM PC got a year. The Macintosh group had two years. Note that the time span of discretion is one kind of deadline. It's not a deadline imposed by the nature of the task, but a periodic checkpoint dictated by the organization. Too often, nascent hot groups are killed by very short time spans of discretion. This is largely because panicky managers, risk averse and fearful of anything that deviates from the routine, stand over them waiting to pull the plug at the first hint of trouble.

The Strategies of Hot Groups: "The Science of Muddling Through"

Hot groups are partial to what one observer called "the science of muddling through."[5] What he meant was reliance on a cut-and-try kind of approach to getting things done, a "strategy" of making a move, seeing if it's taking us in the right general direction, then trying another to take us forward from there. The muddling through strategy is a lot more sensible than it may look, especially when we are trying to go where no one has previously gone. It's a simple way of attacking problems, quite different from the grand, pre-specified blueprinting we usually associate with that weighty and forbidding phrase "strategic planning."

Hot groups do a lot of muddling through. They tend to integrate planning and acting, constantly moving back and forth between them. Conventional teams, on the other hand, characteristically treat planning and acting as two separate processes. They identify a specific goal—a point in time or space—and lay out in advance the precise route they will take to get there. Only then do they go into action.

> Remember, in junior high school history books, the story of young George Washington's attempts to teach British General Edward Braddock about guerrilla warfare? In July 1755, while serving as an aide to Braddock, Washington is said to have urged the general to proceed with stealth and caution as they moved along the shore of the Monongahela toward their objective, Fort Duquesne. Braddock refused. He had a plan and insisted on sticking with it. So, the British marched through the woods in full military formation, their drums signaling their presence, and their red coats providing easy targets.
>
> The enemy, however, composed of 900 French irregulars and their Indian allies, used something more like a muddling through strategy. They moved like ghosts from tree to tree, taking cover wherever and whenever they could find it, changing tactics as they went. The outcome: Nearly 1000 of the 1500 British colonials, including General Braddock, were killed or wounded, seven miles before they even reached Pittsburgh's Fort Duquesne.

More systematic and analytic strategies can work wonders in stable situations, when we know in advance just where we want to go and we have clear charts showing us how to get there. Such approaches carry all the advantages of orderliness. The cut-and-try, muddling-through approaches are messier, but have the benefit of easy modifiability and flexibility. They make sense when we know only roughly where we want to go and when nobody's sure about how to get there or what we'll encounter en route. Those are precisely the conditions that hot groups like best. They like to go places where there are no road maps. And that's just the kind of world that organizations are now encountering every day.

When a Large Organization Becomes a Hot Group

Most hot groups are quite small, but a large organization, of hundreds or even thousands, can become quite hot at some periods in its life. These are some of the conditions under which large groups can heat up:

- Crisis is probably the single most powerful generator of organizational heat. In times of crisis, otherwise bureaucratic organizations will take on much of the flavor of a hot group. Those occasions are rare, and most are short-lived. Johnson & Johnson, during its Tylenol crisis, was a good example. NASA, during the brief but intense crisis of Apollo 13, also seemed to operate as one hot unit.

- A few small start-up companies manage to maintain much of their early heat even as they grow quite large. Intel is one example. Its outspoken and confrontational culture continues (as of this writing) to make it a pretty warm organization.[6] Maybe next year it will cool down, or maybe it won't. Science Applications International Corporation (SAIC), a company we mentioned earlier, even in its infancy several decades ago, quite consciously worked as a loose collection of small, quasi-autonomous, mostly hot groups of scientists and technologists. It has now grown into a very much larger community of similar groups.

- Some large, "protected" subunits of still larger organizations sometimes show almost all the attributes of hot groups. The National Institutes of Health, in its youth, was such an organization. Congress insulated NIH, granting it a long time span of discretion. It was allowed freedom from oversight for several years. During that period, NIH grew into a hot organization, innovative, risk-taking, exciting, and extremely productive. Its standards of excellence were very high. The same was true of Bell Labs (now partially reconfigured into Lucent Technologies) in its scientific glory years, when it was similarly and intentionally insulated from the other units of the huge Bell System.

Organizations, as well as individuals and groups, need those sheltered periods, though they seldom get them. How much warm-up time does the Board (or the media) allow that new top management team before the evaluations and critiques begin? How long do we tolerate our newly acquired subsidiary's insistence on doing it their way before we step in to change things? Sometimes, the criticisms begin even before a new management team has found the restrooms. Remember how one media guru solemnly pronounced President Clinton's administration irretrievably dead within a week after his first inauguration?

Companies in which the search for truth is a dominant, widely shared value often generate a good deal of heat, even though they may be quite formal and rigid in other respects. Bell Labs, in its prime, was a good example. There, the free-thinking values of science prevailed even over the traditional values of that otherwise conservative, hierarchical parent, old Ma Bell. We return to the issue of truth-seeking as a key value in a later chapter.

One can debate endlessly about whether a whole organization is or isn't hot. Wasn't Bell Labs really a cold organization that permitted many hot groups to grow within it? Are organizations like Intel and NIH really large hot groups? Or are they more like those aquatic creatures that, on close inspection, turn out to be colonies of separate, but highly interdependent, small organisms? Some organizations certainly look like that kind of dynamic, ever-changing assemblage of many loosely connected small hot groups—functioning, in fact, much like the whole of American society. The label is far less important than the result.

Currently, many private sector companies are trying to restructure themselves into multi-unit forms, changing from traditional monolithic bureaucracies into clusters of smaller entities. They are trying to change so they can cope better with the volatility of the speedy informational world. New names are even being created to denote such multigroup architectures. Some scholars call them "federalized"[7] organizations or organizations built around "internal markets."[8]

One final generalization: If observers generally agree that a whole organization is hot, then it is also likely that large crops of small hot groups will be found growing inside it.

In Summary

Hot groups' structures are fully interconnected. Anybody and everybody is free to communicate with anybody and everybody else. If communication is restricted in a hot group, it is because the group chooses to restrict it, not because of structural rules imposed from above or from outside. Hot groups' structures are more like egalitarian "Circles" than hierarchical "Stars."

Hot groups are mostly small. Larger groups sometimes get hot, but they have a propensity to break up into smaller ones. When that happens, the breakup is very frequently accompanied by mutual hostility.

Hot groups shouldn't be expected to live forever. They should end, and they usually do, when their task is done. The definition of "done" belongs to the group, not to the parent organization. Forcing a hot group to carry on beyond where it wants to stop is a sure way to cause a big chill.

While wearing their organizational hats, hot group members may hold very specific titles and job definitions. No such restrictions carry over into the hot group. There, roles and responsibilities may change again and again, conferring considerable power on a member one day and none the next. That variation, however, is a function of each person's appropriateness to the particular aspects of the task.

Some large organizations, on rare occasions, become hot groups, especially in times of crisis. Other large organizations become more like collections of small, semi-autonomous hot units. The important point is not their form so much as the degree of heat large organizations can generate as they confront the kaleidoscopic changes of the new world.

In the next chapter, we look at the frequently tense relationship between small hot groups and the large organizations to which many of them are inseparably tied.

9

Hot Groups and the Organization: A Marriage of Inconvenience?

No man—or woman—is an island, nor, in our interdependent global metropolis, is any group. Hot groups may prefer to live in splendid isolation, walled off from the rest of the disturbing world, but that's seldom in the cards. The rest of the world is too much with them. Like every other unit of the modern organization, hot groups must continuously communicate, negotiate, compete, and collaborate. They must work with other parts of their own institution and with all sorts of outside groups. They may complain about the demands that those others make on them, yet they must, perforce, do at least as much demanding as the other guy.

In this chapter, we examine both sides of this marriage of inconvenience. Instead of going on about why modern organizations need hot groups, we consider why hot groups also need their parent organizations. Then, we try to figure out why hot group/organization marriages are so often rocky. We even offer some marriage counseling, outlining a few steps that each might take to help them live more happily together. How can hot groups and organizations get along without either being forced to abandon its core culture and its core values?

Once, if a hot group were unhappy with the way it was being treated, it could rather easily have packed up and walked away. No more! Nor is it any longer wise for an organization just to shove one of its hot groups out the door. Those quickie divorces are pretty much a thing of the past. As the world speeds up, hot groups and their parent organizations are being pressed to stay together, forced into ever more symbiotic relationships. The two may not like living with one another, but they're finding it even harder to live apart.

The 1997 Academy Awards provide an example of that increasing interdependency. After those awards were announced, there was much talk in the industry about how many Oscars had been taken by "indies," small, independent film makers. It seems, however, that those little hot indies aren't as independent as they look. *Fortune* magazine pointed out that many of them are closely tied to major studios.

> Indies, the standard line goes, got 70% of the [Oscar] nominations in the top categories, proving that independents are classier and more intelligent than their crass, studio siblings. Now is the perfect time to ask whether this accounting is correct. In short, it is not. . . . The confusion stems from the fact that [the large] studios have been spending heavily to acquire independent films and studios. . . . Independent studios now routinely produce their own movies with their corporate parents' money. . . . 'Indies', such as Fine Line, Gramercy, and Sony Picture Classics, are also owned by big corporations (Time Warner, Polygram, and Sony, respectively). . . . "I don't really know if there's anything that can truly be called independent right now," says Lawrence Bender, who produces Quentin Tarantino's films.[1]

So, too, in science and technology. Little high-tech startups can go part way all by themselves, but the full completion of their chosen tasks is likely to require facilities, skills, and other resources that only a big organization can provide.

On the other side, the big organizations, undertaking huge projects, find that they also need those little hot groups. They can easily put together a number of bodies and call it a "tiger team," but heating that team up is quite another matter. Groups with "tiger team" labels often behave like pussycats. The problem is to generate heat in groups working in the chilling environments of cold bureaucracies.

What's So Special About the Relationship Between the Hot Group and the Rest of the Organization?

Hot groups' dealings with other units are unusual in three important ways:

First, task-obsessed hot groups typically take a narrow, binary view of other parts of the organization. They see other groups as either task relevant or task irrelevant. There are at least two ways in which another group can be task relevant:

1. *That other group looks like it may be doing things related to our task.* Maybe they've got useful knowledge, or equipment, or skill. That's why Steve Jobs and his little group went to visit Xerox PARC (Palo Alto Research Center) in 1979.[2] They knew that the Xerox people were doing interesting things with PCs. That visit turned out to be the stimulus for what later became the Lisa computer and, ultimately, in 1984, the Macintosh.

2. *That other group looks like a competitor or an intruder.* Those varieties of groups are task relevant because they stir the blood and push already high levels of motivation even higher. They are simultaneously task distracting, however, because they divert attention from the group's task to attend to the threat.

As for everyone else, they're task irrelevant, so hot groups often make the foolish mistake of ignoring them. Although those other groups may not be directly task relevant, many are apt to be strategically, albeit indirectly, important. Just as organizations are too often deaf to the interests of hot groups, hot groups too often ignore the longer term, economic, social, and political interests of other groups. That two-way lack of understanding was illustrated dramatically some years ago in what happened between that isolated hot group at Xerox PARC in Palo Alto, California (the same one that Steve Jobs happened to visit in 1979) and its philosophically and geographically distant parent in upstate New York. It is an unhappy illustration of how the working styles, cultures, and mindsets of little hot groups can clash with those of their large, structured parent companies, causing both to snatch defeat from the jaws of imminent victory. The following case is adapted from Robert Cringely's book, *Accidental Empires*.[3]

In the early 1970s, Bob Taylor, the visionary psychologist who was ultimately its director, established Xerox PARC. He recruited a handpicked group of researchers and set up a lab in the idyllic, oak-studded foothills of the Stanford Industrial Park near Palo Alto, California. The lab's task was to give Xerox a head start toward the office of the future. They envisioned sites where typewriters and copiers would be nothing more than archaic relics. The researchers at PARC were independent and irreverent. They had ideas that broke the mold. Cringely writes:

> They had nothing at all to do with copiers, yet they worked for a copier company. If they came to have a feeling of solidarity, then it was much more with each other than with the rest of Xerox. The researchers at PARC soon came to look down on the marketers of Xerox HQ, especially when they were asked questions like, "Why don't you do all your programming in BASIC—it's so much easier to learn," which was like suggesting that Yehudi Menuhin switch to rhythm sticks.[3]

The PARC researchers, inspired by the mouse and bitmapping work of Doug Englebart, a researcher at Stanford Research Institute, invented the first high-speed computer networks and the first laser printers, and they devised the first computers that could be called easy to use, with intuitive graphical displays. Yet the Xerox Corporation never became a significant player in any of those areas. It is overly simplistic, however, to suggest that Xerox was too hidebound or too bureaucratic to comprehend the enormous potential of that little hot group's creations. It was more complicated than that, on both sides.

> David Kerns, the president of Xerox, kept coming around [to Xerox PARC], nodding his head, and being supportive but somehow never wrote the all-important check. Xerox's on-again, off-again handling of the Alto [the first primitive and expensive prototype for a personal computer invented at PARC] alienated the technical staff at PARC, who never really understood why their system was not marketed [although, as Cringely notes, at a 1973 street price of $25,000, the Alto was beyond the pocketbooks of "mere normal mortals"]. To them,

it seemed as if Kerns and Xerox, like the owners of Sutter's Mill, had found gold in the stream but decided to build condos on the spot instead of mining, because it was never meant to be a gold mine.[5]

Thus, the Xerox Corporation and PARC could not develop a critical linkage between them. Although Xerox had itself been founded on a brilliant technical invention, it missed its opportunity to exploit other technical inventions that might have allowed it to dominate the whole gestating PC industry.

That was not the first, nor will it be the last, failed relationship between a large organization and a little hot group within it. Yet, in the years ahead, those relationships will surely become even more vital. Consequently, it is certainly time for each partner to acknowledge, if not admire, the important role of the other.

Second, as we described earlier, hot groups' propensity to isolate themselves generates frustration, resentment, and envy in other groups. Such feelings are not trivial. They have practical effects. Those other groups soon begin to hit back. They may not protest aloud, but they may slow down support, cut off supplies, and generally bad-mouth the group. By putting too much distance between themselves and other groups, hot groups thus frequently defeat their own purposes. They actually generate, and may eventually have to confront, some of the very intergroup tensions they want so much to avoid.

Third, hot groups can be fickle friends. They can seem capricious and even disloyal. In a certain limited sense, they are both—and more. Let other groups be warned! You may think that a particular hot group loves you, but down deep it loves its task much more. A hot group may come around flirtatiously, all sweetness and generosity, but once it's got what it wants, good-bye Charley! It's really after what it can get from you, your skill, your equipment, or your money. Its heart is always firmly devoted to its own work. Don't count much on a hot group's loyalty, even to those who have been helpful and supportive, and certainly don't count on devotion to the organization. It isn't that hot groups are selfish or malicious. They're just single-minded.

Although such hot group behavior is quite unattractive, it is worth noting that it is also quite businesslike. Described somewhat differently, the same qualities look more positive. How about this alternative description? Hot groups keep their eye on the ball. They're all business. They don't waste time. They know what they want, and they go for it. Nevertheless, many executives understandably view hot groups as loose cannons. They may ask: "Why support such difficult groups? Why ask for all that trouble?" One answer, of course, is that these are not the times to be avoiding "trouble" or seeking solace in the status quo. Nor is it a time for organizational peace and tranquillity. Hot groups, albeit difficult to integrate into many larger systems, offer potential benefits that far outweigh their costs.

A second answer: Because they are enthusiastic, hardworking, and task oriented, hot groups can set a more urgent tone for a lethargic organization. They may get other groups mad, but that can be just the spark to relight the fire of a cooling organization. And a third: Hot groups give their members a *raison d'être*, a chance to do worthwhile things, to ennoble themselves. Shouldn't every organization's people get that chance?

Why Hot Groups and Large Organizations So Often Have Trouble with One Another

Why do those group/organization relationships so frequently go downhill? The answer, this time, lies neither in our stars nor in ourselves. It lies instead (a) in the complex structures of our large organizations, which too often squeeze people into untenable situations, (b) in our human propensity to attribute causality to individuals and groups rather than to situations, and (c) in still another "natural" human propensity—the tendency of groups to distrust other groups, especially unfamiliar ones.

Structural Complexities in Organizations Cause Tensions Among Groups

When two units of an organization can operate entirely independently of one another, the relationship between them may be superficially and cautiously friendly. When the two meet, they say a polite "good morning" and then go on about their business. They don't bother us, and we don't bother them.

In modern organizations, though, that's the rare and exceptional case. Most relationships among units are marked much more by *inter*dependence than by independence. Besides, where there is significant interdependence, there are also bound to be tensions. Indeed, interdependent relationships between groups, whether of similar or different sizes, probably go sour even more frequently than relationships between individuals. In our experience and in that of other observers,[6] mutual *dis*trust among organizational units is far more common than trust. Production people stereotype engineers as impractical, pie-in-the-sky dreamers. Marketers caricature designers as nerds who wouldn't know a live customer if they met one. Researchers see accountants as nitpickers, while accountants see researchers as wastrels. And so on and so on.

Any reader who has lived in a large organization knows how easily such conflicts can arise, even when no one wants them, how enduring they can become, and how quickly they can migrate into personal dislikes and even lasting enmities. Such conflict is part of the day-to-day background noise of all organizational life. And it's also one of the reasons that hot groups and large organizations have trouble meshing.

Not too long ago, one of us encountered this example:

In a large technical company, the R&D/marketing relationship had gotten so bad it verged on the ridiculous. The R&D Division was a major force in the company, employing several thousand professionals. At the behest of R&D's top management, two of us consultants were asked to help design a marketing course for the division's department heads.

We thought the marketing course was a fine idea and attributed great wisdom to the R&D vice president who initiated it. He seemed to be sensing imminent changes in the whole competitive environment of the company. So, he had decided his researchers ought to have a better understanding of the marketing end of their business. Hence, as a first step, he proposed a three-day intensive, off-site marketing course for his senior managers.

Together with a small committee of R&D executives, we went to work designing the course. We helped line up appropriate marketing professors, as well as practitioners from other companies. At one point during the planning stage, one of us suggested something so obvious that it never occurred to us to think twice about it: Let's invite the company's two senior marketing executives for a session in which they could talk about the Marketing Division's plans, problems, and operations.

The reaction from our R&D planning committee was, to say the least, curious. Again and again, our proposal was gently sidetracked. "Well, that's worth thinking about," or "Let's decide that off-line." For several weeks, we simply couldn't get the committee to say either "yes" or "no" to scheduling a presentation by their own company's marketing people for R&D's new marketing course.

In private, we consultants scratched our heads. Why? Why was R&D offering its people a marketing course, but refusing to let them hear about their own company's marketing policies and practices? Over time, we came to understand the situation better. We learned that the relations between R&D and marketing had become so strained that the leaders of the two groups quite literally hadn't spoken to one another for a very long time. As far as R&D was concerned, marketing was a bunch of hack salesmen who didn't know their ears from their elbows. They kept pushing R&D to develop junky, Mickey Mouse products instead of doing serious research and development. R&D certainly wasn't going to have such birdbrains teaching their people about the basics of modern marketing. Inviting marketing professors was OK. Business school professors might not be real scientists, but at least they carried a modicum of respectability.

Still, one question remained unanswered. It was the R&D people who had wanted to put together the marketing course in the first place. Why was the R&D Division even bothering to invest time and money in such a course?

We discovered that we consultants had made a major attribution error. We had ascribed the request for the course to the foresight of the R&D VP, believing that he had sensed his industry's rapid shift toward a market-driven, competitive environment. Thus, to prepare for it, he wanted his people to become more knowledgeable about the marketing process. Or so we thought!

That, we later learned, was hardly the case. The VP, it turned out, was not the real source of the marketing idea. That idea had come down from upstairs, from the corporate COO. Top management had been putting more and more pressure on R&D to come out of its mountain top isolation and get its people closer to the marketplace.

The VP of R&D had made a significant contribution all right. He had come up with the idea of the course. It was his way of finessing the real problem. By putting on a marketing course, taught by outside academics, he could demonstrate to the folks upstairs his division's willingness to think seriously about marketing, while still avoiding direct contact with those awful company marketers.

That R&D Division's effort to steer clear of marketing should sound familiar to hot group members, even though no hot groups were involved in this case. Like the R&D Division, hot groups are prone to self-isolation, so they can get themselves into similar conflicts quite easily. These days, however, no groups, whether hot or cold, can hide out for long. Interdependencies are inescapable in modern organizations. The tensions that accompany the complex designs of large organizations are as inevitable as the interdependencies that generate them. Still, those tensions are not all bad, and things can be done to alleviate the bad ones.

We Attribute Causes to People that Really Stem from Structure

Although a job or a whole organization may be poorly structured, we are still most likely to blame the people, individually or as groups, for its inadequate performance. That's the attribution error at work again. When Harry doesn't perform well at his new job, we conclude that he's just not up to it. Perhaps, though, Harry's job was so badly designed that it couldn't be done by any mortal creature, living or dead.

We know one company, for example, whose chairman hired and fired five CEOs in four years. In the fifth year, he came around to blaming himself, but what he blamed himself for was hiring all those dunderheads. He was still sure that Mr. or Ms. Right was out there somewhere. He went right on looking for the right person for the job. He might have done better to begin looking for the right job for the person.

That attribution process, for good or ill, works in both directions. It can make fools out of heroes and heroes out of fools. When the economy goes into recession, blame the president, but when the economy booms, re-elect him—by a landslide. How many teachers have been told, years later, that some passing remark they made decades ago changed the entire course of a student's life? Usually, the nonplussed teachers can't remember ever having said anything like that. How many consultants have been blamed for disasters or lauded for great deeds that were entirely independent of their actions?

In many, if not most cases, larger situational factors are likely to be the actual forces responsible for the current state of affairs. The team's losing season may have had little to do with the coach and much to do with injuries and schedules. Far off revolutions in oil-producing countries, not presidential decisions, may be what's sucking the economy down the drain.

Some political advice to aspiring young managers follows from that tendency to ascribe causes to people more than to situations:

> Don't let your hubris cause you to wade into a situation that is guaranteed to fail, regardless of the quality of your work. Look carefully at the situation and consider how much of it is beyond your control. Don't forget that if your hot group fails, you may be killing off not only your own future chances, but the chances of other such groups which might follow.

Predatory Groups, Ethics, and the Spirit of Competition

There is yet another reason why hot groups thrive in open, flexible, organizational settings. In this and many other societies, freedom of enterprise is a core value. Relative to traditional hierarchies, groups in those newer, flatter organizations can more readily engage in enterprises of their own making and are freer to innovate, explore, and search anywhere for whatever they may need. In those more open, multichanneled networks, the search for resources, ideas, and people becomes quite easy. There's much less nonsense about going through channels, getting permissions, writing memos. If a group needs something to help accomplish its work, the group itself becomes an avid hunter, not for sport or survival, but for achievement. Members use all of themselves—their skills, connections, reputations, and personalities—to get the job done.

Elsewhere, we have labeled such behavior *personal instrumental* because it involves the use of all aspects of the self as well as the use of others connected to the self.[7] Groups can use that *personal instrumental* style, too, and hot groups often do. They frequently beg, cajole, threaten, or co-opt to obtain whatever resources they need, people included. They use a wide range of goal-oriented behaviors that we earlier described as achieving styles.[8] Hot groups in such organizations remind one of those ever-present characters found in every army—the ones who can always manage, somehow and somewhere, to "requisition" whatever the unit happens to need.

In conventional organizations, such behavior, particularly when laced with casual disregard for others, won't do at all. It is deemed predatory and immoral. In many organizations, if a group acts that way, top management will find itself besieged with complaints—frequently exaggerated—about that gang of raiders who pirate our people, do their own "creative" accounting, and violate all the rules. In more and more of today's redesigned organizations, however, such styles are being viewed more tolerantly, so long as all groups stay within well-defined boundaries. The result? Vitality and productivity, if careful limits have been set and actively enforced. Complete, not organized anarchy, if there are no boundaries at all.

Remember *The Soul of a New Machine* from the 1980s?[9] It's worth another look. That small volume describes a driving, internally competitive organizational style, with all its costs, but also its benefits. Was the hot unit of Data General just an anomaly? A random group of renegades? We think not. We believe it was an early harbinger of organizational evolution just now coming to pass.

In Summary

Modern organizations need hot groups, but hot groups also need organizations. The era of the stand-alone, little startups is rapidly drawing to a close. In the new, interconnected world, it's not just individuals who will be building networks, alliances, and support systems. Small groups and large organizations will require all those as well.

Yet, even though they need one another, interdependent units in large organizations readily tend toward enduring conflicts and mutual distrust. Hot groups hold a certain advantage here. Because they tend to be short-lived and because they are so extremely task oriented, they don't have time for long-term feuds. That advantage, however, also makes them fickle. Their commitments to relationships are short term, with members likely to feel more loyal to their task than to their organizations or their allies.

This chapter outlined some costs and benefits that accrue to organizations and hot groups as a result of their ongoing relationships. There are many sources of strain in that relationship, strains that can lead not only to misunderstandings but to unethical behavior at both ends. Many derive from the needs of large organizations to maintain order and predictability and the needs of hot groups to hang loose and do things their way. But the benefits of modest compromises on both sides can and often do pay off handsomely.

In Chapter 10, we continue to examine the hot group/organization relationship, this time focusing on how hot groups can serve as effective instruments of organizational change.

10

Using Hot Groups to Improve
the Organization:
Some More Marriage Counseling

Most of the accommodation between hot groups and organizations has to come from the organization's side. So, most, but not all, of our marriage counseling in this chapter, will be directed to that larger partner. We shall offer some possible ways that the leaders of large organizations can use small hot groups to help them effect significant and positive change in their organization's performance.

You Can Encourage Hot Groups—and the Whole
Change Process—by Doing Less, Not More

Changing an organization usually means taking clear positive actions, like installing a new information system, or restructuring financially, or moving from a functional to a product line design, or bringing in a new top management team. None of these is likely to do much to lay out a welcome mat for hot groups. To make the organization more receptive to hot groups, it's more often a good idea not to take clear, positive actions. For a highly structured organization to start growing hot groups, it first needs to relax its old rules and constraints. It does not need to install new ones.

Loosening is almost always easier than tightening. If done gradually, the effects are also much less traumatic for all concerned.

Obviously, one shouldn't expect people who have spent twenty years in leg irons to leap into creative action immediately after their release. So both incrementalism and some positive leadership are in order. Yet, all things considered, the opening of closed organizations is likely to be far less difficult than the closing of open ones.

Set Your Hot Groups Free. Change Will Follow

One option for large organizations seeking change is to give birth to some hot infants and then encourage those infants to fend—mostly—for themselves. That tactic, setting up new entities and freeing them from most parental controls, has been used for centuries by many different kinds of institutions. Its advantages are obvious: Older sibling units can go on conducting their usual business, without any niggling from those haloed little newcomers. The new babies will like it, too, because they can then conduct their un-usual business, free from bureaucratic interference and sibling rivalry.

As with humans, though, organizational pregnancies sometimes occur accidentally. Baby hot groups, thus, come in two models: *Intended* and *unintended*. Intended hot groups, while not manufactured, can be desired and encouraged. They're the organization's legitimate offspring. *Unintended* ones are usually surprises, initially unwanted and often disavowed. Organizations are likely to treat the two kinds of youngsters quite differently.

Parenting intended baby hot groups: Supported isolation

Even while living in quasi-isolation, legitimate hot groups receive lots of TLC. Their parents give them space, money, and other resources. Remember, for example, the *intended* group at IBM that developed its first PC? At the time, IBM was in a catch-up mode, well behind the newcomer Apple. So they sent a little group off to Florida to create a great new personal computer. They also gave it lots of parental support, while still protecting it from the rest of the family. It worked. That group heated up and did its job extremely well. Of course, IBM wanted that baby, or rather it wanted what that baby might produce.

Coping with Unintended Baby Hot Groups:
Abortion and Absorption

Unintended hot groups often arise in protest against something their parent organizations have either done or failed to do. For centuries, organizations have tried—sometimes quite successfully—to deal with such groups by using a variant of that same isolation scheme. Almost always the parent organization initially views the deviant, protesting group as an irritant and tries to destroy it. Failing that, it tries to get rid of the group by sending it away, walling it off, or otherwise isolating it. For PR reasons, the parents may publicly bless the child, even while sending it off into the forest where they hope wild beasts will—discreetly—devour it. Sometimes, however, the little group fools everyone. It survives and even does something wonderful, like converting the carnivorous beasts to vegetarianism. In that case, the organization takes a deep bow, congratulates itself on its foresight, and publicly pins a medal on the group's collective chest.

That strategy—try-first-to-abort-them-then-isolate-them-then-absorb-them—is, one might say, "ethically challenged." Nevertheless, it is frequently successful because it allows parent institutions to play it both ways. If the troublesome group doesn't make it, little harm is done to the organization's existing culture. If, on the other hand, the stubborn little group should manage to survive and prosper, the parent organization can modestly take the credit and also, often, the fruits of the group's labor. Here are two examples, adapted from the work of Ruth Love.[1]

In the sixteenth century, the Carmel Order of the Church of Rome used just such a strategy to deal with St. Theresa's small, dissident faction of "discalced" Carmelites, so called because of the simple sandals they wore. Believing that the parent order had become too lax and that nuns were spending more time gossiping than praying, St. Theresa's little band insistently protested, wearing rough garments to symbolize their purpose and relentlessly demanding wide-ranging reforms.

At first, the parent Church responded harshly. It ordered the group to be split in two, sending St. Theresa off to run a distant convent and excommunicating other nuns loyal to her cause. Even in her new setting, however, that irrepressible woman persevered. She organized another small, hot, protest group. She also found a protective patron, King Philip II of Spain, to help sustain her group. The movement grew and gained influence. After an extended struggle, the Church eased up and absorbed the group, finally allowing it to initiate its own order. In 1593, the Discalced Carmelites were granted full autonomy by papal bull. From then on, they reported directly to the Pope.

Another, somewhat more recent historical example, also adapted from Love, reveals the same tactics and essentially the same outcome: Initial rejection, then isolation, then absorption.

In the 1930s, well before the U.S. entry into World War II, General Claire Chennault and a ragtag group of fighter pilots were flying against the Japanese in China.[2] By 1941, when the United States entered the war, that group, by then called the Flying Tigers, had become something of a thorn in the side of the U.S. Army Air Corps. The Tigers complained publicly, constantly, and in no uncertain terms that the Air Corp's fighter tactics were utterly obsolete, useless in contemporary air warfare.

The Air Corps was not pleased. Initially, in keeping with the classic pattern of abortive isolation, it sought to disband the Tigers. Failing that, the Air Corps tried all sorts of ploys intended to eliminate them. They delayed Chennault's recruits in India, to keep them from completing their trip to China. During that time, they also tried to indoctrinate those recruits against the Tigers. The Air Corps even sought to select Chennault's Chief of Staff for him.

Once again, however, an influential patron intervened. This time it was Mme. Chiang Kai-Shek. Using her connections to the U.S. power elite, connections that reached all the way to the White House, she held off the Air Corps so the Tigers could stay alive to help her husband's Kuomintang carry on against the Japanese. She even invited the Tigers to join the Chinese military as a volunteer unit, paid by the Chinese government.

Finally, in 1942, after the United States had entered the war, the military bowed to mounting pressure from Mme. Chiang, President Franklin Roosevelt, and the by then enormous public popularity of Chennault's group. The Air Corps absorbed the Flying Tigers, eventually renaming them the 14th Air Force. The unit was placed under General Stilwell's command, but with specific instructions from Chief of Staff General Marshall to give Chennault whatever he needed.

Let's consider another example, the relationship between the United Steelworkers of America, CIO and a little group led by a great trade unionist, Joseph Scanlon, a trusted veteran of both that union and the United Mine Workers.

The Scanlon Plan,[3] a local union/management cooperation plan, was developed in the 1940s by Joseph Scanlon, together with local steelworkers union officers and the managers of a small steel fabricating company. As with many other innovations, the Scanlon Plan was the product of crisis. In this instance, a factory in a small Ohio town was on the verge of bankruptcy. The plant was sinking rapidly, so both company officials and local union members turned to Scanlon for help. Scanlon was then educational director of the United Steelworkers.

Together, the company's CEO, the local union president, and Scanlon shaped the first experimental version of what later came to be known as the Scanlon Plan. The plan called for setting up worker/manager joint productivity teams throughout the company. All improvements in productivity were to be tied, by an agreed on formula, directly and quickly to everyone's take-home pay. "Everyone" meant everyone, from sweeper to CEO. Increases in productivity this week would show up in higher paychecks next week, not next year.

That first experiment was welcomed by all concerned: Owners, managers, employees, and the local union. It worked. Both productivity and morale rose sharply enough to swing the company back to viability.

At first, the Scanlon Plan was also hailed by the steelworkers' national union. The national certainly wanted its members to prosper, and Joe Scanlon, after all, was a dedicated, long-time union man. The number of companies adopting the plan increased rapidly. Later, though, the national union's attitude changed. In plants in which the plan was operational, local union workers and managers were joining together to work on a common task. They were improving their company's performance and, thus their own incomes. In the manner typical of hot groups, joint work on the task was followed by improvements in the relationships among the participants. Local union/local management relationships began to turn the corner from mutual hostility toward mutual trust. Employee commitment to their companies increased.

That worried the steelworkers' national leadership. Their union's strength, they seemed to believe, lay in an adversarial relationship with management. Scanlon's plan was causing too much collaboration. Gradually, the national began to view the plan not as a positive good, but as just another management ploy intended to co-opt their union members.

Nor were leaders on the management side universally supportive of the Scanlon Plan. Many wouldn't touch it, for fear that it would require them to cede too many "management prerogatives" to their employees. Others probably worried about the feedback they might receive from employees. They might learn too much about the inadequacies of their own managerial practices.

Bureaucracies, on both sides of the management/labor divide, behave like bureaucracies. So, the United Steelworkers, founded with the help of John L. Lewis's United Mine Workers and dedicated to the welfare of steelworkers everywhere, eventually grew into the same kind of turgid bureaucracy as its corporate counterparts. The Scanlon Plan did not die, however; indeed, it is alive and operational in a number of companies in the United States and abroad. Sadly, it never received the wide adoption it deserved.

One moral:

Learn to appreciate and pay attention even to the unintended offspring of your organization. Those unwanted babies may be trying to push you in the direction you really ought to be going.

The behavior of hot group leaders becomes critical in such situations. Whether active conductors, more distant patrons, or KOFs, it's the leader's job to make sure that the hot group's isolation is never absolute. Leaders can serve as linchpins, connecting even an unintended hot group to other groups, keeping communication channels open, informing relevant stakeholders about the group's activities, and generally building relationships throughout and beyond the organization. Then, when and if the hot group accomplishes something useful, its product will not have to be sprung on the whole company as one huge surprise.

Move Toward a Broad, Group-Based Architecture

Organizations still *think individual*. In the past, there were plenty of good reasons for doing that; now, however, it is time for organizations to *think group*. Ironically, thinking group will also encourage individualism. Consider this complicated sentence, which isn't, we suggest, as silly as it at first sounds:

> When an organization focuses on the groups that compose it, the individuals within those groups can act more individualistically than when the organization's focus is only on individuals.

When the organization thinks *group*, organizational controls can be targeted on each group's behavior, more than each individual's. Individuals are then freed up to behave more autonomously than if they must all work within the same standardized, organization-wide rules, regardless of their individual differences. Under the protective umbrellas of certain kinds of groups, individuals can be more themselves.

Not all groups enhance individualism. Many lay their own controls on individual members, demanding that every member conform to that group's particular styles and standards. What then? Aren't peer-group pressures to conform even more powerful than pressures emanating from distant executive offices?

Peer pressures are certainly a real danger, especially for two varieties of hot groups: Those that arise in protest and anger, like the Discalced Carmelites, and those caught in the thrall of a single powerful leader, like the suicidal Heaven's Gate sect. For the majority of hot groups, however, dedicated to their innovative task, the danger of hyperconformity is minimal. Hot groups may share common standards about what constitutes good work, but they almost never set standards about what members must believe or how they must behave. Although one cannot discount altogether the danger of "groupthink," wherein a whole group falls through the looking glass of self-deception and megalomania, it seldom is a serious danger in diverse and democratic hot groups.

To profit from the energy and creativity of both individuals and groups, the organization can apply the necessary—and only the necessary—controls to whole groups, leaving most of the rest to the groups themselves. That's what many scientific and academic organizations have been doing for a long, long time and what many contemporary "federalist" organizations are now doing. That means less uniformity and more diversity across the organization and also more opportunities for groups to invent and innovate.

Risky? Not very, although given all that autonomy, an occasional outlaw group may violate even the necessary organizational rules, bringing pain and humiliation on its parent. Such unhappy events occasionally happen with groups, just as with individuals. Earlier, we mentioned Michael Milken's group at Drexel Burnham.[4] That was a very hot and very secretive operation. It separated itself from its parent's New York headquarters by moving to Los Angeles. That group was certainly innovative. Unfortunately, many of its innovations were illegal.

There is reason to hope that such violations will occur less often in increasingly group-based organizations. Such an organization has to exert oversight over only a relatively small number of groups compared to the much larger number of individuals who comprise them. That change should make it easier for the parent to know what's going on in the total organization, even though it is partially counterbalanced by the propensity of hot groups to keep their internal operations under wraps.

Using the Hot Group as a Change Agent, Consciously and Intentionally

A few hot groups scattered around the system make excellent organizational alarm clocks. They stimulate and agitate. They wake up sleeping units and release frustrated people who have been held captive within them.

Encouraged by senior organizational patrons, hot groups can act as prods to move the rest of the organization from lethargy to vivacity. Hot groups' bravado and passion can stir the organization's blood and increase its pulse rate.

> One of us observed firsthand how a single hot group acted as a change agent to raise the vitality of a whole organization:
>
> A large, conservative engineering firm, let's call it A&B Engineering, was generally considered rather slow-moving, but with a reputation for first-class work. Financially, A&B performed reasonably well, though few analysts touted its stock. A&B's headquarters occupied a moderately new, ten-story urban building. The top floor executive offices were imposing, thickly carpeted, and hushed. Turnover among executives was almost nonexistent, with average managerial seniority well over twenty years. As far back as anyone

could remember, promotions had come entirely from the ranks. For senior managers, A&B was a safe, comfortable place to pass one's golden years, and the food in the executive dining room was worth at least one Michelin star.

Then, quite unexpectedly, the chairman made a radical and unprecedented move. Concerned about his organization's future, he recruited two newly retired military engineering officers directly into the company's upper ranks. They, in turn, brought in a small cadre of their former military mates. This new group, given lots of leeway by the chairman, became quite hot. Its members moved into strategic positions in major divisions of the company. Wherever they went, they infused energy and speed into one field division after another.

Younger, more junior engineers welcomed the newcomers. Long frustrated by the old bureaucracy, they willingly fell in with this lively new crew. They began to take risks they had never dared attempt before, and ideas, long-withheld or ignored, came bubbling to the surface.

The veteran senior officers felt differently. The newcomers frightened and angered them, especially since they marched right past the long termers, largely ignoring them and doing little to placate them. Among themselves, these veteran executives called the new arrivals the "military mafia." Still, their obvious disapproval only seemed to turn up the group's heat.

Despite rising tensions, the company's chairman, the mafia's patron, held his ground, giving the mafiosi lots of room to innovate and experiment. Before long, several vice presidents took early retirement. Slowly, the whole culture shifted, moving in a much more lively and proactive direction. The group itself gradually metamorphosed into an ongoing management team. It lost much of its heat, but its members remained powerful all over the organization.

The chairman hadn't consciously planned this hot-group-as-change-agent strategy. Nor had he deliberately set out to act as patron of a hot group. He just brought in two strong people to help get the company moving. The hot group developed semispontaneously from there. As it evolved, the group was blessed with support from both top and bottom. That support lasted long enough to enable the group to do its thing, despite the stresses generated in the midddle and upper levels of the organization. In this instance, the new hot group was not physically isolated. It infiltrated throughout the organization. Helped along by eager young working engineers, it got things done. Psychologically, however, the group was isolated from the rest of the senior executives. That isolation worked both ways. It disturbed and stimulated the rest of the organization, and it simultaneously added to the newcomers' own sense of cohesiveness.

Rough-riding hot groups make wonderful change agents, especially when nurtured by high-level patrons. Using hot groups that way, however, is a risky option. Such groups are neither gentle nor subtle. They don't nudge or cajole. They more often do their work via confrontation and challenge, generating high anxiety all over the organization, much like rampaging new CEOs. Sometimes the rampage causes so much human trouble that it outweighs the benefits of the change.

In the case of A&B, there was a sharp increase in performance of the company's field operations, but very slow change at headquarters. Since that "revolution," A&B has performed moderately well. From 1995 to the end of 1997, its sales increased a respectable bit over 50 percent. One can only wonder what might have happened if the revolution had not occurred.

Anxiety: The "Bête Noire" of All Organizational Change

Once, as we were about to begin a consulting assignment, our client company's CEO made this double-edged request:

> Feel free to go anywhere you want to go in the company. Talk to anyone you wish. Ask any questions you wish. But there's just one thing I ask of you. Please, make sure you don't cause any disturbance.

Is that possible? Can one separate change from its closest companion, disturbance? We think not. Kurt Lewin, the great social psychologist, characterized change as a three-stage process, starting from an initial "frozen" state, then moving to an "unfrozen" state, and only after that to a new, "refrozen" state. The most important and most neglected part of that "freeze, unfreeze, refreeze" formula is the middle, the unfreezing part. Neither individuals, groups, nor human organizations simply change from condition A directly to condition B. We must first pass through a vulnerable, risky swamp of "unfrozenness." We must give up the security of the old before we can enjoy the benefits of the new.

Individuals, and organizations, too, change much the way lobsters molt. A period of soft-shelled vulnerability intervenes between the past security of the abandoned old hard shell and the new security that can come only when the new one hardens. We don't know whether lobsters feel anxious during that changeover, but humans certainly do. Moreover, lobsters, even if they do feel scared, can't elect to squeeze themselves back into their old hard shells, but humans often think they can. When children try to change from crawling to walking, their frequent falls upset and frustrate them. Periodically, they regress to the security of what they know best—crawling. Sooner or later, though, most kids make the switch. They change. Managers do the same. Confronted with pressures to change their attitudes and behavior, they may feel anxious. Yet, despite that anxiety, they stick their necks out and change. Their interest in new and better ways is too hard to resist.

Groups and organizations are human, too. Their anxiety also increases as they approach the unknowns of imminent change. Right now, in our chaotic world, they have to endure that scary molting much more often than in earlier times. Understandably, they move gingerly out of their old ways, cautiously dipping their toes into the waters of change. Then, they are apt to get scared and try to hightail it back to the security of the familiar shore. For the people in organizations, though, that secure shore may not be there any more.

That's what happened when the military newcomers changed A&B Engineering. We believe they changed it for the better, but it was certainly no free lunch. Some of A&B's people paid a very high price. Lives were disrupted. Those veteran executives—the ones who were ignored and bypassed—had spent their careers in that company, building it, sacrificing for it, giving it their full loyalty. In the twilight of those long careers, should they have been subjected to all that humiliation and anxiety? Clearly, they did not deserve such unhappy endings. Could some other less painful option have worked? Certainly—but those alternatives would have caused other anxieties and distress, too.

We are not touting the hiring of renegade hot groups to toss hand grenades into sleepy organizations. We are simply suggesting that any significant human change will have important human costs and organizations should be ready to take responsibility for coping with them.

The lessons:

1. Significant change invariably causes disturbance and anxiety. So, the presence of moderate anxiety should not be read as a sign of failure, but an indication that change is actually underway. Don't turn off a hot group simply because it makes its own or other people feel anxious, any more than you would turn off a new CEO or a consultant for disturbing the status quo.

2. The presence of a little anxiety is likely to improve human performance. Modest amounts of anxiety increase our energy and productivity. Excessive amounts, however, can cause paralysis or explosion in both individuals and organizations.

3. Anxiety hurts. So, although you can't avoid anxiety during periods of change, you can and should do your best to prepare for and ameliorate its pangs and pressures.

Look Forward, not Backward

Looking forward is easier to suggest than to do. It's hard to orient oneself toward the space age if you've lived your whole life in a sixteenth-century Venetian palazzo. Working in outmoded structures, no matter how elegant, drives one to look backward toward the proud past, not forward to the uncertain future. Although failure to learn from the past can be dangerous, inability to shake free of it can be fatal. The Victorian poet Matthew Arnold offered that wisdom a long time ago. He recommended keeping the best of the past and discarding the rest. He urged each new generation to integrate the valued residue of the past with the best of their own new ideas. We would then have a continually appropriate approach to each new era. Hot groups are a piece of the future, as surely as the World Wide Web. It is time to integrate them into the best of the organizational past.

In Summary

How can large organizations utilize hot groups without entirely abandoning their core cultures and traditions? The first step involves relaxation of existing constraints more than imposing new ones. That can be done incrementally.

Hot groups can also be used in active, intrusive ways, as agents of organizational change. They can awaken dozing organizations and raise organizational pulse rates. Such actively instigated changes, however, generate anxiety and emotional pain. Organizations should consider how best to deal with those human costs before opting for such invasive approaches.

Thus far, we have said very little about the downsides of hot groups, their weaknesses and failings. Chapter 11 examines the causes of such failures, as well as their effects.

11

Why Some Hot Groups Fizzle While Others Sizzle: Four Cautionary Tales

Not all hot groups manage to maintain their sizzle all the way to the completion of their tasks. In fact, without the right nutrients, even a very hot group can fizzle out, leaving its distraught members helpless and frustrated. So, although we are enthusiastic about hot groups, we must also acknowledge their fragility. This chapter looks at some sources of that vulnerability, factors that can spell disaster for a hot group.

Case 1 — An Epitaph: The Premature Demise of a Productive Hot Group

We begin with a sad case from the publishing industry, one that illustrates many, if not all, of the elements that can prematurely douse a hot group's sizzle.

The company, which we'll call New Press (NP), is actually an old press with a long and revered history. Of its seven divisions, the Management Books Division (MBD) had become the company's real engine, accounting for more than half of NP's total profits and perhaps even a larger percentage of its respected reputation.

MBD's vision was simple, but powerful: It sought to publish quality books that would significantly improve the art of management. Driving that vision was a small, hot group. One member of that group recalls:

> We honest to God believed that the reason the entire NP existed as a publishing house was to influence the way management was practiced by the quality of the books we published. The four of us had this shared vision about what it meant to be publishing such books and that sense of incredible responsibility for contributing to publishing works that people were, we assumed, going to read and sort of take as gospel. And then (we believed) they were going to take this and do something with it. Their behavior would be influenced by what we had helped the author create.

This all-encompassing purpose became the focus of that little group within the MBD. The group's four core members were the acquisitions editor and leader of the group, Jack Right; Jack's administrative assistant, Ben Fellows, whom Jack was grooming to become a second acquisitions editor within the group; the production editor, Jennifer Lindsay; and Harriet Silvers, the marketing director. Although there were other members who worked with the group, these four continuously fueled the group's furnace.

Jack was truly an "author's editor," a charismatic, dynamic Max Perkins type for management writers. Jack admired the way Perkins, in earlier decades, had coached so many young novelists, like Thomas Wolfe, bringing shape to their often cumbersome and inchoate manuscripts. Jack was also a superb acquisitions editor. He successfully signed up excellent new authors and charmed many older ones away from their previous publishers. Authenticity was a major key to Jack's success. He developed deep, honest, and loyal relationships with every writer he nurtured. Authors felt they were handing their beloved babies to someone who understood and loved them as much as the proud, but edgy, parents did themselves.

Ben, eight years younger than Jack, was much quieter. He tended to work in the background, but the other group members understood the vital importance of his role. He was the stabilizing force that often kept this little group from self-destructing by spontaneous combustion. Harriet described a typical situation:

While the rest of us would be off ranting and raving about one thing or another, and sometimes at each other, Ben would just sort of be there, the voice of reason, the person who would keep the home fires burning.

Jennifer, by contrast, was a complex, intense young woman of thirty-something. Everyone considered her an absolutely top-notch production editor. Other members of the team held Jennifer in awe, despite her very different, sometimes abrasive style. On occasion, spectacular conflicts erupted between Jennifer and Jack, largely based on the way that Jennifer would "challenge the process." Harriet explained:

> It was because she was so incredibly good at what she did that there was never ever a question about the integrity of Jennifer's work or her intent. It really was just a style issue. . . . The one difficult thing sometimes about teams in general is the group mindset—the Abilene Paradox—where you get going and things almost get too smooth. You start going down a road, and all of a sudden there isn't anybody to be that real difficult person, to say, "Wait a minute. We really did-n't want to be here," or in plays and literature, the village idiot, the bearer of truth, when no one else will say it.
>
> There were times—I remember one particular instance—when it became so clear to me that that was Jennifer's role on the team. When the rest of us would be advocating for the market and the sales reps, Jack would be advocating for the author; so that sometimes the whole perspective of the quality of the house, of the publishing house itself, [was getting lost]. Then Jennifer would step in and say, "Wait a minute. When this is done, are we really personally going to be proud of what we did? Our markets might be satisfied, and our authors might be satisfied, but are we personally going to be proud to say that we published this book?"

Harriet, the marketing director, always spoke her mind, directly, vigorously, and often humorously. Before joining NP, Harriet had worked in several ad agencies, marketing consulting firms, and corporate communications divisions. She, too, was first rate at what she did. Initially, Harriet and Jack often found themselves in conflict, largely because Jack remained skeptical about whether Harriet could make the transition to marketing in the publishing business. Harriet recalls:

Jack and I had the strongest personalities, which of course caused tensions. The upside is the creative energy; the downside is the conflict. And I think Jack and I both appreciated the fact that without conflict, you also can't have the creativity. I think it plays itself out through a real sense of passion about what one is doing and the sense of passion that you bring to your own contribution to a team. And sometimes Jack and I would simply have different ideas of the way that quality should be executed.

Harriet understood she had to earn her stripes with Jack. She described the sometimes painful process that ultimately forged a bond of trust between them:

> In a publishing house, . . . the role of an editor is to advocate for the author, and the role of a marketing person is to advocate for the market. And what happened was that Jack and I finally realized that those were our roles. And he felt safe in the sense that I was not going to try do his job. He also learned . . . that I would do my job. He didn't have to do it for me. And I don't think that he ever had that experience with a marketing person before.
>
> I had to convince Jack that he really could trust me implicitly, . . . that I was not ever going to do him any harm. I was never going to be disrespectful to his authors; that they weren't going to be just his authors, but that I was going to take them on as my authors, too. . . . And once we got past that . . . then there was almost nothing that he and I couldn't work out. . . . We could at least always come to the table and come to some agreement about what the ultimate goal was and come to terms with the fact that it really was my domain to decide how we got there. It took a while.

Although there were sometimes up to six other members who worked on the periphery of the MBD, these four individuals were the nucleus of this hot group. Between 1991 and 1995, according to one member, "Ninety percent of the work was done by those four." During this time, like much of the publishing industry, NP's parent company, let's call it Koch and Kincaid (K&K), was undergoing a seismic shift in philosophy and strategy. Ultimately, MBD and the entire New Press would feel the impact of those changes. At the heart of that looming crisis lay a near-reversal in editorial policy. According to Harriet, the change moved from publishing more books to make more money to publishing fewer, but more blockbuster books. The greatest impact of that shift in philosophy on a publishing house is on production, because, if there are not as many books, you obviously don't need as many production editors. So the call went out for volunteers to be laid off. At the time, we actually had two full-time production editors, Jennifer and Connie, both of whom opted to take the severance package. That was a shock. I was devastated. I felt a tremendous loss for Jennifer. . . . I really didn't try to convince Jennifer to stay. She was just really burned out. She needed to leave for her own sake, but I think I knew instinctively the impact that her absence would have.

As part of the restructuring at K&K, an orphan imprint, focusing on scholarly books, was unloaded on NP. The people upstairs were talking to Jack about heading up that operation. In many ways, he liked the idea. It was to be a small academic press encompassing many scholarly fields. In such a setting, the editor could work closely with authors, without the growing pressure for producing blockbuster trade books. Increasingly, Jack became distracted, trying to decide between heading up the new imprint (which meant abandoning the excellent division he had helped to shape) and dealing with the demand for fundamental and less *simpatico* changes in MBD. He also knew that there were more than a few embers of sibling resentment smoldering within the other six divisions, which perceived his group—not necessarily incorrectly—as a spoiled, outrageously demanding, but highly productive and creative brainchild.

Under the old philosophy, MBD could do no wrong, although both Jack and Harriet occasionally had been advised to tone down the "noise"—the attention that the group called to itself. They recognized, however, that the group's creativity and noise level were conjoined twins, not easily separated. Of course, Jack's division knew they carried a lot of clout, and they rarely hung back from making special demands, whether for new laptops, more staff, or a move to arrange all the group's offices on the same corridor.

The new philosophy focused much more attention on the bottom line. NP had, in the past, produced mostly research-based books. Most of those books didn't sell in huge numbers, but, by carefully managing their production and marketing, Jack's group had been able to make the list quite profitable. Those relatively narrow margins, however, were not part of K&K's new strategy, one requiring more "accountability," including more written justifications for the group's proposals. That new way of life was stifling. Harriet analyzed the coming changes:

> The more reports that were necessary, the farther away I was going to get from the things I liked to do and the less time we would have to operate as a team. Eventually there was a lot of pressure from K&K. Our one team was producing the lion's share of the profits for NP. That was dangerous—too much reliance on our books. Four of us were making it work for 150 employees. K&K was trying to push the other six publishing divisions to carry their own weight. The result was perhaps what they anticipated: It killed off our group. The strategy of trying to create more balance of sources of revenue was right, but it was done wrong.

To replace Jennifer and Connie, a new production editor, Decatur, came on board. Completely unflappable, Decatur, whose competence was unquestioned, maintained a low-key presence. The rhythm of the group began to change. Harriet lamented,

> Decatur's work was certainly on a par with Jennifer's, but we had lost that extra personal component to really creating that kind of high-energy, creative sense.

Eventually, with some misgivings, Jack decided to accept the job with the new imprint. He assured himself, as well as his authors, that his leaving wouldn't change anything, that the division's operation was a "team effort," that Ben would step into his shoes, that the changeover would be totally seamless. Jack had already added new people to the group, in corporate sales and publicity. The half-dozen outer circle members of the hot group were still there, and things would work out. In fact, he argued, there would be more muscle than ever before.

Ben, who had been the perfect balancing member of the hot group, stepped into the leadership role for which Jack thought he had groomed him. By now, Ben and Harriet were the only remaining core members of the original group.

Ben, scanning the horizon for new books, spent a lot of time on the road at conferences and with individual potential authors. By that point, it was clear that the hot group had fizzled. It simply did not exist.

Harriet reminisced:

> After Jack left, it just wasn't as much fun. I need a lot of creative tension to do my best work. To this day, there is one other person, maybe two others, I feel I have had this with. It's been so perfect in terms of my doing my absolute best, stretching myself, delivering beyond what I thought I was capable of. One is Jack Right. Jennifer was another. Jennifer and I talked about this several times. It wasn't only Jennifer's qualities, but the dynamic of the team. I know people who've worked in publishing for fifteen years who don't know what I know about production and acquisition. There was learning that went on in that group that was really mind boggling when the group was hot. It was the same for Jennifer, who also learned.

Within six months of Jack's departure, Harriet quit to join a marketing agency 1500 miles away. Several years later, with another shift in K&K policy, Jack finally left the company to start his own small publishing firm.

Some Lessons from MBD

What can we learn from the dissolution of this particular hot group?

- *Even "golden calves" can be sacrificed.* MBD's four-year lifespan was longer than many. Maybe this fizzle was just a natural event. Yet, we believe this group's demise came earlier than necessary. MBD was cut down in its prime; its task was changed in midstream, not by the hot group itself, not even by NP, but by the distant parent organization, K&K. The group was caught off-guard, lulled into complacency because they believed they were the "golden calf" of NP. Even golden calves, however, can be slaughtered "for the good of the organization."

- *Monitoring the environment.* This case underscores the importance of monitoring any hot group's environment, something hot groups too often ignore. Caught up in the passions of the task, group members frequently forget that the organizational environment, as well as the wider world outside the parent organization, can change swiftly, creating currents that an unprepared group will find hard to navigate. Unless someone is continuously monitoring what's happening out there, the group may find itself swept away by those powerful, unanticipated events.

- *Monitoring the folks next door.* A hot group must monitor more than the larger world. It also needs to scan the smaller, close-in boundary between itself and other units of its larger organization. Most hot groups, like the MBD, are noisy, creative, resource guzzlers, who—from the perspective of those on the outside—appear arrogant and selfish. Someone—whether the conductor/leader or the patron/leader—needs to mediate between this hot group and other organizational groups, both hot and cold, and also up and down the hierarchy.

- *Dealing with crises.* Jack's group was confronted with a sudden and major crisis. It had been going great guns, and then—before it had completed its task—an organizational meteorite crashed into its insulated world. Hot groups have a complex relationship with crises. Some crises actually serve as midwives to hot groups, helping to deliver them so that they can make the quick, vital responses that could not come from other parts of large, unwieldy organizations. Other crises, like this one at MBD, become hot groups' executioners.

  Should that crisis have come as such a complete surprise? The entire publishing world had been in turmoil for close to a decade. Who, if anyone, at or close to MBD was scanning the horizon for signs of danger? Connective leaders, who see the connections among everyone and everything, usually build vast networks of associates. They can act as natural magnets for the organizational and environmental intelligence needed to avert or otherwise cope with impending crises. In this case, Jack, a fine leader in other respects, did not perform that intelligence function, nor did anyone else.

- *Losing a leader.* If a respected leader leaves, the group is in serious danger of a terminal tailspin. In theory, at least, the leader should have already prepared an appropriate successor, but that is easier said than done.

  If we look once more at MBD, Jack's leaving spelled the very end of the hot group, even though he had presumably readied Ben to take over. Group leadership, especially hot group leadership, is not something that can be passed on easily. Some ineffable qualities of both person and situation are irreplaceable. Leadership in a hot group is "organic." A new leader may emerge, but only rarely can one be implanted.

  Jack, as we saw earlier, also tried to manage the meaning of "the team effort" after he decided to move to the new imprint. The team, he assured everyone, would go on as before. Despite his sincerity, those words always hung unconvincingly in the tense air—even to the untrained ears of a newly recruited author anxious about the impending turnover.

  Although Jack thought of Ben as his alter ego, virtually everyone else saw them as opposites who, nonetheless, made a good team. Jack's dynamism and vision had charged up the group and generated creative sparks. As the new leader, Ben, quieter and more introspective, simply couldn't fan the flame. He tried to keep the dream alive and actually believed he could, but there was little fire left in the ashes.

  Perhaps this is a good example of the transient quality of hot groups. Rather than expect to revivify the old group, we might better mourn its passing and run the shop in a more organizationally traditional way until the seeds of a new hot group can be helped to sprout.

- *Coping with burnout.* Burnout may be rare in hot groups, but it can happen. When any member begins to burn out, prompt first aid is absolutely required. Unattended burnout of one or more key members seriously intensifies the fizzle factor. It is not just a question of helping one person as he or she begins to falter. Burnout in one member usually signals impending burnout in others. Moreover, burnout, like suicide, is contagious.

In the MBD case, the most clearly declining member was Jennifer, but others were also experiencing various degrees of exhaustion. Ordinarily, when one member begins to suffer such depletion, others step in to relieve the wounded member. Yet despite her own anxiety about Jennifer's departure, Harriet, perhaps wisely, never tried to convince Jennifer to remain with the group. Harriet recalls:

> Jennifer just burned out. That took a couple of years. . . . I didn't try to convince her to stay. I think I knew instinctively the impact her absence would have, but she needed to leave.

Burnout prevention is worth a thousand cures. Although prevention is sometimes not possible, in most cases, early detection can certainly help. So let us offer a few strategies that might either prevent or at least reduce the chances of burnout in a hot group:

1. The leader, as well as every individual member, must be on the lookout for early signs of burnout in other group members and also in themselves. Constant monitoring is absolutely essential for strengthening the immune system of an individual or the whole group.

2. The simplest cure for exhaustion is rest and relaxation, for individuals and for groups as well. R&R is a good mechanism for preventing serious burnout, but it is also useful once the blahs have begun to set in.

3. Perhaps the key to minimizing burnout is the ratio between fatigue and satisfaction. Increasing satisfaction, via explicit rewards, including social approval and appreciation, can certainly help keep burnout at bay.

4. Using hard and soft markers to take stock of accomplish-

ments helps restore people's energies. A confident, but realistic, reassessment of how far the group has come can often prove a welcome relief.

5. Group therapy sessions are fine, too, if fatigue and petulance have set in, so long as they don't become a permanent substitute for the original task.

6. Individual therapy may also be in order. Sometimes, because of the group's zest, individual members may be reluctant to air publicly their own doubts. Providing a private space for the expression of misgivings can be a powerful medication. Purging the soul can be restorative.

7. It is often useful to introduce and encourage other tension-releasing mechanisms, for the group as a whole and for any member who seems particularly vulnerable. We wrote earlier about the seemingly infantile antics one often sees in hot groups. We want to reiterate that there can be wisdom in such foolishness.

8. If the task and the talents of the various group members permit, think about urging the burnout candidate to change focus, at least temporarily. A shift in focus often reduces tension and sparks new creativity.

9. Finally, if a member's burnout really requires that person to leave the group, then facilitate a gracious exit. Don't, however, forget to bind the group's wounds and institute some ritual to mark both its regrouping and a renewed beginning.

Case 2—The Difficult Newcomer: A Hot Group's Near-Death Experience

One of us once led a small, hot research group of graduate students. The introduction of a new member almost capsized the group, but luckily—and not because of the leader's skill—it managed to right itself. Here is a first-person account of the case:

The little group, composed of three graduate students and me, as instructor, was already in full swing when a faculty member from the Economics Department of our university telephoned to ask if I would permit one of his students to join the group. I was a little reluctant, primarily because I worried that the economics student might not have the methodological training necessary for this particular project. My colleague assured me that this young woman was familiar with our work to date and was fully prepared to assume her load.

At the same time, I, perhaps naïvely, felt I shouldn't refuse any graduate student entry into a group for which students received research course credits. So, with misgivings, I agreed to admit the new person into our, by then, lively, even sizzling little group. I guess I should have attended to my own radar.

Julie joined the group several weeks after the semester had begun. She called to tell me how excited she was about joining and how much she had read about our research. I felt somewhat heartened.

When I announced to the group that we were going to get a new member, there was some low-level grumbling but no serious resistance. After all, they, too, were graduate students who could have been in the same situation.

Meeting 1. At the first meeting Julie attended, things went about as one would expect. Julie said little and listened, and, while there was distinct wariness on the part of the regulars, they gave it their best shot. Most of the session was spent briefing Julie, bringing her up to speed. I felt slightly more encouraged.

Meeting 2. The night before the next meeting, Julie telephoned me at home. She commuted more than fifty miles to the university and her car was out of commission. She wouldn't be able to make tomorrow's meeting. The regulars—Frank, Marcia, Jim, and I—met, and the heat began to build. The group was full of ideas and excitement—much to my relief. Things, I thought, would work out after all.

Meeting 3. Julie, her car repaired, showed up on time. The members took turns patiently explaining what we had accomplished at the meeting Julie had missed. Julie listened, a serious look clouding her features, eyes narrowed, mouth downturned. When Frank finished describing our progress, Julie nodded slowly and thoughtfully. Then she began to speak. For ten minutes, Julie questioned every point the group had made. She disagreed with our methodological decisions. She felt our conclusions were dubious at best. The atmosphere palled. The group began to sag.

Meeting 4. No Julie. When it became clear that she was not coming, the group began its work. One could almost see the group shrugging off the previous meeting's depression. We worked longer than usual. The ideas just seemed to flow. The enthusiasm—mine included—mounted. At the end of the session, everyone just hung around. It was as if no one wanted the magic to end.

As you have probably surmised by now, a pattern was emerging. Julie would miss a meeting, the group would work well without her, then spend most of the next session bringing her up to speed. She would respond by criticizing everything that had been done in her absence. Soon, the regulars were in near revolt. They sought me out, individually and then as a group. Julie, they complained, was ruining the group's momentum. They all felt Julie's criticisms were neither valid nor helpful, that they were her weak but destructive defense against having missed the previous meetings. I had to agree. Clearly, action had to be taken.

I called Julie at home to set up an appointment. Her schedule was very tight. We agreed to talk on the phone then and there instead of face to face. I tried to explain that her on-again off-again participation was really slowing down the group. Julie protested that she really enjoyed the group and wanted to remain in it. She promised more regular attendance. Several additional meetings were held. Julie appeared only once more.

When it became evident that Julie had pretty much departed the scene, a palpable resurgence took place in the group. The energy level rose. The excitement returned. Unfortunately, much time had been lost, and we were under a tight time constraint. The semester would soon be over, and we were nowhere near our goal.

That little band of four dug into the task with unbelievable vigor. We not only reached our original objective before the deadline, but also solved another rather complicated research problem.

We've all kept in touch with one another since then, even though the three students have long since graduated. Whenever we meet, we talk nostalgically about that group and our superhuman accomplishments. From time to time, I have asked the other three what happened to Julie. Why had she dropped out? What had transpired between Julie and them? No one could or would offer much of an explanation, but I suspect that the group, in its own way, had taken more effective action—consciously or unconsciously—than I had.

There were, obviously, things that I, as leader of that group could have done to mitigate the situation. None, however, was likely to have been entirely satisfactory—none, that is, save keeping Julie from joining the group in the first place.

Here are some other imperfect options that could, and perhaps should, have been tried but weren't:

1. If someone new must be introduced into an ongoing hot group, clearly the leader should take pains to prepare the group well in advance of the event. Together, the leader and the group can plan a conscious strategy for incorporating the new person.

2. The leader should fully clarify the group's norms and expectations for the neophyte member. If, as leader of that research group, I had sat Julie down at the front end and again as the trouble began to brew, Julie would have had a better chance of integrating herself into the group.

3. If I had put the issue on the table for the entire group, including Julie, either Julie would have been able to participate more effectively or she would have withdrawn sooner. In either case, the group would have been better protected, a first-order responsibility of the leader.

4. As leader, I might have specified a trial period, during which both sides could decide if the fit was right. That is a reasonable procedure, even when the new person is someone who is actively sought by the hot group. It may be difficult to negotiate such an arrangement when the new member is unavoidably foisted on the group, but it's certainly worth a try.

5. The "deviant" member (Julie) could have been given a specific subtask that required little interaction with the rest of the group. She probably would have seen that ploy for what it was, but it may have been better than nothing. We know of one such case in which the group isolated the intruder, giving that individual a separate and separated

task. But that isolation took its toll. The leader spent much energy keeping the isolate sufficiently busy and content so that he did not resentfully undermine the hot group.

Basically, trying to operate a hot group with one off-center member is like trying to run a marathon wearing a too-tight shoe. Maybe you can finish, but only with much more than the usual pain. The misery, moreover, might get so bad that you would have to give up and drop out. The best idea is to start the race wearing shoes that fit.

Case 3—The Government Injects a Resident Director to Control a Newspaper's Hot Editorial Group

Once, when one of us served as a consultant to the largest newspaper group in an Asian country, we had a chance to observe this situation:

> By any journalistic standard, the newspaper we'll call the *National Tribune* was a first-rate daily. The editors and reporters had been trained in the finest schools of journalism in the United States and the United Kingdom. Their journalistic standards of excellence were just that. The Prime Minister took a paternal pride in the paper, but, like many demanding fathers, he and other government ministers also reacted swiftly whenever the *Tribune* published material even mildly critical of government policy.
>
> The Prime Minister, a larger-than-life figure, was universally regarded as a brilliant, benign autocrat. The young Harvard-educated editor had grown accustomed to warnings from the PM and to irate phone calls from one cabinet official or another. He handled them as diplomatically as possible. He also had to transmit the complaints to his editorial staff, who reacted strongly, viewing them as threats to their journalistic integrity. Nevertheless, the paper managed to walk the tightrope between full freedom and full control.
>
> Finally, however, the PM concluded that more than telephone calls were in order. He decided to implant a trusted cabinet minister and career diplomat into the *Tribune* organization as a Resident Director. Mr. Edward Chen moved full time into an office at the *Tribune* building. No one quite specified what Mr. Chen's duties were, but it was clear to all that he was there to protect the government's interests.

At first, everyone, from publisher to editor to reporters and staffers, was on the alert. Richard Ho, the young Editor-in-Chief, worried about the impact that Mr. Chen's presence would have on his small very hot editorial group, a group that worked literally around the clock to put out a paper that made them all walk a little taller. Ho, a straight shooter who communicated his own core integrity to everyone, wasn't quite sure what would happen. Ho knew one thing though: He was determined not to compromise the journalistic excellence of his paper nor would he abandon his loyal staff.

Some members of the editorial group thought the best way to deal with Mr. Chen was to isolate him, not to let him in on the "real stuff." Ho thought that strategy would be not only dishonest but self-defeating as well. Instead, true to his own nature, Ho decided the best plan was simply to include Mr. Chen in everything, make him a real part of the team, let him see the problems they faced from the inside.

Surprised and pleased at his positive reception, Mr. Chen, a long-time diplomat, listened and watched. He attended staff sessions, even meeting separately from time to time with Ho and others all along the line. He soon understood that no one was trying to hide anything.

Ho and the rest of the hot group never lobbied Chen to plead their case with the Prime Minister. That had been a conscious and deliberate decision of the group. On occasion, they asked Chen's opinion, but not his advice on editorial matters. Gradually trust and respect grew on both sides. The staff recognized that when Chen gave them his opinion, he was simply predicting how this ministry or that one was likely to view their proposed actions. He was not trying to pressure them, just telling it like it was.

Mr. Chen, for his part, began to understand the paper's concerns, the dedication of the editors, the hot group's struggle to report the full story, even at the cost of some embarrassment to the prickly government. Quiet, unobtrusive, but broadly experienced in the ways of diplomacy, Chen quite naturally took a diplomat's perspective: to get the two parties, each concerned with the nation's health, to see one another's points of view. Over time, Chen became virtually a full member of the hot group, so much so that when we visited the *Tribune* one year later, Chen was invited to the lively luncheon the inner core of the hot group held in our honor. Tensions between the Prime Minister's office and the *Tribune* eased, although, from time to time, the paper crossed the government's line, leaving Mr. Chen to smooth feathers on both sides.

In this case, the uninvited and initially unwanted member was co-opted, not by artifice, but by actuality. Chen, offered an unadulterated look inside the workings of the hot group, was wise enough to see at least part of the world through their eyes. As a result, he gradually assumed the role of patron, a leader who could use his diplomatic skills to mend the group's fences with the outside world. Of course, the co-optation worked both ways. Skilled negotiator Chen also succeeded in slightly softening the editorial group, so the number of government complaints began to fall.

As we have already seen in previous cases in this chapter, not all uninvited hot group members work out this well. A large part of the reasonably satisfactory outcome was due to Mr. Chen's style. He remained patient and understanding throughout. Another part was attributable to the group and especially to its leader, who never compromised his own or the group's integrity.

Case 4—The Hard Life of a Hot Group of Bulgarian Entrepreneurs

Throughout, we have emphasized a dilemma: Hot groups tend to be great consumers of resources, thereby often creating resentment and consternation elsewhere in the organization. When resources dwindle, however, the hot group may begin to falter. The following case, reported to us by a Bulgarian colleague, is about that dilemma and its sometimes sadly humorous aspects.

> Shortly after Bulgaria's transition from socialism, a small group of scientists began to form around a talented physicist/engineer whom we'll call Sascha Dimitrov. Dimitrov had developed a new laser technology that would allow surgical intervention in cases previously considered inoperable.
>
> In 1990, immediately after the political transition, Dimitrov registered a private company that we'll call LASELLA Ltd. He gathered around him a group of other scientists to work on the development of his device for laser surgery. According to observers, the most salient characteristics of each member were (a) acknowledged expertise in a scientific area, (b) similar scientific values, and (c) a reputa-

tion for honesty, reliability, and a strong sense of ethics. Moreover, Dimitrov's personal opinion of each member was the most important criterion in the selection of the team.

As our informant described it:

While they had been colleagues at a research institute, the group had often discussed the theoretical possibilities for making such a device. In fact, even before the transition, they had wanted to start this project in quite a different organizational form. They were highly motivated because they knew that their product was unique. It would offer a surgical cure for some patients with diseases of the eye, the liver, the intestines, etc., who now had no hope through ordinary therapies.

Bulgaria's new post-communism conditions provided an extra stimulus for the group because they believed that they would now be independent and free from bureaucracy. They would be able to choose any organizational structure they wanted, and they would own their device. The new market environment would inspire interest in such innovations as theirs, and that, in turn, would increase the size of the market.

The group had studied two foreign companies that were developing similar apparatuses and concluded that theirs had more options and several better features. By this time, the group was indeed hot. They were working at fever pitch, confident that their device would have many other unforeseen applications. They were certain that the new range of products they wanted to develop would help with even more difficult and specialized surgery. LASELLA Ltd. then signed a contract to sell and install the new device at one hospital attached to the Ministry of Health. The laser was delivered, and the hospital's physicians began using it. All reports were positive.

Then came the hooker: The hospital did not pay its bill, nor would it return the product, claiming it was essential to its work. Without that payment, LASELLA could not afford to continue its work, even though they had fifteen other products on the drawing board.

An ironic twist resulted from all this: The members of the hot group, anxious to carry on their work, then became fund-raisers for the hospital. They began persuading members of the community to make donations to the hospital so that the hospital would pay what it owed and they could then continue their work. Needless to say, they also began exploring other ways of earning a few *leva* to support their families and their research.

Our informant continues:

> Almost six months have passed from the time the hospital adopted the device, and the work of the group has ground to a halt. Nonetheless, the dedicated members continue to plan their future work. They meet frequently in one apartment or another—since they no longer feel they should use the Institute's laboratory—to discuss the theoretical issues involved in such new devices. They have developed plans so that they will be ready to go into production as soon as sufficient resources are garnered.
>
> For Dimitrov, it has become much more difficult to travel around Sofia to consult with other members. It takes more time and effort, but he and the rest work at it. Now that they have created the device, they are full of energy to continue. It seems that organizational, political, and financial barriers—not scientific difficulties—have just motivated them all the more.

Talk about entrepreneurial perseverance! This hot little group just won't give up. Even the lack of space, equipment, and money, which might well have discouraged many an individual entrepreneur, cannot stifle the élan of this embattled group. What they need is a patron or two. Any volunteers?

In Summary

This chapter has examined four cases in which groups started out hot and then lost, or almost lost, their sizzle. Many things can drive the fizzle factor: intrusions by outsiders, departures of leaders, unforeseen changes in the external environment, loss of resources. Monitoring the external environment, tending the boundaries, carefully preparing new members for the group and the group for new members, keeping an eye out for incipient burnout, seeking patrons—all become key tasks for the leaders of hot groups.

In the next chapter, we move on to a related set of issues: organizational conditions that can thwart the development of hot groups and ways to change those conditions so they will foster, rather than inhibit, hot groups.

12

Hot Groups and the Individual: What's in It for Me? And What's Not?

Until now, we have insisted that individuals will no longer be kings and queens of the hill, no longer the only protoplasm from which to construct human organizations. In matters organizational, we have argued, the primacy of the individual is being seriously challenged by the rise of the small group. Here, somewhat paradoxically, we focus on the place of the individual in our new organizational world—the same individual we downplayed in earlier chapters.

To propose that the individual must make way for the group is not to suggest that the individual must thereby lose value, dignity, or status. It is certainly true that several kinds of groups suppress individualism. Some demand mindless conformity and uniformity. Hot groups, however, and many other varieties of groups, do quite the reverse. They enhance individualism. Besides, with or without groups, individualism will remain alive and well as long as humans populate the earth. The American sociologist Charles Cooley said it eloquently nearly a hundred years ago:

> Each man must have his "I"; it is more necessary to him than bread; and if he does not find scope for it within existing institutions he will be likely to make trouble.[1]

Individuals, with all their idiosyncrasies, will remain our center-piece. The shift will be from individuals as faceless "factors of production" within massive organizations toward individuals as diverse and unique participants within small groups. In the new organizational architectures, those groups, rather than their individual members, will become the primary elements of those organizations. Still, it is within those groups, we believe, that individuals will find much more room for individualism than they did in the lockstepped giants of the past.

A Bit of History: How Past Organizations Focused on Individuals, Yet Suppressed Individualism

Early industrial planners certainly treated the individual as the key unit in their designs; individuals, but not individualism. They needed uniform, standardized individuals. Yet, the individuals who showed up at the plant gate always arrived in a wide variety of shapes, sizes, and colors. Planners therefore tried to cut and trim all the individualistic bits, leaving only the "useful" common denominators—arms, legs, and eyes. Then, everyone could be expected to do identical work, at the identical pace, in the identical way. That initial focus on the individual served much more to de-individualize people than to enhance their individuality.

All that repressive cutting and trimming, however, didn't look very moral in our Judeo-Christian society and could easily be read as oppression. A scramble then ensued to provide it with some moral justification. To accomplish that, meaning had to be managed. A colonialist sort of white man's burden theory was promulgated to redefine that social evil into a social good. The theory ran something like this:

> There are two kinds of people in the world: Those primitive, rather brutish Type 1 people, mostly immigrants who don't speak our language but to whom we give employment in our mills and factories. Then there are the Type 2 people, like us, more educated gentlefolk, who own those mills and factories.
>
> The discipline we Type 2s impose on those Type 1s via tightly timed, narrowly repetitive labor is really a social good, a worthy act of social welfare. Putting Type 1s to work at those repetitive jobs is

right for them. They need that tight control. It keeps them on the straight and narrow.

Exaggeration? Perhaps, but here, for example, is how Frederick Winslow Taylor, the brilliant father of industrial engineering, described the immigrant pig iron handlers he studied at the Bethlehem Steel Works, back in the first decade of the twentieth century:

> The pig iron handler is not an extraordinary man, difficult to find; he is merely a man more or less of the type of the ox, heavy both mentally and physically.[2]

In that same piece, Taylor went further. A small increase in wages, he said, will make those Type 1 laborers

> not only more thrifty, but better men in every way; they begin to live rather better, begin to save money, become more sober, and work more steadily. When, on the other hand, they receive much more . . . many of them will work irregularly and tend to become more or less shiftless, extravagant, and dissipated. Our experiments showed, in other words, *that for their own best interest* [italics ours] it does not do for most men to get rich too fast.

Almost a century later, that kind of thinking may seem nothing more than a quaint relic of things past, like the Model T Ford. Taylorism worked, but it also didn't work. Its transparent attempt at moral justification didn't wash either. Organizations of the day certainly got enormous increases in productivity out of their standardized, routinized workers, but they later had to pay some huge human bills. Eventually, most managers learned that you really can't—to use a phrase common until about the 1950s—"hire a hand." Like it or not, the irrepressible brain always tags along for the ride. Decades later, that same unwanted brain was to look more and more attractive as we moved into the information age.

In the "enlightened years" after World War II, organizations began treating people more sensibly. The human relations movement entered the scene and radical new techniques were invented, like sensitivity training and organizational development. Just about every one of those techniques was very deeply group-based. In business schools, courses in personnel management faded away, while those in human relations took their place. New ideas about "participative management" and "industrial democracy" were initially applied almost exclusively to hourly workers in manufacturing organizations. They were implemented there in the service of the industrial engineers because management was encountering more and more "resistance" from overly Taylorized employees. This "human relations stuff" looked like a low-cost palliative. "We've planned a change in the way we set up the assembly line," the engineers might say, "but we're running into a lot of resistance. Will you human relations guys get those people to like it?"

That "human relations stuff," however, turned out to be much more than a simple anesthetic, as the research began to reveal. Many readers are probably familiar with several of those early research efforts, among them the pioneering studies at Western Electric's Hawthorne Works in the 1920s,[3] followed, a couple of decades later, by McGregor's Theory Y,[4] Blake's and Mouton's Managerial Grid,[5] the Scanlon Plan,[6] and many others. Most of those experiments, however, eventually ran into massive resistance from both management and unions—their implications were too radical. A few companies tried to apply the new techniques, but most shop-floor jobs continued as before, time-studied, motion-analyzed, and boringly de-individualized.

Then came the unexpected rise of that new phenomenon, the middle manager: marketers, staff planners, engineers, the forebears of those we now call "knowledge workers." They entered organizations in droves after World War II. Once in, they created a new problem: How does one manage and control these new people who use their brains much more than their biceps? At first, personnel managers and industrial engineers tried to apply the old control devices, time clocks and stopwatches. Not surprisingly, those tools backfired. They had been designed for people who did things that one could see and measure. These new folks didn't "do" anything. They just sat around at desks and lab benches, thinking and playing with little gadgets. Nor could organizations get far by preaching to them about how discipline was good for their souls.

In this expanding new white-collar market, human relations methods found their real niche. Participative ideas offered an alternative to the old screw-tightening controls. Give the knowledge-based new arrivals more autonomy, even more authority to make decisions. Let's set up management education programs and leader-ship training seminars—not for hourly workers, but for our new, up-market knowledge workers. One unforeseen cost evolved from all that: a wider-than-ever gap between the folks in overalls on the shop floor and the suits at the next levels up the hierarchy. Hourly employees continued to work under tight, Tayloristic controls, while middle levels were managed quite differently, via more partic-ipative techniques. Meanwhile, the "Personnel Manager" was going down the tubes, to be replaced by the new "Human Resource Manager."

Another, even more dramatic new arrival also appeared in the 1950s and later in the 1960s, information technology (IT). Initially, IT reinforced the old top-down approach, injecting new vigor into the weakening concept of centralization. Information technology made it possible for seniors to exercise tighter real-time controls, even over complex organizations. Now, middle-level individualism could be squeezed into the uniformity of the gray flannel suit.[7]

Still another related event occurred in those innovative postwar years: the emergence of the completely remodeled graduate busi-ness school and its popular new product, the number-crunching MBA.[8] Although later to be accused of suffering from "paralysis by analysis," those analytical MBAs fitted perfectly into organizations where hard logic was taking precedence over imagination. Their flashy new rationality was much different from the simple rationali-ty of Taylorism. Organization charts and spans of control were out; linear programming and forecasting were in.

As all those changes of the postwar decades swirled around them, individuals continued to be the organization's pivotal unit. Individualism, however, remained an organizational outcast until a sharp awakening hit the West in the early 1980s. Suddenly, or so it seemed, the Japanese invaded us. This time they didn't attack Pearl Harbor; they just flooded us with high-quality, low-cost TVs, VCRs, watches, and automobiles. Moreover, the Japanese were doing it all without MBAs and without elaborate performance appraisals, but with lots of small groups.

That incursion from Japan was just one manifestation of rapid change in the organizational world. New technologies of information, transportation, and communication were blowing up a huge storm of change. Radical social movements—including the sexual and student revolutions, the womens' movement, as well as the rise of religious fundamentalism—were also upon us. Those new winds were too powerful for any organization to deny. They were tearing classical organizational "principles" up by their roots. Even given their new technological power, the old hierarchical architectures couldn't cut it. Those fresh technologies were spawning new problems as fast as they solved old ones.

Some observers thought those ferocious winds would blow over, that things would settle back to the way they used to be. No chance. As some gales dissipated, other more violent ones gathered. Hanging on to the old structures might continue to provide a semblance of internal stability and orderliness, but those were no longer the critical requirements for growth or even for survival. Agility and flexibility became the names of the new game. Now, we are trying to learn to live with the uncertainty, volatility, and diversity that accompanied those gusty winds. Impermanence, we have come to realize, is a permanent condition and one that may bring individualism back to the organization.

Organizations Need Effective Groups, and Effective Groups Need Individualism

One way for organizations to cope with that impermanence is by making more effective use of the human group. Why? Because the lone individual, no matter how clever, is no more likely to make it in the new world than the lone organization. For the individual, the new tasks are too big and too connected with other people's tasks. For the organization, the new tasks are too fast-changing. Groups provide an intermediate answer. They're big enough to take on many tasks that individuals can't handle and flexible enough to respond to the changing environment.

As the whirling world causes organizations to shift toward groups, what will become of individualism? Will most individuals simply remain uniform cogs in organizational wheels, or will they finally be welcomed, in all their diversity, in all their different styles of knowing, thinking, and acting, in all their variations of ethnicity, race, and gender? The answer, it seems to us, is reasonably clear. Our new era is already becoming an era of liberation for more and more individuals in more and more organizations. Unrelenting uniformity is on its way out; diversity is on its way in.

Unhappily, as every reader knows, we aren't there yet. Consider, for example, this recent *Wall Street Journal* report:

> Nearly two-thirds of 641 managers and 773 hourly workers surveyed by consultant Kepner-Tregoe Inc. in Princeton, N.J., said their companies don't use more than half their employees' brainpower. More than 70% compared their organizations to a slow-moving truck or a ho-hum car, blaming failure to involve employees in decisions and lack of training or rewards.[9]

Despite such unhappy news, the freeing up of the employee mind has begun. Labels like "blue-collar worker" and "knowledge worker," after all, are not about varieties of workers, but about varieties of work. It's repetitive, mind-numbing "blue-collar" work that's on the decline. Many of those blue-collar workers have already metamorphosed into knowledge workers, simply because their jobs have changed to include knowledge work.

Beyond Knowledge Workers to Total Workers; Beyond Individuals to Groups

Even that phrase, "knowledge worker," is no longer an adequate descriptor of the new world of work. In this era of impermanence, people will work with more than their minds and more than their muscles. They will be "total workers," working with all of themselves—their imaginations, intellects, characters, personalities, and their relationships, too.

They will not, however, work alone. The individual's individualism will be maximized through interaction, not isolation. Few hermits will inhabit the new organizational world, but lots of groups will, and many of the hottest ones may well be *temporarily* hermitic. That's such an optimistic picture, it deserves a counterargument:

> If individuals cannot find their individualism in large, hierarchical organizations, why should we expect them to find it in small groups? Groups, after all, whether street-corner gangs or trade unions or boards of directors or new product teams, all know powerful ways to

pressure their members into conformity and to punish those who dare to deviate. Indeed, many small groups are far more skilled than organizations at suppressing individualism. Organizations are out there, distant and impersonal. Groups are close in and very personal, ready to climb on the backs of any individuals who dare to think for themselves. How, then, can any sensible person argue that groups promote individualism?

Response:

Groups certainly can do all those awful things. They can squeeze the juice out of both individuals and individualism. Groups, however, can also do the opposite. They can provide extra *lebensraum*, space for individualism. They can protect individuals from capricious bosses and that impersonal big brother, "the system."

In group-first organizations, "they," up at the top, will have to cede to the group much of the control they now exercise over the individual. Whether those groups will really foster individualism or suppress it will then depend upon the nature of the groups, which in turn, will stem largely from the attitude of the organization toward its groups. Does this organization support and reward hot groups or only cold ones? Does it insist on trying to manufacture its groups, or will it have the good sense to farm them? Will it repress its groups, thereby generating the aggressive, anti-organizational conformity that follows from frustration? Or will it allow its groups to let members ennoble themselves by providing opportunities for the ennobling of all?

We must not forget that organizations are under pressure, too. Their decisions about how they handle groups are not entirely free. They must respond to the howling winds that characterize the age of impermanence. Those disturbances are pressing organizations toward continuous innovation, toward flexibility, creativity, and urgency. These pressures are driving organizations toward more wild ducks and more hot groups—translating into enhanced opportunities for individualism.

Hot Groups Let Individuals Be Themselves

Hot groups, more than most other varieties, give their members lots of personal space. Hot groups don't care about how you look, speak, or dress. They don't care whether you're fat or thin, tall or short, young or old, male, female, or somewhere in between. They don't even much care if you have an oversized ego. They'll put up with almost any of your less attractive qualities, as long as you contribute to the group's task. Nor do they demand that you become buddy-buddy with everyone, on or off the job. If you want to socialize, go ahead. If not, that's OK, too.

Yet, simultaneously, hot groups, like all groups, will indeed press their members to conform to a few inviolable rules. Hot groups may not care about your haircut or your shoes, but they do care very much about how you work and how you think. Hot groups are intolerant of shirkers, so they're likely to exert strong pressure on those who don't carry their load. Although hot groups certainly don't demand that their members think alike, they do demand that members meet implicit and sometimes explicit standards about the *quality* of their thinking. In that regard, hot groups are elitists. Always focused on their task, they think they know a good idea when they meet one, a sensible argument when they listen to one, and a skillful act when they see one. They do not suffer fools lightly. People who consistently come up with bad ideas, nonsensible arguments, or inept actions are likely to be quietly clobbered.

The Upside: What a Hot Group Can Do for You and Me

Hot groups, thus, leave space for individualism, but do they actively encourage it? If "each man must have his 'I,'" will a hot group help the individual find it? We think so. This book is not a treatise on the psychology of individuals, whether in groups or organizations.[10] Nevertheless, the psychology of the individual is relevant here. We have to ask basic questions: What do we humans really want out of life? What makes us feel fulfilled? Why does each of us want so much to be valued by others as unique and significant individuals?

Psychologists, among others, have tried to approach such questions by positing concepts like *needs, drives,* and *motives.* David McClelland long ago measured individuals' three "basic" needs for achievement, power, and affiliation.[11] Abraham Maslow offered his hierarchy of needs: physical needs, safety needs, social needs, egoistic needs, and needs for self-actualization.[12] More recently, Mihaly Csikszentmihalyi developed the concept of *flow,* the urge in individuals to move forward, to accomplish things worth accomplishing.[13]

"The best moments [in life] usually occur," he writes, "when a person's body or mind is stretched to its limits in a voluntary effort to accomplish something difficult and worthwhile."[14]

Hot groups give individuals an opportunity to stretch toward those limits, a chance to achieve, to move forward, voluntarily, in a collegial effort to do something great. Hot groups don't help individuals satisfy all their needs, drives, or motives, but they can certainly give us chances to strive toward those "best moments."

Here, in summary, are some benefits membership in a hot group can have for you:

- *Hot groups can give you the opportunity to ennoble yourself.* We talked, in Chapter 2, about the potential for ennoblement as a distinguishing characteristic of hot groups. Many kinds of groups can offer their members emotional support. Many groups can act as educators, trainers, and mentors. But few groups—and few organizations—offer people the chance to do something so intrinsically fulfilling and extrinsically worthwhile that their members feel themselves personally elevated and ennobled. Hot group members move forward, exercising all their faculties, striving, thinking, creating. They do not march in place. They tap into the depths of their beings to undertake ennobling challenges.

- *Hot groups protect you from some common forms of organizational injustice.* Hot groups are a force for truth in organizations. They help protect the vulnerable lone individual from victimization by manipulative peers and bosses. When your group knows you do good work, enemies will have a hard time proving otherwise. With a hot group looking on, good work cannot easily be redefined as bad, nor can credit easily be pilfered from those who deserve it.

- *Hot groups offer you a refuge.* They do not offer the lotus blossom refuge of tranquillity, but an oasis of opportunity, a haven from the wheel-spinning routines of "normal" organizational life. Hot groups give the individual—in ways large and small—an escape into adventure, a chance to set sail with a small crew of committed others on uncharted seas in search of a wondrous grail. To the outside world, some of those quests may seem trivial, others earthshaking. That's not the relevant issue. In the eye of the hot group beholder, it's always a glowing grail.

- *Hot groups provide you with an antidote for the anomie generated by traditional organizational life.* They compensate for the organizational loneliness and cynicism so often depicted in cartoons, novels, and stand-up comedy routines, caricatures of catch-22 bureaucracies, insensitive bosses, meaningless work, and overly competitive colleagues. Scott Adams's capacity to pinpoint the absurdities and bitter honey of organizational life has landed the Dilbert books on so many best-seller lists.[15]

- *Hot groups supply you with community.* Of course, some other kinds of groups can do that, too. Like other groups, hot groups may also give you opportunities to satisfy needs for power, safety, and security. Those are positives, but they are not what distinguish hot groups from the current crowd of teams, task forces, and other organizational groups.

In sum, hot groups protect and enhance individualism. They provide a modest opportunity for individuals to find what all of us want—some meaning in our lives. They offer the possibility of satisfying the symbolic part of our nature, of leaving behind a meaningful trace even after our physical selves have departed.[16]

The Downside: What a Hot Group Can Do to You and Me

Legend has it that once upon a time a Tammany Hall politico noticed a saloon sign advertising a pitcher of beer for just five cents, with a free lunch thrown in. This caused him to utter those insightful words: "There ain't no such thing as a free lunch!" He was right.

One way or another, sooner or usually later, we have to pay for those "free" pickled eggs and pigs' knuckles. Hot groups don't give away free lunches either. Here are some of the several problems they can cause for you:

- *Working in hot groups can be physically and mentally taxing.* Hot group members work at high intensity, for long hours, often for months on end. They get tired. Yet, working very hard at something you love, then feeling exhausted at day's end, isn't all bad. It's not nearly as bad as feeling exhausted from the boredom of working all day at something you hate. Can't that kind of exhaustion—the kind that follows the exciting-job-well-done—be deeply satisfying, even exhilarating?

- *Hot groups can be addictive.* After a hot group experience, you may find it hard to return to normal work routines. Though weary, you may miss the verve and titillation of your hot group. Or, you may feel ambivalent. "Never again!" you may insist, and yet, simultaneously, "Let's get started on a new project!" Feeling weary, yet wanting to re-enter the game, isn't that also part of the positive human flow? Is it a failing, an "addiction," to rest a while and then—because you actively wish it—to pick yourself up and dive back into the fray? Is it a failing to fall in love all over again? Or, is that the way lives ought to be lived?

- *Some hot groups fail.* They fall flat on their faces, and that hurts. The customer suddenly cancels the contract, or the test model explodes, or a competitor just plain beats us to it. When a hot group encounters failure, it becomes much like an athletic team that has just lost its biggest game. Pain, sadness, and perhaps some recriminations are likely to follow. "If you hadn't dropped that easy pass, we'd have won that game." Still, some learning also follows, some adjustments, some new ideas, and, with the help of conductors, patrons, and keepers of the flame, eventual recovery and growth.

  The critical factor is the larger organizational culture in

which your group's failure occurs. In your organization, is it a disgrace to fail? Even if your group gave it a good try, will your senior officers strip off your brass buttons? Or, does the culture expect to lose a few? Indeed, does it even have the wisdom to applaud the occasional good failure?

Moreover, when your whole group fails, it is generally less painful than your individual failure. Unhappiness is spread across the whole group. It is not all piled on you, the lone loser. When others are there to help us mourn, it just feels better. Misery does, indeed, love company.

- *The most serious issue of all: Hot groups can have negative effects on your family and other relationships outside of work.* Working in a hot group can cause major stress in your nonwork life. When you are fully committed to a group's task, friends and family may feel abandoned, left out, slighted. "He doesn't come home for dinner." "She works every weekend." "He doesn't spend any time with the kids." Those complaints from home are usually echoed by similar complaints from inside the organization: "He doesn't answer our phone calls." "We can't find her to get a signature on this report." "Customers are getting PO'd." Hot groups, of course, are not the sole culprits here. Lots of us work too hard and put in too many weekends, usually for less worthy reasons. The fact, however, that many other kinds of work also cause stress at home certainly doesn't vindicate hot groups.

Whether those close to you can tolerate or even positively enjoy such peaks and valleys depends on a whole host of other variables. It can hinge on the solidity of family bonds as well as on the lifestyles and stages of others in the family. It is also related to how much family members and significant others can be included, at least during tension-relieving breaks. It can depend, too, on the extent to which you feel personally enriched by the hot group experience. If you are really on a roll at work, perhaps you may actually bring home an infectious sense of exhilaration and vitality.

It is not our intent to minimize or trivialize the issue of hot groups' effects on members' families and other close ones. We have seen the troubles such stresses can cause between spouses, as well as between parents and children. It's a serious issue. We just don't know how to turn back the tide. All we can do is search, like the inveterately optimistic Dr. Pangloss in *Candide*, for upsides that may partially compensate for some of the downsides.

In the impermanent new world, it is quite conceivable that the relationship between the family and its breadwinners will actually improve. When some things change, other things must also change, often in unexpected ways. New technology may do some real good by moving more work, even hot group work, away from the office and into the home. Such changes may permit even passionate hot group members to spend more time at home—and that is bound to ease some of the pressures that build from physical separation. On the other hand, one can also imagine some new pressures arising from an excess of proximity. Much of that home time is likely to be spent at the computer terminal, with a "Do Not Disturb" sign pinned to the study door. Time at home won't necessarily mean more time spent shooting baskets with the kids.

In Summary

Overall, what you are likely to get from a hot group has to be well worth the price you must pay. Indeed, the costs can be fairly minor compared to the enormity of the rewards. Too many of us in organizations still live out lives of quiet desperation, putting in time, waiting for weekends and vacations. We, however, subscribe to the premise that human beings become more complete when they move forward. Whether one describes that forward movement as "self-actualization," "personal growth," "flow," or ennoblement doesn't matter. The important point is that membership in hot groups is a step in that right direction. Hot groups are vehicles that can carry us forward in our search for meaning in organizational life.

It seems appropriate, therefore, to devote the next chapter to the other end of the spectrum, to ask what kinds of organizations enhance and encourage that search for meaning and which ones cause it to shrivel and die.

13

The Organizational Surround I:
Where and When Do
Hot Groups Thrive?

Hot groups go blah in the dull, dog-days of regularity and routine. They flourish amid atmospheric Sturm und Drang. Paradoxically, that statement may appear to contradict some advice offered in an earlier chapter. There, we proposed that one way to encourage hot groups was via relaxation, by loosening organizational rules. There's no conflict though. First step: Relax constraints. Second step: Agitate the organization, so it will utilize its new freedom. Stir it up. Instill a sense of urgent purpose. Open its doors and windows, so its occupants can hear, see, and feel the turbulent winds of change blowing out there. Entice the organization's people out of their offices, into the storm. Get them out where the action is, among customers, suppliers, potential allies, and competitors. Then, things will happen. Ideas will generate and so will hot groups. That's what this chapter is about, the organizational conditions that make hot groups flourish—and those that don't. We'll start with those that don't.

The Gentlemen's Clubs of the Past and Why Hot Groups Were Seldom Members

Most older Western organizations were built on the assumption of permanence. Things changed slowly back then, so organizational houses were designed for durability, not modifiability. Organizational "principles," presumably universal and timeless, governed both the design and management of human enterprises. Those principles included mantras like "authority must equal responsibility" and "the span of control can be no more than seven." Textbook after textbook defined managing as a fixed, orderly process, consisting, almost invariably, of exactly five steps: planning, organizing, controlling, staffing, and a fifth that varied with the text's author. Ideal managers were envisioned as near-monarchs, enthroned atop their enormous, perfectly symmetrical pyramids, pushing the buttons on their high-tech consoles. Those buttons would set their human dynamos ahumming each morning and shut them down cleanly at the closing bell each night.

Of course, actual managing of real-life organizations wasn't like that then, and it isn't now. That ideal of a clockwork organization was an extension of our Western faith in planfulness and rationality. Disorder, irrationality, power politics, and other messy human realities have always been ubiquitous in organizations. Back then, however, they were tagged as managerial failings. Disorder meant managers weren't doing their jobs.

Organizations also shared an implicit norm of "gentlemanliness," at least on the executive floors. Operationally, that meant control over one's emotions and avoidance of open confrontations. Think of some of the common shibboleths of the past: "Let's be businesslike!" "Let's keep personalities out of this!" "Let's not get emotional!" We don't hear those phrases much any more. That kind of almost ritualized behavior had good points and bad ones. It reflected an underlying commitment to a certain honesty and integrity in dealings with others. A handshake was as reliable as a written contract. It meant decency, in the old British colonial sense. One helped subordinates when they were in need and rewarded loyal service.

Gentlemanly behavior, however, also meant suppressing organizational tensions. So, when managers had to cope with intergroup conflict, they often began by publicly denying its existence, while privately—in a gentlemanly way—chastising the protagonists. Those actions would sometimes suffice to push a conflict underground, but they seldom either eradicated or usefully exploited it. Simply ordering warring parties to stop fighting has never been a very effective tactic for making peace break out. As soon as Mommy and Daddy leave the room, the kids begin pulling each other's hair all over again. Only this time, they do it quietly.

Given such attitudes, one can easily understand why old organizations quickly stomped on nascent little hot groups. Those groups were exactly what such organizations didn't want. Hot groups were noisy, intrusive, organizational ruffians.

New Clubs, New Members: Welcome to the Ungentlemanly Age of Impermanence

There are many quite different kinds of organizational conditions under which hot groups are likely to sprout. We have previously mentioned some of them and now want to spell out three in greater detail.

- First, hot groups like open, informal, and not-too-orderly environments—but not casual, lackadaisical ones. They need environments bubbling with excitement.

- Second, hot groups frequently arise in times of crisis, when the usual organizational rules and methods simply won't work.

- Third, hot groups often form in response to real or imagined enemies and competitors.

Let's examine those conditions one at a time.

Hot Groups Grow Where the Organizational Soil is Loose and Rich.

Hot groups, like truffles, are not easily domesticated. Thoroughly organized organizations stifle them, while looser organizational soil gives them room to grow. So, if one wants to design, from scratch, an organization whose primary objective is to encourage the growth of hot groups, a good way to begin is to do just the opposite of what the usual organizational manuals have so long prescribed:

- Don't organize more. Organize less.

- Don't tighten controls. Loosen them.

- Don't reduce each manager's span of control. Expand it.

- Don't check people's work once a week. Check it once a month.

- Don't conduct elaborate, individual performance evaluations. In fact, don't conduct any formal individual performance evaluations at all.

- If you want an organization chart, make it look more like a map of Boston than a neat triangle.

- Don't always keep the throttle on cruise. Periodically, push it to full speed!

If you do all those, hot groups may grow profusely, though some other less desirable aspects will probably grow along with them. Consequently, we are not recommending such an immediate, all-out attack.

Looseness and openness, by themselves, are not sufficient. Some loose, open organizations are laissez-faire places, casual and unhurried. Hot groups don't do well in such summer resort cultures. They prefer the tension and exhilaration of the bobsled ride to lying around by the pool. So it is not surprising that they frequently pop up in new, still-pliable, do-or-die, young organizations, only to disappear as success generates feelings of safety and venture capitalists insist that it's time to "get organized." Routinization is a systemic poison for hot groups. It kills both their freedom and their fight.

We have used Apple computer as an example more than once in

this book. Until now, though, we have always talked about Apple as it used to be, when it was young and vital, in the 1970s and 1980s. Now, in the late 1990s, that hot little Apple is gone. It's been supplanted by a rather large, bumbling, middle-aged Apple, struggling to regain its footing. Except for their common logo, the two would hardly recognize one another, although the final score is not yet in on Steve Jobs's dramatic efforts at resuscitation.

Young Apple's culture was wide open and passionate, "on a mission from God." Anyone over thirty was old. Apple was blessed by the irrepressible pushing and prodding of the young. It was a vibrant place then, flamboyant, defiant, ready to take on Big Blue and everybody else. Once, back in those euphoric days, one of us gave a talk to a meeting of Apple's financial managers. These are notes on how it went:

> Suited and necktied, got off the plane in Phoenix. Met there by a limo from the resort where the meeting was to be held. So far, so good. Arrived at hotel just after dark. Met again, this time by an Apple person in full cowboy regalia. Immediately presented with (1) a cowboy hat and (2) a yo-yo with a picture of Albert Einstein on each side. Then driven, in a microbus, over dirt roads to a desert hilltop. Huge bonfire blazing. Masses of people milling around, dancing, shouting, eating, and drinking. Removed tie and jacket. Band playing bluegrass—loudly. On rough stage, turbaned Sikh acted as MC. Learned later that he was from Apple's Singapore operation. Nothing like the sedate, well-mannered Singaporeans I knew.
>
> Toward 3 A.M, began to worry. Party going full blast. Scheduled to speak in five hours, at 8 A.M. Searched for a ride back to the hotel. Finally found reluctant driver. Clear he felt I was a terrible party pooper.
>
> Caught a three-hour nap. Arrived at appointed conference room just before 8, expecting audience of perhaps five sleepy people. Instead, the place was jammed. Crowd bubbling and lively, gulping coffee and chatting animatedly in little groups. During my spiel, most didn't sit in available chairs. Some stood, some squatted on the floor, some were lying down.
>
> Made my presentation and, surprisingly, they listened. Asked good questions and debated some relevant points among themselves.
>
> As I departed, John Sculley, the COO, was just arriving to speak. Hung around to listen. Lively session. Sculley, lucidly and sincerely,

trying to convince audience that Apple needed to get organized. Talked about stockholders and marketing. Several in audience complained that they hadn't come to Apple to worry about stock prices and marketing strategies. They'd come to build computers for the millions. On way out, heard loud applause—for questioners, not for Sculley.

That young Apple culture blended nicely with its surroundings, the equally youthful, 1970s culture of Northern California. Remember Berkeley in the seventies? The People's Park uprisings and the Black Panthers and sensitivity groups? In that surround, hot groups fitted into Apple's organizational milieu like bowler hats into the city of London. It seems very doubtful, indeed, that a company like young Apple could have come to life in, say, Zurich or Tokyo, let alone Venice or Natchez. In fact, several years later, we tried an informal test of that proposition.

In the late 1980s, one of us played a video about early Apple and its culture to a group of dark-suited, middle-aged Swiss businessmen in Geneva. The tape showed excerpts from Apple's 1984 annual meeting at which the first Macintosh was unveiled as well as the famous one-time-only Super-Bowl Sunday commercial about "1984."

The video was loud, musical, colorful, humorous, and brash. Fast-talking, young Steve Jobs, then CEO, spoke audaciously, challengingly, envisioning Apple as an intrepid pioneer opening the way to a brave new world. The whole show was a revival meeting. The large crowd reacted enthusiastically. They climbed on their chairs, applauding, shouting, cheering.

The smaller crowd watching the video in Geneva certainly did not react that way. When the tape ended, the meeting room fell silent. We asked, a little nervously, "Well, what did you think of that video?" Silence. People shifted in their seats. Finally, someone rather hesitantly offered this: "Well, to us Swiss, it looked very American." Someone else then added, "Not just American, Californian!" The ice was broken. Still another voice, clear and firm: "That sort of thing might work in the States, with all that boasting and yelling, but it would never work in Switzerland!" The test results were coming out as predicted. That boisterous Apple culture was looking more and more like a uniquely Northern California phenomenon.

That wasn't the end of it, though. After another long pause, one of the participants rose, turned to his colleagues, and asked this question: "Wait just a minute. We may not like it, but how would our teenage children feel about that video?"

A cacophony of noisy, rather un-Swiss discussion erupted. An overall consensus soon emerged: A slightly embarrassed admission that their own Swiss sons and daughters would probably just love to join that Apple culture. They would jump at a chance to work in such a vital, challenging environment.

We believe those conservative Swiss businessmen had it quite right. Apple was not for gentlemen, and it was not for their generation, but neither was it just a Northern California aberration. It was a culture of and for the young, be they in the Bay Area, or Geneva, or Lima, or Beijing.

In the old days, some observers put down Apple, calling it "The children's crusade." That epithet was not far off the mark. Young Apple was, indeed, a bunch of arrogant kids, untutored in the ways of the grown-up organizational world, thumbing their noses at the old folks and the old rules. Yet, they did something, as Steve Jobs put it, "insanely great." For a few years, that intrepid little company, led by its charismatic conductor, proceeded to change the face of computing and the whole modern world. Characteristically, the hot group that did most of it was turned on by the ennobling and expansive challenge of building small computers for the masses. Let great big (and bad!) IBM make those monstrously huge machines for the elite. Apple would occupy the moral high ground, promising an agile, inexpensive little computer for every man, woman, child, and chimpanzee on earth.

Of course, Apple's heat couldn't last forever. Middle-aged Apple now seems tepid and tired. As the company evolved, it made several foolish product and policy decisions. Worse than that, it grew up and got organized. Currently, Wall Street analysts are skeptically watching Apple. Many think it won't survive. They may well be right. But so what? Where is it written that it is in society's interest for organizations to live on and on, as bounded, separate entities? Young Apple, let us remember, when it was vital and "unorganized," did the impossible. That it later grew into a middle-aged duffer can in no way devalue the magnificent accomplishments of its youth. Age has a way of making duffers of us all.

Those Wild Kids Did More Than Build Computers for
Everyone. They also Ushered in the Age of Impermanence

Unintentionally, Apple and its upstart peers accomplished something much more insanely great than the creation of the Macintosh. Together, they ushered in the whole new era of organizational impermanence, one that is likely to be with us more or less permanently. Those young rebels didn't cause the new era, but they caught its wave long before most other organizations even caught their breaths. As that new wave moved in, with its forceful, compelling styles and informal, flexible organizational designs, the era of stable, rigid organizations began to crumble.

In the past, we treated permanence and stability as major indices of organizational quality. We assumed that organizations should and would live on, growing bigger and better as they aged. Any deviation from a steady course was, and often still is, treated as a disaster. *Fortune* magazine, for example, in April 1996, wrote an almost gleeful article about the difficulties being encountered by Anita Roddick's company, The Body Shop. Beneath the story lies an archaic implicit assumption, the assumption that a "good" organization must go on growing and prospering, on and on and on. The Body Shop, like most of today's and tomorrow's organizations, may or may not do that. It may reinvent itself, or merge with some other organization(s), or be gobbled up by some giant of the cosmetic industry, or it may just get sick and die. Apple, too, may be absorbed by Sun Microsystems or IBM or some newcomer. Or perhaps, at some far-off time, a revivified Apple will swallow giant IBM.

We must not, in this day and age, equate excellence with immortality. Can any of us any longer identify organizational players without an ever-changing scorecard? For example, here is a fairly typical set of items from the "What's News" column on the front page of the *Wall Street Journal*:

- SBC is near an agreement to acquire Ameritech in a stock swap valued at more than $5 billion. . . .

- Seagram is close to an agreement to acquire Polygram, the world's largest record company. . . .

- Baker Hughes is expected to announce that it has agreed to acquire Western Atlas. . . .

- Stone Container agreed to merge with Jefferson Smurfit. . . .

- Con Ed has agreed to acquire Orange & Rockland. . . .

- Telxon rejected an unsolicited $38-a-share offer from Symbol Technologies. . . .[1]

Unusual? Then try the front page of the *Journal* the very next day:

- DuPont plans to shed Conoco. . . .

- Monsanto agreed to buy two crop-biotech firms. . . .

- Boston Properties agreed to buy San Francisco's Embarcadero Center. . . .

- Publicis agreed to buy San Francisco ad agency Hal Riney & Partners. . . .

- Citibank purchased Confia. . . . becoming the first U.S. lender to buy a troubled Mexican bank.

- Nissan confirmed that it is in talks with Daimler-Benz about the possible joint production of commercial vehicles. . . .[2]

The new organizational world resembles the fluid sea much more than the solid mountains. Organizations rise and fall, merge and emerge, consume and are consumed. It is time to evaluate organizations in the same way we try to evaluate humans, by their contributions, not by their life spans.

Crises: Lightning Bolts Spark Hot Groups

Hot groups thrive in urgent, challenging situations. They often keep company with crisis, as we have already seen. By definition, a crisis is a threatening situation for which existing coping mechanisms are not sufficient. We cannot find answers in the instruction manual, so we must rely on our own intelligence and imagination. Too often, though, we don't. Instead, we turn to our leader for the answers.

Leader Take Charge! The Number 1 Crisis Script and Why Organizations Have Been so Wedded to It

When a crisis strikes an organization, we tend to think individual, not group. We are likely to turn first to the Great Leader: the president or the king or the senior officer present. That omnipotent leader scenario was around long before those Saturday afternoon movies of our childhoods, the ones in which the bank's gold has been stolen by bad guys. They are now holed up in the livery stable, firing at anything that moves. How can we recapture the gold and bring the evildoers to justice? Do we turn to a group? No way. Only ineffectual weaklings turn to a posse. Bring on the hero! Bring on Gary Cooper or John Wayne or Wonder Woman.

The heroic individual appears in the nick of time, striking just the pose in which his or her posthumous statue will later be cast. Radiating confidence, the leader makes instantaneous decisions, never missing a shot. Just by being there, she gives the terrified citizens new heart. Their confidence restored, the followers rush to obey the sharp, definitive commands. They are ready to give their all—because the leader has told them exactly what to do. With such a powerful, decisive leader, how can they fail?

Readers may remember a partial real-life version of that oft-replayed script, when, some years ago, President Reagan was wounded by a would-be assassin. The President was rushed into surgery, but Vice President Bush, his legal successor, was in Texas, far away from Washington. At that point, ex-General Haig, the Secretary of State, stepped in, assuming just that kind of I-am-in-command posture. He mounted the rostrum and declared, "I am in control here in the White House. . . ." His intent, of course, was to allay anxiety, to reassure the nation that order would be maintained. In a private company, Haig's approach might well have worked. In a democratic society, it didn't. That "I am in control" assertion turned out to be a classic CLS, a "career-limiting statement." His inappropriate eagerness to take charge violated the script and seriously undercut General Haig's subsequent presidential aspirations.

That leader-take-charge script probably remains so popular because both leaders and followers usually like it, albeit for different reasons. Too frequently the cry that "time is of the essence" has been invoked by panicky or egocentric leaders to justify precipitous action. Too often, as well, anxious followers, seeking reassurance, take the same route. In times of crisis, after all, fear and anxiety sweep across our emotional screens. To rid ourselves of those terrible feelings, we turn to Big Daddy.

A Number 2 Crisis Script: Go, Group, Go!

Consider another script, one only now being acted out in some large organizations, a script whose real-world advantages are becoming ever more obvious. Although it is a far less muscular script, it still carries a stiff front-end requirement. It requires that those involved, whether leaders or followers, be personally courageous. When a crisis arises, this scenario calls for brief, focused discussions among the relevant participants, plus autonomy for small units. It expects those closest to the crisis to think and act on their own, without waiting for the leader to tell them what to do, but always keeping the leader posted on what they are doing.

In this increasingly frequent scenario, groups play a central role, despite pervasive organizational prejudice against them. For many of us, words like "committee" and "task force" have so long evoked images of inaction and bickering that using them in the context of a crisis would seem a sure recipe for disaster. Small groups, however, by whatever name, often do tough jobs very well, especially in crisis situations. Consider, once again, the critically dangerous 1962 Cuban Missile Crisis.[3] That event has been frequently cited as one international crisis that the United States handled correctly. We know, from recently declassified material, that the situation was far more complex than any of the participants believed. The world actually came even closer to Armageddon during those thirteen days than most of us had imagined.[4]

This is roughly what happened:

President John Kennedy, after viewing incontrovertible photos of Soviet missiles being positioned in Cuba, was convinced that we were confronting a major and imminent threat. Some of his advisers, among them Air Force Chief of Staff General Curtis LeMay, recommended immediate surgical air strikes to take out the missile sites before they could be completed.

Despite such pressure for decisive action, the President chose to set up an ad hoc group, an Executive Committee, informally called the "ExComm." The ExComm was composed, intentionally, of extremely bright but also extremely diverse people, including Dean Rusk, Robert McNamara, McGeorge Bundy, Ted Sorensen, General Maxwell Taylor, and JFK's brother, Bobby, then Attorney General. Others, among them U.N. Ambassador Adlai Stevenson and Vice President Lyndon Johnson, participated intermittently. The President, however, deliberately kept his distance, joining in only occasionally.

That group met in the cabinet room, secretly and more or less continuously, day and night, for what turned out to be the thirteen-day duration of that crisis. Thirteen was neither a scheduled nor a magical number. Crises seldom provide us with unambiguous end-points. The missile crisis, and much of the world, might have lasted fewer than thirteen days if some of the more take-charge, bomb-hell-out-of-'em advisers had prevailed.

The ExComm's mission was to generate and evaluate possible courses of action. It did just that. For example, Soviet Premier Khrushchev had sent two letters to President Kennedy, one quite belligerent, the other considerably less so. From the ExComm came the suggestion that the President ignore the hostile letter altogether. The committee guessed it had been generated by the Soviet bureaucracy. They proposed that Kennedy respond only to the one that offered more room for negotiation, which they believed had been written by Khrushchev himself.

By all accounts, the ExComm displayed most of the characteristics of a hot group. Intensely focused on its challenging task, it was short-lived, egalitarian, and full of debate. Internal discussion was passionate, wide-ranging, and frequently chaotic. In fact, audiotapes of those discussions reveal that many people were often speaking at the same time. In the midst of the crisis, as we noted earlier, the ExComm even engaged in some "exercises," such as dividing itself into two groups, each independently putting together arguments for opposing alternatives.

Like many hot groups, the ExComm operated largely in isolation. It was sponsored, in absentia, by a valued and powerful patron, the President, who intentionally kept to a "business as usual" schedule.

Ultimately, in the crucible of the crisis, that ExComm experience even built warm personal relationships where none had existed before. Robert McNamara allegedly later recalled that his membership in the ExComm permanently changed his negative impression of Robert Kennedy, eventually leading to an enduring friendship between the two.

Finally, in a manner also characteristic of hot groups, when that terrifying crisis finally ended, the exhausted participants simply parted and returned to their normal roles.

The ExComm made no final decisions. It provided options for the President. In most of our institutions, we still lay final responsibility on the shoulders of single individuals. In this instance, it was President John Kennedy, all alone, whom our form of governance charged with the awesome task of making a decision that could easily have decimated our planet. There is nothing in the Constitution, however, that disallowed him from making good use of a hot group's counsel.

We close this section with one more example of the effective use of a number 2 group script in a crisis situation.

Remember the Tylenol crisis that occurred some time ago, when several people died from poisoned Tylenol capsules? In that crisis, the whole of Johnson & Johnson, Tylenol's manufacturer, heated up. A top executive group, working as a crisis management team, debated options for long hours. Almost overnight, a PR group produced videos for network use. An engineering and design group quickly repackaged the product to make it more tamperproof. Moreover, in the ensuing months, thousands of employees made more than a million personal visits to physicians, hospitals, and pharmacists around the nation.

Despite experts' assertions that the product was irrevocably dead, Tylenol soon returned to the land of the living, regaining and then surpassing its previous market share.[5]

Individuals obviously played major roles in both of those crises, but so did groups.

In Summary

Hot groups grow best in free, open, interactive environments. They thrive on urgency. They can work miracles in times of crisis.

Given commitment to the task, hot groups don't need more than a very few externally imposed rules. They will usually develop for themselves whatever operating regulations and controls they need. They are nourished by freedom and challenge. Once committed, the rest usually falls into place.

In sum, hot groups thrive in organizational surrounds that are loose and free, yet urgent and lively. They wilt in the stifling climate of tight hierarchies and lose their verve in the cool and correct atmosphere of country clubs.

14

The Organizational Surround II: Hot Groups Also Grow in Unexpected Places

Hot groups sometimes turn up in very unlikely, even counterintuitive situations, not just in open and urgent organizations. This chapter examines four of those kinds of situations.

Task-First Hot Groups Prefer People-First Organizations: Do Opposites Attract?

In Chapter 6, we suggested that organizations that focus much more on people than tasks are likely to spawn hot groups that focus much more on tasks than people. The explanation for that seeming paradox is straightforward. Organizations that initially devote major efforts to selecting their people, but then give them lots of elbow room, are likely to generate innovative groups that will build challenging tasks for themselves. Examples: some film, theater, and musical groups, some TV production companies—like Carsey-Werner—some universities, some research labs, a variety of large companies—such as Hewlett Packard and 3M—and many younger and smaller organizations.

Despite their current tribulations, universities are the seedbeds of many hot groups and therefore provide a useful model. They continue to maintain a broad, people-first orientation, as they have for centuries.[1] Universities put enormous effort into recruiting new faculty. Later, they expend further effort in deciding whether or not to keep those they recruited earlier. Senior faculty members examine each potential recruit's research, teaching, and professional activities in exquisite detail. They read the candidate's written works. They collect evaluative letters from knowledgeable colleagues at other universities. Hours, sometimes days, of meetings may be spent debating the qualifications of even a junior candidate. Every senior faculty member gets into the act. Nor would any sensible dean risk vetoing the faculty's nominees without first calculating the stressful consequences likely to ensue from such authoritarian behavior.

Then, there is the much maligned university tenure rule. Once tenured, a professor cannot be fired, except for some grievous or scandalous behavior. Whatever tenure's other strengths and weaknesses, it clearly drives toward greater freedom for tenured faculty. It permits them, if they so choose, to do their work singly, in near isolation, or to join up with others within or among departments of their own or other universities. It also permits a few to do almost no work at all, despite powerful peer pressure. The great majority of tenured faculty, however, like the great majority of all human beings, do not choose the do-nothing route, even when it is an available option. They search, they explore, they interact with others, they connect with people who hold related interests. In this free-ranging context, at random intervals, hot groups are born, groups that work intensively and productively for a few weeks, months, or years, then fade away. Some of their work also fades away, but some bears rich fruit. Here's an example of one such instance.

> Readers at all familiar with the history of American business schools will remember the innovative role played in the 1950s and 1960s by Carnegie Institute of Technology's Graduate School of Industrial Administration (GSIA). That hot little school was instrumental in revolutionizing and upgrading the quality of management education throughout the world. Its faculty, composed of bright, mostly young, very diverse mavericks, set out to make their business school a first-class educational and research institution.
>
> It would be first class in at least three ways:

1. It would undertake systematic and analytic research, relevant and useful to the practice of management, but also relevant in a broader sense. Business schools weren't academically "respectable" then, but GSIA's work would meet or surpass the quality standards of other respectable academic disciplines, such as economics and psychology.

2. It would help bring evolving ideas and new technologies, like then brand new information technology, into management and management education.

3. It would develop new methods for educating both students and experienced managers.

Carnegie Tech's GSIA accomplished all that, even though that new school was embedded in an institution with little repute in fields related to management. Dean Lee Bach, the quintessential patron leader, set high standards. He began by collecting a group of unusual, young academics, several of whom were "too difficult" for their previous institutions. Their names were not familiar then, but many are now. Among them were Herbert Simon, Franco Modigliani, and Merton Miller, each later to win a Nobel Prize, along with Professors William Cooper, Richard Cyert (later president of Carnegie Mellon), James March, and several more. All became eminent contributors to their multidisciplinary fields.

That little enclave rapidly heated up into a lively, creative, and intensely task-focused group. It generated seminal research and transferable new teaching methods. It developed eager and well-trained young managers, as well as top-notch new Ph.D.s to teach in other schools. One index of hot group activity: Just about every publication emerging from GSIA—and there were many—carried multiple authorship, often three authors or more. At many more hidebound institutions, still focused on the individual much more than the group, such multiple authorship would have been—and often still is—frowned upon, treated as a possible sign that the authors might be incapable of doing "independent" work.

The people at GSIA shared several interests, standards, and attitudes. They wanted to understand how organizations worked and how to make them work better. They sought to do that in a systematic, objective way and to lead management practice, not follow it. Otherwise, they were extremely diverse, in training, age, social background, and more.

The search for truth, however, was a core value. It was shared by just about everyone in that Carnegie group. The intellectual atmosphere was more than just lively and confrontational. Plenty of spirited discussions took place at other schools, but too often in a "House of Commons debate" style. Seminars elsewhere were frequently of the slash-and-burn variety, with questions meant more to display the questioner's wit than enlighten the issue. At Carnegie's GSIA, during its hot years, debate was also continuous and intense, but it was almost always aimed at discovering right answers rather than clever ones.

GSIA was no love-in. Tensions ran high. Even though interpersonal competition, jealousy, and jockeying for position certainly existed, they were largely obscured by the furious pace of work. As with all hot groups, that group's heart was in its work.

Externally directed competitiveness, however, was quite another matter. Like so many hot groups, GSIA saw itself as an embattled enclave, hemmed in by three partially self-enacted enemies. Harvard and other big, exclusively business-oriented B-schools were one set of bad guys. The nose-in-the-air, traditional university disciplines were another, and the "you're too theoretical and too impractical" business community was a third.

Initially, the other elite business schools brushed off GSIA, treating it as an irritating fly buzzing about in the Pittsburgh smog. Who had ever heard of Carnegie Tech? So, too, did the "respectable" academic disciplines, like economics, psychology, sociology, and mathematics, which had long viewed business schools as crass servants of Mammon. The same was true of big-time company recruiters. Why should they pay any special attention to this little gang from a not-quite-first-rank technical institute?

Did the big business schools or the disciplines or large companies really spend much time looking down their noses at GSIA? Not likely. It was in GSIA's self-interest, however, to perceive the world as though the big boys really disliked it. GSIA met Andy Grove's criterion: It was just a little paranoid. So, those mostly imagined and occasionally real snubs served to intensify the challenge. It made GSIA try harder to show everybody that its pioneering work was about to change the world. As usual, that energy and bravado were widely viewed—by anyone who happened to notice—as insolent and arrogant. Consider this little illustrative episode from that same setting.

A group of GSIA faculty and students had invited a senior sociologist from a major university to give a talk. That professor wrote back a rather snippy letter of refusal, suggesting that business school people knew so little about sociology that they couldn't possibly appreciate his research. That misfired missile naturally stirred the blood of the GSIA crew. Characteristically, they immediately undertook a quick quantitative analysis of citations in recent sociological journals. (Citations by other writers are a frequently used index of the importance of a book or a paper.) It turned out that works by GSIA authors had been cited much more frequently—in sociological journals—than those from the writer's own highly touted sociology department.

Victory for the white hats! Little business-oriented GSIA was turning out more "respectable" new sociology than that whole respectable old sociology department! The offending professor of sociology was so informed—with appropriate charts and tables!

Gradually, but only gradually, GSIA gained some attention and a modicum of grudging recognition from other schools and from the business community. Student applications increased. More good young faculty wanted to join up, and GSIA's doctoral and master's graduates began to get good job offers. Even the Ford Foundation turned to GSIA, using it as the primary model for a large new program of grants aimed at upgrading the generally poor quality of management education.

That hot group at GSIA came and went in about a decade, longer than most, but also long enough to help make modern, university-based MBA, doctoral, and executive education a significant part of the world's academic landscape. Eventually, the core group broke up, its key task finished, a victim of its own success. Some faculty members were seduced away to other schools. The leadership changed. In our age of impermanence, even GSIA's parent, the Carnegie Institute of Technology, got a new name. It became Carnegie Mellon University

Was GSIA a people-first organization? Yes, but not in the usual sense. It wasn't the least bit touchy-feely. It wasn't warm and loving. It was, however, embedded within a people-first place, a university, where such pioneering undertakings had a reasonable chance of surviving. To boot, GSIA was constructed people first.

Dean Lee Bach was GSIA's chief patron. A soft-spoken, rather taciturn midwesterner, he knew how to locate and recruit people with ideas, mavericks, innovators, people intrinsically interested in solving tough problems. One leading faculty member, for example, had never received his Ph.D. His doctoral committee at another university's department of economics had felt that his work wasn't "real" economics. That work subsequently pushed the whole field of operations research into prominence.

Hot groups must be people first because their people are their only asset. Finding the right people is the *sine qua non* of their existence. It is also close to being the *sine qua non* of universities' existence. Despite all the pickiness and internal politics that plague many aspects of life behind ivied walls, universities' underlying people-centeredness still provides a rich milieu for both hot individuals and hot groups. To go a step further, is it not via great people, rather than great job definitions, that all great organizations—academic, political, social, and industrial—succeed?

Few Other Kinds of People-First Organizations Also Support Hot Groups

Those same people-first considerations are also key in some commercial sectors where temporary organizations are the rule rather than the exception.[2] Independent film producing companies—those that are still independent—provide an example. There, people have to come first. A producer must assemble, for any project, a collection of writers, directors, actors, cinematographers, financial backers, and more. Most often, those temporary groupings do not blossom into hot groups. Frequently, they explode before they accomplish much of anything. Yet, the probability that such an assemblage will click into an exciting hot group is considerably higher than in many more rigidly structured institutions.

In Chapter 1, we briefly quoted TV and film actress Barbara Babcock's description of the exhilaration shown by the company doing the TV series *Hill Street Blues*. That group, Babcock told us, remains in her memory as one of the high points of her illustrious professional life. Her further comments catch the spirit of that hot group even better:

> I was brought in the first time after they'd already done the pilot. The pilot was screened for me so I could get an idea of what it was going to be like, because it was going to be totally new, in concept, in camera work, everything. So, they put me into a little room in front

of a TV monitor and closed the door and said, "Come out when you're ready." I still remember what that room looked like.

I'm getting goose bumps right now as I tell this story. I sat on the sofa first, and then, as the thing progressed, I found myself getting on the floor and working my way toward the television set until I practically had my nose in it. . . . I realized I was watching something utterly new. It was so exciting! I knew it was going to be something extraordinary, and I was a part of it. I thought I was only going to be a part of it for two or three episodes. I didn't know I was going to be in it [much longer]. . . .

The show was not a commercial success by any means. It was a critical success. Every single well-known reviewer gave it rave reviews. They had coupons for readers to send in if they liked it because NBC was having a hard time keeping it on the air because the ratings weren't good. And the show was about to be canceled. Only Fred Silverman, the head of NBC, before the Emmys even came out said, "I'm standing behind this show. It's going to come back next year." And then the nominations came out, and we got more nominations than any other show, and then it went on to win more than any other show that year.

But we all knew, we just knew. . . . We were all such a family back then, so connected and so committed to making it work. It didn't become a "what can I get out of it for myself"—not until several years down the line, which is always what happens in a series, ultimately. All we were concerned about was making that show work.[3]

Why did that particular group heat up when many others didn't? Babcock, who won an Emmy for her portrayal of the sex-hungry lover of a police sergeant, ascribed much of its vitality to the conductor/leader of the group, Stephen Bochco. It was his drive to do outstanding work, she felt, and his encouragement of others to do likewise that raised the whole group's temperature.

Sometimes, in the entertainment industry, larger production companies include several smaller groups, each doing a different show. The Carsey-Werner Company, producers of many popular TV series including *Roseanne*, *The Bill Cosby Show*, and *Third Rock from the Sun*, is a good example. Many of their different shows erupt into very hot groups, though, obviously, some don't.

Marcey Carsey, Co-Chairman and Executive Producer of Carsey-Werner, emphasizes the important role of "fun" as a major contributor to her firm's success. She wants that sense of fun to permeate everything the company undertakes, believing it sparks the creativity that is the lifeblood of her organization.[4]

Many other organizations in the arts combine those temporary and hot characteristics. Jazz and rock bands, both professional and amateur, are, in a near literal sense, hot groups. Most are self-generated, passionately devoted to their task, and often quite short-lived. Some, of course, try frantically to remain hot, sometimes resorting to chemical supplements to fuel their heat. Often, they fail.

What about the effects on such hot groups of those revered prizes, such as Nobels and Oscars and Emmys? Most are presented to individuals, not groups, even though many of those individuals are members of small hot groups. What happens when one particular individual within such a group is singled out for such special recognition? Certainly, those Nobels helped the reputation of Carnegie Tech's GSIA. They were certainly worth boasting about in the promotional literature. We don't, however, think they helped the GSIA group to remain hot. We also asked Barbara Babcock about the effects of those individual Emmys on the *Hill Street* company. Those awards to individuals, she felt, though applauded by all, had actually done more to divide the group than strengthen it.[5] Awards granted to special individuals, and thus visibly not granted to others, must necessarily release some small spores of group-polluting jealousy, causing it, at least momentarily, to take its collective eye off its task.

Where Truth Is Valued, Hot Groups Also Grow

People-first organizations are not the only ones in which hot groups thrive. We mentioned earlier that another place to find them is in institutions with strong, truth-seeking traditions, places where learning and knowing are valued for their own sakes. Research centers and universities are obvious examples, but many other kinds of organizations also give high priority to such values.

Once again, we encounter a seeming paradox: Many industrial and governmental research organizations are quite large, quite traditional in their management styles, and quite hierarchical. Thus, they would seem unlikely places in which to find hot groups. Yet, in many of these organizations, truth-seeking values and norms continue to prevail. The spirit of open inquiry is certainly still alive in most universities and many research organizations. Such institutions place high positive value on freedom of thought. Although focused mostly on individuals, that freedom also extends to groups. Those basic values, coupled with the realization that frequent failures are an inescapable feature of the creative and research processes, can make even rather authoritarian organizations quite supportive of both hot groups and hot individuals.

As we noted in Chapter 8, Bell Telephone Laboratories provides a good example. Now, of course, in this age of impermanence, it has been restructured for the nth time, and a large chunk of Bell Labs has been incorporated into Lucent Technologies.

> Both of us used to work with Bell Labs before the AT&T breakup. BTL was no small, bluejeaned, Silicon Valley parvenu. A mature company with more than 20,000 employees located in central New Jersey, BTL was, in most respects, a conservative, even bureaucratic unit of old Ma Bell. We counted nine levels in the BTL hierarchy. At one point, one of the senior managers used to station himself at the entrance to the main lab on random mornings, taking note of employees who arrived late.
>
> BTL was also a polite, gentlemanly place, even to its euphemistic language. No on was ever "fired" from Bell Telephone Laboratories. They were "stimulated"—to go elsewhere.
>
> This would seem the wrong soil in which to grow hot groups, except for one pervasive attribute: BTL's widely shared and tenaciously held truth-seeking values. Those core scientific values underlay every aspect of the company and were ingrained into everyone. From its beginnings, BTL had been designed as a house of science, operating almost independently of its corporate parent, AT&T. It was also deliberately insulated from its corporate siblings, the several regional phone companies and Western Electric, AT&T's manufacturing arm.
>
> Despite the fact that those relatives paid its bills, BTL was carefully sheltered from them. It was given an extended time span of discretion before it had to demonstrate "practical" results. Its managers could take a fairly long-term perspective doing their research and development without excessive concern for next quarter's results.
>
> In other respects, BTL carried all the trappings of a classic bureaucracy. It was steeply hierarchical and tightly controlled. Yet, its core

values and its operating style were closer to those of a graduate department in a first-rate university than to the values and behavior of most other private sector organizations. One positive consequence: A new Ph.D. in electrical engineering or physics, fresh out of Stanford or MIT, could blend into Bell Labs with hardly a ripple. Their universities and BTL both valued intellectual excellence and integrity. Those recruits' new bosses were not managers in the usual business sense; they were much more like the professors back at the university. They were outstanding engineers and scientists, with credentials at least as impressive as those of their academic peers. Like their professors, these new patrons demanded discipline and responsibility, even as they encouraged excellence, creativity, and intercommunication.

Interestingly, the nontechnical, administrative managers at BTL were an underclass, viewed by the technical staff as a necessary, but ancillary and occasionally troublesome adjunct to the really important work. Staff executives—finance people, accountants, HR managers—were there only to serve the technical side of the house. Indeed, to make sure that everyone understood who ruled the roost, the chief administrative officer was always a senior technical person, someone who had already earned his or her technical stripes.

We once asked a group of Bell Labs middle level technologists to tell us what they would most like to achieve in their lives. Not one person wanted to become CEO or even a vice president of BTL (or of any other company). What they wanted was to write the definitive paper in their field or, better yet, to win a Nobel prize. Moreover, the highest status in the organization went to the people in basic research, the ones doing the most far out, "impractical" work. In many other companies, these folks, if there were any, would have been pilloried as "nerds" and "longhairs," irrelevant to the real power structure of the organization.

Overall, BTL was certainly not a hot organization. Yet, despite its rather stodgy traditionalism, hot individuals and hot groups flourished under its umbrella, and so did major scientific and technological breakthroughs. That odd culture gave birth to modern information and communication theory, the transistor, and a myriad of other major developments. We believe it was those deeply rooted truth-seeking values that provided the growth medium for those accomplishments and for the presence of hot groups as well.

Some Hot Groups Just Show Up at the Front Gate. When They Do, Invite Them In

Some groups grow spontaneously, regardless of the organizational surround. In fact, people don't necessarily have to be presented with an intriguing, ready-made task to form a hot group. It can work the other way. Small sets of people, with overlapping interests and shared values, can discover one another, create tasks, and then develop into hot groups. Such spontaneous conception is a common genesis for hot groups. If we turn our memories back to our teen and preteen years, we can surely recall the imaginative projects our little friendship groups created, projects to which we dedicated ourselves with all-out passion and energy. We organized camping trips, theatricals, dances, and bake sales, with all the verve and creativity worthy of the greatness with which we endowed those tasks.

That spontaneity needn't end with adulthood, although it often does. We encountered such a spontaneous event among some quite adult executives of Singapore Airlines.

> In anticipation of SIA's fortieth anniversary, a small, informal group of employees, members of the company's Flying Club, hit upon the idea of locating and rebuilding the very first commercial transport flown by Malayan Airways (the original name of Singapore Airlines). No one in the group even knew whether any of those planes—five-passenger, twin-engine Consuls—even existed any longer. Nevertheless, using their own resources and on their own time, those volunteers undertook a worldwide search, a search that ended a few thousand miles away in Manchester, England. There, they located the decrepit shell of an old Consul.
>
> From that point, they moved on, overcoming difficulty after difficulty. They advertised for needed parts in aircraft magazines. They located some of the few remaining skilled craftsmen, including a "doper," an expert in an almost extinct craft, who still knew how to coat properly the plane's canvas fuselage. The group's enthusiasm was contagious. Volunteers appeared. People from distant places donated parts. Working posthaste in their off hours, nights and weekends, the group managed to meet the deadline for SIA's anniversary celebration.
>
> That beautifully refurbished Consul now sits in a place of honor in front of SIA's Training and Development Center, the pride of a small, short-lived, spontaneous group.

Note that modern information technology and the proliferation of alliances among organizations can lend a large helping hand to that self-generating process. It may be very hard to find a critical mass of people who share interests, values, and thinking styles even within a large single organization. In our new, soft-boundaried world, however, our world of computer networks and instantaneous communication, the birth rate of cross-organizational and even cross-national hot groups should rise. We suspect that, even in these early years of its development, the Internet has already germinated a large number of such virtual hot groups.

In Summary

Hot groups don't thrive just in lively open organizations. For good reasons, they also prosper in several other settings. Even though they are, themselves, highly task oriented, they often grow in strongly people-oriented environments. They are also likely to flourish where truth is highly valued, as, for example, in scientifically based institutions and in settings where artistic standards and values are high.

Many hot groups also just grow spontaneously, outside organizations or even in inhospitable ones. From the Manhattan Project scientists working in the surreal atmosphere of Los Alamos to your teenager's rock group endlessly practicing in the very real atmosphere of your basement, hot groups may simply sprout. We recommend welcoming them, so they can do their innovative things, then disappear.

In the two chapters that make up Part IV, we take an optimistic view of the organizational future. We propose that organizations are entering an era of managers' liberation; an era that will unleash the creative power of those two very natural resources, the individual mind and the hot group.

IV

AN OPTIMISTIC VIEW OF WHAT'S AHEAD

15

Things Change at Different Speeds

Prediction: For people who inhabit organizations, as well as for hot groups and entire organizations, the future will not just be different. It also will be bright. That sanguine statement hangs mostly on this rather simple notion: *Different things change at different speeds.*

Organizations will have to free their people more and more to meet the demands of these differential rates of change. Then those people will, as is their nature, respond by working harder and smarter. They will tackle challenging and important tasks and will pursue their work, often in small, hot groups. Consequently, the new ideal manager will be a more complete and natural human being than the old one, much less distorted by years of bureaucratic sandpapering. Those new managers, moreover, working in their new self-motivated groups, will not only do more innovative and useful work for the organization; they will also create challenging and ennobling opportunities for themselves and their workmates.

We want to begin by spelling out that rate-of-change idea.[1]

Rates of Change: Slow, Fast, Faster

There are no speed limits in natural law, nor is there any requirement that all traffic must move at the same pace. Over time, some things change fast, some slowly, and some hardly at all. Here are three bald assertions about organizationally relevant rates of change:

1. The world around organizations is changing very fast.

2. Organizations themselves are also changing, but much more slowly.

3. People in organizations are hardly changing at all.

Those three, we propose, add up to much more good news than bad, so let's examine each a little more closely.

The World is Changing Very Fast

That the world is changing faster and faster is the easiest assertion to document. In fact, it hardly needs documentation. We all have been witness to the enormous changes of the last decade, the last year, the last week, even the last hour. For example, only yesterday we learned that the average temperature in American cities has increased significantly over the last decade.

- *The world is changing fast technologically.* Consider just a few of those changes: the information and communication explosions, genetic engineering, exploration of our sister planets, and much more. The fancy new PC we bought last month is already "retro." A corded telephone? How ancient! First, researchers cloned a sheep, then mice and calves. Scientists set a little six-wheeled robot wandering across the Martian landscape.

- *The world is also speeding up geopolitically.* The last decade has seen the breakup of the USSR, the enormous economic expansion of Asia (and its difficulties), the ubiquitous reemergence of nationalism, the differential rise in population growth rates, and so much more. Map makers are breathless trying to keep current. West Germany is still struggling to digest reunification with its eastern half. Hong Kong has been absorbed back into China. Poland, the Czech Republic, and Hungary are now NATO members.

- *Our world is changing fast socially, too.* We have all observed (and perhaps participated in) the sexual revolution, the rise of religious fundamentalism, the AIDS epidemic, the decline of the nuclear family, urban chaos, sharpening ethnic, gender, and racial divisions, and more. Expectations are escalating in all parts of the world. People everywhere want—indeed expect—a reasonable chance at the good life. Some political leaders are being brought down because the media are exposing their amorous peccadilloes, but everyone else's romantic dalliances are viewed more tolerantly than before. Crime rates are up in Russia, down in the United States, but we Americans still don't walk out alone at night.

- *Individuals are too small, organizations are too big, but hot groups are just right.* All these developments are creating highly complex new problems and opportunities for organizations and their people. The *complexity* of many of those changes makes it difficult for single individuals to deal with them; their *speed* makes it difficult for large, slow organizations. Hot groups, however, look like just the right-sized operational units for coping with this volatile and complex new world. Hot groups are fast, and hot groups have plural brains. Obviously, groups encompass individuals, and organizations encompass groups—all three are inseparable, interactive parts of the larger circus.

Organizations Are Changing, too, but Much More Slowly Than the Big World

For the last decade, organizations have certainly been changing, probably faster than ever. Relative to the pace of their environments, however, they aren't breaking any records. Nevertheless, they have been cost-cutting, downsizing, restructuring, and reengineering. They also have been team-building, flattening, empowering, and federalizing. Consultants and academics try to facilitate the changes by offering up a host of programs, books, and counsel about how to go about altering organizational cultures, structures, work processes, and just about everything else. Organizational change is certainly happening and will accelerate in a continuing effort to catch, if not outrace, the speeding world.

For organizations to change, however, they must first "unfreeze." They become caught up in an ongoing process of abandoning old ways and then trying to settle into new ones. It's the settling into new ones that is now the hard part. There will be scant opportunity for repose in the new world. New ways will become old ways too soon. Unfrozenness has become a steady state. So all kinds of new organizational cuttings and tryings have been occurring all around us. Some are quite wonderful. Others, unfortunately, are rather depressing.

Not too long ago, for example, a character named Al Dunlap (a.k.a. "Chainsaw Al") was named CEO of the Sunbeam Corporation. He published a book called *Mean Business*.[2] Chainsaw Al is purported to have cut 11,000 jobs in five months while in his previous post as CEO of Scott Paper Company. He undertook similar actions at Sunbeam. Most disconcertingly, his behavior was initially reinforced by applause from the marketplace:

> Since Dunlap's July [1996] arrival as chief executive, Sunbeam stock has risen 133 percent and now sells for more than 100 times this year's projected profits. . . . Stocks as a group sell for only about 18 times profits.[3]

Add this to the picture: *Fortune* magazine reports a Cornell University survey indicating that 60% of MBA students admire Dunlap's "slash-and-burn" style. They see it as "results oriented."[4]

The adulation heaped upon Dunlap makes even us feel less upbeat about the managerial future. The consequences of organizational meanness and leanness, after all, are much more than just economic. In addition, there are long-term pragmatic effects on, for example, the ways young people think about careers. Quite rationally, many of the new generation recognize that security no longer lies in snuggling into the protective bosom of mother company. Safety lies in maintaining autonomy, along with multiple escape hatches. Those changes will have lasting impacts, well beyond making business school professors reconsider the content of their ethics courses.

There is an optimistic footnote to all this, however. By mid-1998, Sunbeam's stock price had dropped precipitously, and Dunlap was unceremoniously fired, but for the wrong reasons. He was fired by major investors on the board not because he represented the worst kind of managerial inhumanity and shortsightedness, but simply because the stock had fallen. Was it Dunlap, who had been quite up-front about his chainsaw style? Or was it those who hired him, focusing exclusively and disastrously only on the financial side of the whole equation?

- *Big organizations now want to act small, and small ones, big.*

Now, organizations, large and small, are reaching toward one another. The new generation of large organizations is taking aerobics classes to lose weight and add muscle, so that it can become as agile as its smaller confreres. Some of that new muscle is coming from small, hot groups. Large organizations are also abandoning steep hierarchies in favor of flatter, more multifaceted, "federalist" networks. They are trying to become more spherical, less pyramidal, and, we should add, they are also getting more "groupy." Of course, they aren't about to give up any economic power. In economic terms, after all, the race still goes more often to the elephant than to the bee.

At the other end of the spectrum, the small, ninety-pound weakling organizations aren't just sitting around, waiting to be gobbled up by some predatory giant. They're doing their own kind of body building by figuring out ways to develop some of the muscle of size without giving up speed and quickness. Some are forming alliances to muster the physical and human resources they need to stay in the race. Others are trying for the best of both worlds by offering themselves in marriage to Sumo wrestlers. Of course, many of the small ones are already quite groupy. All of which is to say that ours is an era of unprecedented organizational counterpoints, a time of largeness coupled with smallness and diversity with interdependence.[5] Those oddities translate into a period of multiple groups, large and small, interconnected and interdependent, yet diverse and often temporary. In such a lively milieu, hot groups should feel quite comfortable.

People, Fortunately, Are Hardly Changing at All

In these times, when almost any kind of change is highly valued, the flat assertion that managers don't change may sound like a put-down of all manager-kind. It isn't. It's a *kudos* for the managerial species. Managers have been a tribe of movers and shakers for a thousand years, and, just below the surface, they aren't any different now.

That so many managers have hung onto their spirits, despite decades of obedience training, bespeaks their heroic obstinacy. Even in the face of bureaucracies' massive efforts to tame them, managers—many of them—have remained true to their natures. They're still, if you give them a chance, ready to be at least wildish ducks. They may have undergone some wing clipping, but many haven't been tamed. Managers are ready, we believe, to start doing what needs doing just as soon as their cage doors spring open. Obliged as they have been to spend much of their energy clearing paths through the bureaucratic jungle, managers have, nevertheless, tried their best to do good work.

Many older organizations have done just the opposite of what they should have. They have rewarded orderliness and conformity, while punishing independence and risk-taking. In so doing, they frequently cut out much of the live wood in their organizations, while leaving the dead and even some petrified wood in place. In their tireless quest for the "team player"—a phrase that is often nothing more than a euphemism for passivity and obedience— some organizations have made it extremely difficult for their managers to do good work.

All Organizations Are Prisons

Happily, organizations don't always succeed in doing what they try to do. Granted that most managers, most of the time, obey the rules. They do what the organization demands. Still, they also manage to do at least some of their work the way they know it ought to be done, and damn the torpedoes. Moreover, new youngsters are forever entering the system, and, at least for a year or two, they don't understand the rules well enough to be ensnared by them.

We noticed this a long time ago when we used to begin executive development seminars by asking participants to think about two questions: "What makes it easy for you to get your job done?" and "What makes it hard?" The answer to the first question was almost always about people. "What helps me get my job done is my colleagues. I work with great people." To the second question, managers occasionally replied with complaints about their overwhelming workloads, or about long hours, or excessive travel. The bulk of the answers, however, were about the organizational roadblocks they had to get past to do their work. They talked about all the bureaucratic "junk" that obstructed their efforts: the useless meetings, the myriad reports, the floods of "urgent" requests for nonurgent information, and that damn performance evaluation system.

One of us once invited a wise HR vice president to speak to our MBA class. He was a man of wide experience and great integrity. In the course of his talk, that thoughtful veteran of both government and industry said something like this: "After many years of working in them, I've come to the conclusion that all organizations are prisons. It's just that the food in some is better than in others."

The students didn't like that. They hadn't thought of themselves as studying to become career prisoners. His assertion was radical, perhaps exaggerated. Fundamentally, though, he was right. It is in the nature of organizations to limit and constrain their occupants' freedom. They wouldn't be organizations if their members could do whatever they pleased, whenever they pleased.

Of course, that VP gave that talk a few years ago, when things weren't changing as rapidly as they are now. Although organizations are still organizations, does that prison metaphor remain applicable? We think it's somewhat less applicable now and will become even less so in the years ahead. We believe many—but not all—of those organizational prison walls have either already come down or soon will. Some organizations still exercise the kind of tight controls that were driving reasonable employees to distraction at the beginning of the 1900s and will probably continue into the 2000s. Charlie Chaplin's classic film *Modern Times* caricatured the human consequences of a job on the assembly line. The little tramp emerges from the factory at workday's end, still mindlessly and endlessly tightening imaginary bolts with imaginary wrenches, one in each hand. As he walks down the street, Chaplin tightens the buttons on a policeman's uniform and those on the ample bosom of a shocked matron. Charlie, fortunately, was irrepressible. He bounced back from that machine-driven insanity. Not everyone has the same resilience.

Those times should long since have passed, but they haven't—at least, not quite. Nowadays, it may be a computer programmer instead of an assembly-line worker who is driven up and over the wall by the maddening system. The *Los Angeles Times* reported this story not too long ago.

> Computer game programmer Jacques Servin can't quite put his finger on what it was that drove him to insert random scenes of studly males kissing each other into the recently released game *SimCopter*—without informing his supervisors. . . . Maybe he had spent too many late nights designing little people for helicopter enthusiasts to rescue from riots and natural disasters. (His requests for time off were denied.) "Ultimately I was kind of pissed off," said Servin, who was fired last week. "It was the accumulation of a lot of things."
>
> Maxis, the Walnut Creek, Calif., game manufacturer that has built a franchise around its fabulously popular (and non-violent) SimCity simulation game, discovered it had become the victim of a SimSabotage only after 78,000 copies of the CD-ROM had been sent to stores. . . . The incident underscores how difficult it may be to *control* [our italics] a rogue programmer who understands the technology better than his corporate masters. . . . On Friday the 13th and on Sept. 30th, Servin's birthday, the affectionate swim-suited men are programmed to come out in force, he said. "Then, every-where you look, muscle studs kissing everything in sight, especially one another," Servin wrote in his own news release. . . . "On top of police stations and hospitals, kiss-ins! Instead of riots, instead of tuba bands, queer PDAs [public displays of affection]! Instead of shoppers and criminals, wild boys!"[6]

Did the Maxis Corp's control systems just push Servin a little too far? And will Maxis, operating in the new world, learn to loosen up?

Much research supports the view that managers are, by nature, movers and shakers

Managers' propensity for action hasn't changed in at least fifty years. One research study after another has shown that to be true. It is a fascinating fact that many observations of all sorts of managers, carried out by different investigators, at numerous times, in various parts of the world, all keep coming up with essentially the same findings.[7] Since the early 1950s, those researchers have used the same straightforward method to study how managers actually behave. They have simply followed selected managers around, one at a time, noting everything they say and do from their arrival at work until their departure. Variations on these themes regularly appear:

- Managers work relentlessly, at an extraordinarily fast pace, week after week, year after year. They're busy all day, every day, trotting from meeting to meeting and crisis to crisis.

- Managers don't deal with one or two big issues each day, they deal with twenty or thirty issues, some big, some small.

- They do their work in real time, with very limited information. In addition to the elaborate information systems now available, they do it mostly via brief face-to-face encounters with colleagues, customers, suppliers, and others.

- They work all day, then go home, where they often work some more. They return to work the next morning—unless they have to jump on a plane to work elsewhere. At the end of each long day, if they're lucky enough to have a concerned spouse or companion, that person ritualistically empathizes, "You look exhausted. You've got to stop working so hard."

- The process is repeated, albeit with somewhat variable content, daily for forty years, until the manager finally retires to play golf or teach at the local business school.

Maybe executives work that hard because they're constantly under the cold, fishy gaze of their bosses. We think that's the rare case. Both senior managers and junior managers behave that way, with many different kinds of bosses, in large organizations and small, across many cultures, from Boston to Bangkok. Moreover, they have acted that way for at least fifty years, and that's as far back as the research goes.

We think this behavioral consistency occurs because managers are pre-selected from an action-oriented population. Perhaps they even have a genetic propensity in that direction. They simply like to accomplish things. Individual managers have much in common with hot groups. They are both strongly task-oriented.

The New Age of Impermanence Will also be an Age of Managers' Lib

The Maxis situation is fast becoming the rare case. Impermanence creates all kinds of problems for older organizations as well as for older people. It also, however, drives toward an organizational climate conducive to freer individuals and more hot groups. Now that so many companies have gotten much leaner, we doubt that they will also become much meaner. Quite the reverse. The same atmospheric gales that caused the inhumanity of downsizing are also forcing a new freedom for those individuals who remain.

Humans are naturally active and imaginative. Many people who look difficult or lazy just appear that way because of that attribution error we described earlier. When we squeeze people into tight, limited jobs, adaptive human beings adapt. They figure out ways to protect themselves, and they begin to look—to outsiders—like they are indolent, hostile, or rebellious. Change the conditions, and generally people's behavior will change, but their natures' haven't. People just naturally like to do things. If it weren't in humans' natures to create and build, where did we get all the world's ships, bridges, and computers?

When we are hindered from doing what we think should be done, we're likely to complain a lot. When we have the time, space, and opportunity to do work that we feel is worthwhile, then words like "discontent" and "burnout" almost disappear. They metamorphose into "excitement" and "good, healthy fatigue." By impeding that natural human motivation, many traditional organizations couldn't have frustrated the human spirit any more if they had tried.

In Summary

This brief chapter has proposed that the world is changing faster than organizations, that organizations are changing, too, but more slowly, and that organizations' managers are, fortunately, hardly changing. The consequences of those differential rates will be positive for both organizations and their people. The days of organizations as prisons, and employees as long-term prisoners, are both fading fast. In their place, we foresee an era of managers' liberation, in which naturally proactive people will be given much more freedom to take initiatives, even within large organizations.

The next and final chapter draws some conclusions and predicts (and also urges) a more humane and fulfilling organizational world.

16

Differential Rates of Change Augur Glad Tidings

So the world is moving fast, organizations slower, and managers hardly at all. What does all that mean for organizations, for individuals, and the central concern of this book, hot groups? We think several tentative conclusions can be drawn, and most of them look promising for all concerned.

Those Differential Rates of Change Will Kill Off—Once and for All—the Fruitless Old Search for the Orderly Organization

To bring themselves up to speed in a fast-moving world, organizations must first expunge three pervasive managerial myths, myths that have blocked their progress for a long, long time. Some organizations are abandoning those myths; most are still not quite able to let go.

Myth 1: *The myth of the individual as the basic unit of organizational construction.* We've already talked enough about that one.

Myth 2: *The myth of the orderly organization.* That one, for decades, has had managers trying to catch the ring of the seamless, glitch-free operation.

Myth 3: *The myth of the happy camper.* That younger myth, aimed at turning work into joy, has been made more pervasive by people like us: organizational behavior people, human relations people, and organizational development people. It's done some good and a lot of harm.

Both Myths 2 and 3 have caused endless and fruitless searches for those two unreachable grails: orderliness and happiness. Right now both myths are moving away from us at the speed of light—which is fortunate because both are entirely inappropriate for our age of impermanence. Even if we could achieve orderliness and happy campers, they would do us more harm than good.

The Myth of the Orderly Organization

Consider Myth 2, the hoary notion that goes something like this: *A well-managed organization is orderly, predictable, and rational. The manager's job is to keep it operating smoothly, like a fine watch.* One of the many destructive side effects of that idea has been to identify hot groups as pesky weeds and intrapreneurial managers as trouble-makers. If job descriptions are fully specified, that old myth goes, and if the organization chart has been drawn correctly, then unplanned-for problems will not occur. If such unforeseen aberrations should occur, it's management's fault.

In executive seminars and meetings, when we report the research results showing the frenetic real-world picture of their actual behavior, managers always respond with a mixture of discomfort and recognition. Reluctantly, they acknowledge that the reality of disorder is far more accurate than the myth of order, but they don't like to be reminded of it. They've been too imbued with the notion that orderliness should be a major goal. If they were really good managers, they seem to feel, they would be in control. Their desks would be clean, and their units would purr like a Mercedes engine. Given such an impossible standard, the jumbled reality of their own shops is something of an embarrassment.

Unfortunately, that embarrassment has for years pushed managers to head in the wrong direction. They have used their natural drive and energy to make everything shipshape, to impose regularity on an irregular world. Perhaps that's why we have so many annual, and usually ineffectual, restructurings and reorganizations.

Gaius Petronius, called Arbiter, is credited with seeing the short-comings of that kind of "reorganization," even back early in the first century A.D. His description is as relevant and familiar today as it probably was then:

> We trained hard . . . but it seemed that every time we were beginning to form up into teams, we would be reorganized. I was to learn later in life that we tend to meet any new situation by reorganizing, and a wonderful method it can be for creating the illusion of progress while producing confusion, inefficiency, and demoralization.

Incidentally, having dared to speak so bluntly, Petronius was charged with treason and forced to commit suicide.

Human organizations have never been orderly. They've always been full of conflict and disorder. All human organizations—nations, governments, companies—are, and always were, beset with internal dissonance. They may look solid, like serene, snow-capped mountains, but inside they're live volcanoes, forever on the verge of eruption. The rumblings inside those seemingly imperturbable institutions have gotten louder with each passing day.

That problem is not the private sector's alone. Public institutions do not escape such internal battles. Attorney Marcia Clark, for example, reflecting on her role as prosecutor in the O. J. Simpson criminal trial, points out how her case was weakened by the long-term, ongoing conflict between the Los Angeles Police Department and the Los Angeles District Attorney's Office. She writes:

> There had never been any love lost between the D.A.'s office and the LAPD. Invariably there are disputes on the big cases, where everyone starts grabbing turf. But never before had I encountered a flat-out stonewall. This could seriously damage our chances for prosecution, if and when we got there. The resistance wasn't coming from Phil [Detective Phil Vannatter] and Tom's [Detective Tom Lange] level. Nor did it seem to be coming from the office of the Chief. From where, then? The LAPD was such a labyrinthine hierarchy that it's almost impossible to tell who's accountable for any order.[1]

In business firms, too, conflict can run rampant. One division battles another. Subunits want more freedom. Key people threaten to join competitors. Senior executives squabble. In family companies, siblings feud over the fruits of their parents' and grandparents' labors.

Much of organizations' disorderliness is, of course, hidden, never quite spoken aloud. That helps preserve the myth of orderliness. Thus, in his fascinating book about the auto industry, *The Reckoning*, David Halberstam tells this story of just such hidden "irresponsible" acts by production managers, fearful of retribution if they should dare to tell the truth. This one took place at a Ford Motor Company assembly plant:

> The name of the game was Screw Detroit. . . . They had learned to cheat Detroit as best they could in order to preserve the integrity of their own operation. . . . Were there too many parts left over at the end of a model's life? Detroit hated that, so each year the plant people faithfully reported to the home office that they had only sixty-one of one part remaining and only forty-eight of another. . . . Meanwhile they dumped thousands and thousands of useless parts into the nearby Delaware River. Detroit loved how little waste there was, how well the numbers had matched out, and the people in Chester joked that you didn't have to swim the Delaware, you could walk across on the rusted parts.[2]

Organizational leaders, as we suggested earlier, are always faced with two major duties. Their more visible and dramatic job is to make their organizations prosper. Their less visible, less dramatic, but equally vital job is simply to keep their organizations glued together, to hold all those centrifugal forces at bay. In the new era, that second responsibility will become even more difficult. We shall not be able to maintain our institutions by encircling their perimeters with Berlin walls. Nor can we do it by trying to reach the golden goal of the orderly organization. We must elasticize the total institution, so more members and more groups can form temporary groupings, coalitions, and alliances among themselves and with outsiders, while still maintaining a reasonable amount of internal coherence.

Will new technology finally bring order to disorderly organizations? We think not. As the world has become more chaotic, many planners and strategists have turned once again to clever old Professor Technology to provide a cure. Maybe new therapy via computer systems and up-to-date information technology will help us reach that ideal of good order. Past experience suggests that it probably won't. This is not the first time technology has been called to the rescue. Organizations have given themselves large injections of technology several times before, with considerable short-term success. Those successes, however, have always been accompanied by the reverberations of unforeseen longer-term side effects.

A century ago, Frederick Taylor tried to bring order and uniformity with the simple technology of his "scientific management" and the stopwatch. Henry Ford soon followed with the assembly line. Both worked rather well, but they also generated huge new problems. The powers of modern technological medications certainly dwarf those of the past, yet they seem to eventuate in very similar outcomes. New technology, especially information technology, is once again increasing productivity and bringing more orderly control into organizations, but also at a considerable price.

Technology, after all, has always been something of a con artist. It promises to solve all sorts of tough managerial problems, and that promise is frequently fulfilled—initially. In the process, however, that medicine also seems to generate whole new sets of symptoms. These invariably further disrupt the organization, speeding things up, shrinking and complicating the world, spawning unexpected new competitors. Then clever Professor Technology peddles more of the very same medication as a cure for the new ailments that he, himself, has introduced. "Try a dose of today's technology. It's guaranteed to cure the ills caused by yesterday's."

Still, there is hope. More and more organizations are realizing that the original diagnosis was incorrect. They've been trying to cure the wrong disease. They are sensing that orderliness is not what they need. They are turning their energies, instead, to other, perhaps more fruitful and more relevant pursuits.

What we really need is more FUM. Orderly organizations and lively human beings just don't quite mesh, no matter how hard we try to integrate them. Yet, somehow, intrepid people manage to get work done, even in the organizations that make it so difficult. Warren Bennis tells a relevant autobiographical story about his days as a young infantry lieutenant in World War II:

> After a month or so in combat, . . . in the time-honored army fashion, I began grumbling [to my captain]. . . . We had inadequate air

cover and tank support, incompetent "forward observers" from the artillery, delays in getting reserves, unspeakable rations, and so on. Each day my voice became more strident. . . . One day . . . I blurted out, "I, for one, don't know how we're going to win this f——ing war unless. . . ." Finally the [veteran] captain spat out his plug of Red Man, looked at me through sad, beagle eyes, and said, "Shit, kid, they've got an army, too."[3]

Many executives, when they let their hair down, may well feel as that captain did, that their organization succeeds because it's just a little less ineffectual than its competitors. These days, however, they would not necessarily be right.

How about an almost contradictory argument? Our company has about as many foul-ups as its competitors, but it is more successful because we're just a little better at FUM, at "foul-up management"? Rather than trying to become glitch-free, doesn't it make more sense, in today's turbulence, to become glitch-competent? Ingenuity, innovativeness, and self-modifiability are far more appropriate grails for the modern organization than the elusive and inappropriate search for good order.

Those Differential Rates of Change will also Lay to Rest the Myth of the Happy Camper

The third myth, a more recent arrival than that of the orderly organization, dates mostly from the 1950s. It goes something like this: The manager's job is to build a happy organization, one that is warm and supportive, an oasis in which every individual can receive tender loving care. In return, everyone will work very hard and remain very loyal.

A great manager, by this view, not only runs a taut ship, but also a happy one. That ideal is, by now, almost as deeply ingrained into the managerial psyche as the image of the orderly organization. If your people aren't happy, you aren't managing right. Every year, for example, *Business Week* publishes ratings of American business schools.[4] One factor in those ratings is students' satisfaction with the quality of the teaching they receive. Some schools with otherwise fine reputations often receive rather poor ratings on student satisfaction. Those low marks pull the school's overall ranking down, and that means student applications will shrink. On the surface, that kind of survey sounds sensible enough, but we think it isn't. In our experience, good students are seldom happy. They are restless and generally dissatisfied. They want to probe deeper and move faster. Teachers in better schools are also likely to be more demanding, driving students to work harder. So, in combination, it may be that schools with better students and, perhaps, better faculty receive lower ratings because they're less idyllic places, not because they provide less adequate educations.

Academics, themselves, are mostly responsible for this search for the magical fountain of happiness, albeit unintendedly. The innovative and important ideas of early people-oriented thinkers, like Douglas McGregor, Rensis Likert, Abraham Maslow, Fritz Roethlisberger, and a few who came well before them, like Mary Parker Follett,[5] are finally having some real and positive impact on the practice of management. Many of those fine ideas, however, have been both oversold and overbought.

Back in the 1950s, someone at the Harvard Business School coined the phrase, "the happiness boys." He used it to attack the soft-headed human relations newcomers who were then beginning to invade business schools, including Harvard's. It was a taunt that caught on, often accompanied by derogatory bits like, "We aren't in business to make people happy." Whoever coined that epithet was basically right, except that he shouldn't have lobbed it like a hand grenade. The phrase maker was correct in asserting that the human relations movement was at least as concerned with happiness as with productivity. That concern also caught on among managers. Managers still value morale, satisfaction, and well-being as just-beneath-the-surface sine qua nons for a "good" human organization.

At first glance, one might guess that proponents of hot groups—like us—would like that myth. It's a very groupy idea. But we don't. Certainly, high morale and high levels of job satisfaction are worthy and decent values, and we won't for a minute propose that managers or scholars abandon them. Managers who emphasize the goal of happiness, however, may be confusing causes with effects. For a long time, both academics and managers generally believed that high morale in organizations *caused* high productivity. Thus, if we could raise our people's morale, they would work harder. That conclusion, it turns out, just ain't so. Sometimes, as morale climbs, productivity also increases, but sometimes it drops. Conversely, lower morale doesn't necessarily mean lower productivity. A lot of workers in the old days were quite unhappy when the time clock and the stopwatch were laid on them, but productivity increased enormously. As we have come to understand the morale/productivity relationship better, it has become quite clear that morale can go up while productivity goes up, down, or sideways, depending on other situational conditions.

High morale is certainly a good in its own right, but directly trying to make people happy doesn't usually make them so. Morale, we now understand, is mostly a by-product of other actions. It is a positive accompaniment to things like being involved in interesting work, participating in planning, decision making, and profit sharing. Such factors usually build both morale and productivity.

Happiness is as difficult to understand as love. It is fleeting and dynamic. Hot groups are sometimes happy, sometimes not. The Jet Propulsion Laboratory group that put Sojourner down (or up?) on Mars in mid-1997 was ecstatic when their little, airbag-cushioned mini-car landed safely. Yet, during the five years or more of that vehicle's development, we will give anyone long odds that there were many periods of worry, fear, anger, and misery. Moreover, we doubt that their project could have been successful if things had skipped along totally happily, day in and day out.

Hot groups do not search for happiness, though they'll certainly take it when they can get it. They are focused on their tasks. If happiness should come along for the ride, all well and good, but that's not what the ball game is about. What really occurs in many hot groups is a sense of exhilaration and excitement, kissing cousins to happiness and a lot more real.

Hot groups, we tried to show earlier, are not typically warm and fuzzy havens. During much of their lives, they can be internally tense and confrontational, only occasionally delighted with a forward step here or a glitch straightened out there. So organizations in search of happy campers, like those in search of the orderly organization, are not likely to generate many hot groups. Exhilaration, on the other hand, often does characterize hot groups. Exhilaration bespeaks a state of headiness, stimulation, intoxication, refreshment, and elation, all associated with the state of mind found in hot groups.

For Organizations, Those Differential Rates of Change Add Up to an Enormous Opportunity

If our environment is changing fast and our managers are not, then organizations would seem to be caught in a pincers movement, a squeeze between the pressures of the whizzing world and their stubbornly change-resistant people. Isn't that the highly pessimistic conclusion any sensible organization should draw? We don't think so. It's not a squeeze at all. If necessity is the mother of invention, opportunity is its father. The world is forcing organizations to change. They can't do much about that side of the squeeze. It's the other side, those "change-resistant" managers, that presents the opportunity. Those managers have only resisted what they should have resisted—their imprisonment within rigid bureaucratic structures. The ones who held out are still, just under the surface, lively, innovative human beings, and so are the new ones coming along. Released and backed up with a little support and encouragement, they're just what organizations require. Older managers may need more help to unlearn those myths their mentors taught them, and younger ones may need to recover from the brainwashing they got during their MBA educations. Beyond that, managers can become total human beings again, ready to do the kinds of work the new world requires.

At this point, some readers are surely shaking their heads and muttering a few expletives. They may agree with the notion that most managers spend too much time and energy fighting the organizational "system," but they may not be completely certain that the managers they've observed deserve halos and wings. "Many of the managers we know," they may insist, "are anything but models of unsullied virtue. A lot of them look more like goof-offs than good guys, just spinning their wheels until it's time to retire. Some are stubborn and inflexible. They haven't had an idea or taken an initiative in fifteen years." Yet, when the conditions are right, we aver, most managers—not all—will opt for meaningful, challenging work over lazing around in the lounge. It is in managers' natures, we repeat, to behave proactively. And proactivity is certainly what organizations need to stay apace of the changing world.

If we let our imaginations run on a little, a Breughel-like painting of the new organization begins to emerge. The whole busy canvas is dynamic, lively, peopled by all sorts of active little groups, each working like the devil. Some are deeply into competitive games, some battle monstrous enemies, others work and play together in collaborative alliances, and still others are just parting company, following yesterday's success or failure. The new organization becomes a vital human panorama, urgent, flexible, mobile, the whole quite egalitarian, loosely coupled, and only vaguely bounded. It stands—or rather it moves—in dramatic contrast to the grim, massive, and fixed monoliths of the past.

As for the people who work in those organizations, they are quite like those who preceded them, with one major difference: They are freer, less controlled.

Those Differential Rates will Provide Fertile Soil for Hot Groups

Organizations, we have said again and again, need hot groups. Now, we are proposing that if organizations continue to open up, hot groups will follow—naturally. Why?

First, managers' natural styles blend with hot groups' styles. That recurrent pattern of managerial behavior—fast-paced, brief, largely face to face (though technology may be modifying that)—is very similar to the pattern of hot group behavior, also fast-moving, intense, and here and now. So one of the reasons for our optimism is that managers' natural behavior seems to jibe nicely with hot groups' natural behavior.

Second, as internal barriers in organizations come down, communication among diverse people and groups becomes much easier. Individuals will no longer have to go up the down staircase to connect with someone in the next department. As organizations like 3M have demonstrated, easy access across specialties and internal divisions allows hot groups to arise spontaneously and frequently.

Third, new communication and transportation technology have made new kinds of hot groups possible. In many respects, technology may be a con artist, but it has also helped to create a fertile environment for hot groups. Cheap, fast, easy communication makes it possible for hot groups to function, even while members are distant from one another. Recently, for example, we encountered a small firm, Edge Microsystems, that has exploited that ease of communication in a novel way. Its CEO and sole full-time employee is Moshe Becker, an electronics engineer. Edge Microsystems is a kind of virtual firm, simultaneously a one-man operation and a company of temporary, often hot groups. This is how Becker describes his "organization":

> I have a consulting firm that specializes in bringing new products to market, industrial electronic products. . . . It's basically a virtual corporation that assembles a team for the job at hand. . . . The group . . . is usually comprised of clients' employees plus people I bring in to fill the gaps, so to speak, in talents and specialties that are nonexistent in the clients' companies.
>
> I think the thing that . . . gives me the competitive advantage is that they [the clients] are more or less structured into functions. They have marketing, sales, engineering—things like that. . . . And the way I look at things is process-oriented. The team that I assemble usually consists of specialists in each of the areas.
>
> The team has multiple phases. It's not that you group ten people together at the same moment . . . and then at the same exact second they all disperse. It doesn't work like that. . . . So at the beginning . . . to understand the market better . . . I create the initial team that has the expertise that's needed for that, the sales guy, the marketing guy, etc. [You don't want] to have a bunch of people doing nothing.
>
> Q. *And can your group really be described as a company?*
>
> Yes, but the people are far reaching. . . . It's not in theory; it's in practice. I work with people in Europe, in Israel, obviously, in the U.S. . . . So it's really a far-reaching kind of team.[6]

Becker went on to point out that some of those groups get quite hot, but that face-to-face meetings still remain preferable for building real heat:

> In some cases, as I said, I have a person, a software engineer who works for me on design in Switzerland. . . . He needs to come here, but there's also a story behind how you do telecommuting. . . . Bottom line is it's never as good as having the person just next to you, but it can get very close, depending on how you do it. . . . I mean you have to bring him in . . . so everybody feels as a group. If people are

just over the phone, it doesn't create that group atmosphere.

Q. *So sometimes everybody has to get together?*

Yeah, for a while at first, and then they go back, and then they come [here] occasionally.[7]

Becker's company, we believe, is developing one of many new varieties of hot groups. It is probably also one of the many new kinds of firms that will soon evolve. Like Becker's Edge Microsystems, these emerging organizations will be fluid and variable in shape, size, and over time. They will be made possible by innovative technology, and they will also contribute significantly to the development of more advanced technology. They will couple individual freedom with group membership in ways that previously have been extremely rare.

Fourth, in the fast new world, freed-up managers will discover for themselves that they need hot groups. Even lively, newly released managers can't cope, all by themselves, with the complexities of our turbulent world. They need help. They need one another. They also need hot groups. All those observational studies show that managers have, for decades, spent large amounts of their time in groups, in face-to-face meetings of one kind or another, mostly cool, and mostly with small numbers of other people. Many of those groups have been of their own making. They've been doing that without thinking much about it. Now, their new situations will provide opportunities to form and work together in hotter groups, groups that can both solve critical problems for the organization and give managers a chance to reach forward, to reap the psychological profits of involvement in things worth doing.

Fifth, both groups and individuals will have more opportunities to work on their own, rather than on other people's, problems. Managers have traditionally spent a huge proportion of their time responding to other people's problems. Joe and Susan want to talk to you about handling a recent complaint from a big customer. You call an ad hoc meeting to discuss how you can help the law department handle a lawsuit that's just been filed. A new piece of equipment isn't operating properly. Can you and a couple of engineers get over there with the operators to see what you can do to help? The boss needs a report on customers' reaction to our new product, and she wants it ASAP. Will you have it on her desk in the morning? Obviously, working on other people's problems is not, in itself, bad. People in organizations have to help one another. Still, should one always be working on issues initiated by others? Many research organizations allocate a percentage of their people's time to allow them to work on problems of their own choosing. In Chapter 3, we saw that Eric Pollard, at Rain Bird, knew that the chance to work on problems of their own would spur his team to great productivity. In the new world, everybody will be doing that quasi-R&D. In a world of continuous change, our people had better be problem originators, not just helpers on work originated by others. Besides, ironically, those others were probably promoted to their jobs because they were very good at finding and working on their own problems.

Calendars can too easily be filled with other people's problems. One can thereby avoid the harder and more risky business of taking initiatives. How many items on your calendar today represent your own or your group's forward-moving initiatives? How many originated elsewhere?

Mostly, and almost by definition, hot groups prefer problems that they, themselves, are excited about. Of course, in crises and other situations, they will willingly work on others' problems, but they much prefer their own. That's another reason that hot groups had such a hard time in cold, old organizations. There, other people's problems were usually the only ones on the menu.

Those Differential Rates of Change Also Promise Good Things for Us Regular People

In new millennium organizations, regular folks, especially knowledge types and middle managers, will be freer, but they will have to take more responsibility. They will also have to work in groups more than previously. They will have to be imaginative, agile, and flexible. Some may view such changes as negative. More work? Harder work? That's good? Yes, that's good. Those belong on the plus side of the human ledger. Hard work is consonant with the nature of human nature. We aren't pushing the traditional Protestant ethic, the belief that work is duty, that it helps us control our baser instincts. Instead, we're advocating new kinds of hard work because they will help us fulfill our not-so-base instincts, instincts that organizations have controlled far too much and far too long. New organizations will provide opportunities to fulfill some of those highly positive "instincts," to grow, move forward, achieve, create, reap the pleasures of a sense of "flow." In the course of providing room for those, organizations will also be making space for "instincts" of trust, friendship, and even a little altruism.

"OK," says the thoughtful reader. "Those are nice words. In this world of impermanence, all I have to do is use my new freedom to become more responsible, more creative, to work better in groups, and learn to be imaginative, agile, and flexible. Fine, but just how am I supposed to do all that?" We can't write the formula, but here are a few suggestions:

1. A good way to begin is by discarding any residual guilt from your enduring "failure" to make your organization more orderly and more thoroughly "organized." Many sensible organizations and managers right now are working hard to move their units in the opposite direction, to *un*organize them.

2. It is time to come to the happy realization that how you already behave, though you may not fully appreciate it, is very close to how you *should* behave. You *should* be juggling twenty balls in the air. You *should* be out there managing in real time, under conditions of high risk and uncertainty. You *should* be connecting with many other individuals and groups, inside and outside the organization. You should, however, also be doing much of that to help solve your own hot group's problems, not just everyone else's, and you should be learning more about how to do it better and better.

3. Look around for those executives in your organization who seem to do the best job of handling uncertainty and complexity, the ones who not only handle such things well, but aren't stressed out by them. We all know a few people like that. Talk to those people, study them, emulate them. Modeling effective others has always been a fine way to learn almost anything.

4. Look carefully at the people in your own unit. Any wild ducks? People with ideas? Nascent hot groups? Are you helping them? Joining them? Supporting them? Are you recruiting new ones? If not, isn't it time to start?

5. Are you connected? Are you close enough to people in other relevant parts of the organization and other organizations to get the real dope? Do they trust you and vice versa? Do you know your customers, suppliers, competitors? If not, how about starting that, too?

6. Practice working in groups. In the new world, no one will manage by giving orders, even low-key orders, nor will anyone manage alone. Life will be full of peer groups, and peer groups will be full of life. Hot groups, especially, will be needed to perform the endless stream of innovative and responsive acts that are already becoming the daily diet of contemporary organizations.

7. Locate a really hot group and watch it carefully. If it has a conductor, watch how that person conducts. Figure out why its members are so exhilarated. Then, see if you can help some new groups get started.

8. Take a walk on the beach or in the hills or the desert, alone. You're freer now. You have choices. Think ahead toward what you'd like to do with the rest of your life. That's not easy, so you may have to take a second walk, or even a third, or maybe a few months off and away from your "normal" routine.

9. Take another walk, this time with your colleagues. Make it a no-agenda bull session. Try to get everyone to relax and imagine. If the group could try to do anything it wanted, what would it try to do? Can those dreams be achieved in the real world?

Trying a few things like that *might* help to increase your own and your group's agility, flexibility, and creativity. They might even help induce that hot group state of mind.

It's Time for a New Grail: A Search for the Ennobling, Challenging Task

It's time for managers to set a new standard for themselves and their organizations. Let's not altogether abandon those two old myths, let's just push them onto the very back burner. It's not anarchy we're looking for—it's *organized* anarchy. We still need a modicum of order, and we still want people to feel good at work. Now, however, it's time for organizations to give higher priority to the search for challenge, achievement, innovation, and, yes, ennoblement.[8] Actually, that's a very old search, as old as humankind. It has certainly not, however, been a fruitless search. That drive has, since time began, caused human beings to extend themselves, to go out there and just do it, and to feel personally enriched by the process. There's no ambiguity about the value of this third grail. It is unequivocally good for all concerned, for the manager, for other people in the organization, for the organization itself, and, often, for the whole world.

Although this new search is an old one for humanity, it's a new one for old organizations. Only in special, off-center parts of the organization, like R&D and creative departments in advertising agencies, were such novel and challenging tasks likely to be tolerated. Usually, those who performed such tasks were also isolated, lest they infect the whole organization. Even R&D managers, whose activities were, by definition, novel and risky, have often had to fight for their chance to operate differently from the rest of their organizations. Some did it by bending the rules a little, perhaps doing this year's work on next year's budget or putting a little money aside in a secret cookie jar to fund hot projects the brass might think were foolish.

The sages who designed the old Bell Laboratories must have been acutely aware of that problem. As we described earlier, they intentionally isolated BTL from the rest of AT&T, giving it a long time span of discretion, a five-year cushion before it had to show results. That way, without its parent on its back, BTL could go on to do its great, "impractical" works.

Now, all organizations are becoming like those R&D and creative units. Everybody has to create and innovate, not just computer jocks and laboratory scientists. Production people, marketing people, finance people, and HR people had all better be ready to abandon last week's products and processes and continuously go hunting for new ones.[9]

Although most of the new search for the challenging task will be done in groups, those groups will not be the spit-and-polish, command-and-control squads of the past; nor will they be the painful, endlessly bickering committees in which many of us have squandered so much of our time.

The new groups will be good for people. They will be keystones of a psychologically more positive, healthier organizational world. It can be, and we hope it will be, an intellectually and emotionally challenging organizational world, one in which every individual can find adventure, learning, and personal development. It will also be a much more connected and connective world, more diverse, more interactive, more entrusting, more collaborative. It will also be a more open, more debate-filled world, yet much less argumentative, less internally competitive, and less manipulative than the organizational world most of us have known. Many organizations will fade away in the new era of impermanence, but organizations as a class certainly won't.

The people inside those organizations will work hard, perhaps harder than ever. They will not be able to hide behind bland walls of obedience and passivity, nor lose themselves in the befogging world of evasion, bombast, and pretense. Work will be more varied and challenging, frequently pushing people beyond their previously imagined limits. Connective leaders will dedicate themselves to meaningful enterprises and incite their hot group colleagues to follow suit. A good portion of that work will, we believe, be ennobling and elevating, exactly what every human being deserves. Moreover, much of that significant work will be done in task-obsessed little hot groups. The sum of all this: a new organizational state of mind.

Notes

Chapter 1

1. Cringely, Robert. (1996). *Triumph of the Nerds; Impressing Their Friends*, volume 1, New York: Ambrose Video Publishing, Inc.
2. Personal communication, February, 1998.
3. Personal communication, April, 1998.
4. Levy, S. (1994). *Insanely Great: The Life and Times of Macintosh, The Computer That Changed Everything*. New York: Viking.
5. Kennedy, R. F. (1971). *Thirteen Days: Memoirs of the Cuban Missile Crisis*. New York: Norton, p. 24.
6. Meyer, Karl E., and Tad Szulc. (1962). *The Cuban Invasion: The Chronicle of a Disaster*. New York: Praeger.
7. Duimering, P. R. (1997). "The Role of Image and Language in Formal Hierarchical Communication in Organizations." Ph.D. Research Proposal, Dept. of Management Sciences, University of Waterloo, Ontario.

Chapter 2

1. Pinchot, Gifford. (1986). *Intrapreneuring: Why You Don't Have to Leave the Corporation to Become an Entrepreneur*, 2d ed. New York: HarperCollins.
2. Ouchi, William G. (1981). *Theory Z: How American Business Can Meet The Japanese Challenge*. Reading, MA: Addison-Wesley. See also Pascale, Richard T., and Anthony Athos. (1982). *The Art of Japanese Management*. New York: Warner Books.
3. Whyte, William H., Jr. (1956). *The Organization Man*. New York: Simon & Schuster.
4. Lipman-Blumen, Jean. (1996). *The Connective Edge: Leading in an Interdependent World*. San Francisco: Jossey-Bass.
5. See, for example, Chennault, Anna. (1963). *Chennault and the Flying Tigers*. New York: P. S. Eriksson.
6. Watson, J. D. (1968). *The Double Helix*. New York: Mentor Books.
7. Rewald, John (1973). *The History of Impressionism*, 4th rev. ed. New York: Museum of Modern Art, p. 7.

8. Ibid., p. 9.

9. Hillary, Sir Edmund. (1955). *High Adventure*. New York: Dutton.

10. Tenzing, Norkay. (1955). *Tiger of the Snows: The Autobiography of Tenzing of Everest*. Written in collaboration with James R. Ulman. New York: Putnam.

11. Marcinko, Richard. (1992). *Rogue Warrior*. New York: Pocket Books.

12. Cringely, op. cit.

13. Festinger, Leon. (1964). *Conflict, Decision, and Dissonance*. Stanford, CA: Stanford University Press.

14. Cialdini, Robert. (1984). *Influence: How and Why People Agree to Things*. New York: Quill.

15. Levy, op. cit., p. 142.

16. For a discussion of the human development sequence and the leader's role in the followers' commitment to ennobling enterprises, see Jean Lipman-Blumen, op. cit., Chapter 12.

17. We are not the first to make the impermanence argument. Bennis and Slater made it years ago in Bennis, Warren G., and Philip E. Slater. (1968). *The Temporary Society*. New York: Harper and Row. Tom Peters echoed it, loudly, in his *Liberation Management* (1992). New York: Knopf.

18. *Wall Street Journal*. October 24, 1996, p. 1.

19. *Wall Street Journal*. July 17, 1997, p. A4.

20. *Wall Street Journal*. March 13, 1997. "Four Stocks to be Changed in Dow Industrials," Section C, p. 1.

21. *Wall Street Journal*. May 28, 1996. "A Century of Investing," p. R45.

22. Collins, James C., and Jerry Porras. (1994). *Built to Last: Successful Habits of Visionary Companies*. New York: Harper Business.

Chapter 3

1. See, for example, Bass, Bernard M. (1985). *Leadership and Performance Beyond Expectations*. New York: Free Press.

2. Janis, Irving L. (1972). *Victims of Groupthink*. Boston: Houghton, Mifflin.

3. Siu, Ralph G. H. (1978). "Management and the Art of Chinese Baseball." *Sloan Management Review*, 19, 3, pp. 83–89.

4. Adams, James L. (1979). *Conceptual Blockbusting: A Guide to Better Ideas*. 2d ed. New York: W. W. Norton.

5. March, James G. (1971). "The Technology of Foolishness." *Civiloekohomen*. (Copenhagen), 18, 4, pp. 4–12.

6. *Washington Post*, January 26, 1998, p. A3.

7. See, for example, Tracy Kidder's classic (1981). *The Soul of a New Machine*. Boston: Little Brown. See also Levy, op. cit.

8. Janis, op. cit.

9. Ibid.

10. Reported in Neustadt and Allison's afterword to R. F. Kennedy's *Thirteen Days*, op. cit., p. 132.

Chapter 4

1. Sato, Ikuya. (1988). "Bosozoku: Flow in Japanese Motorcycle Gangs." In Csikszentmihalyi, M., and I. S. Csikszentmihalyi (eds.). *Optimal Experience: Psychological Studies of Flow in Consciousness*. New York: Cambridge University Press, p. 113.

2. Handy, Charles. (1995). "Trust and the Virtual Organization." *Harvard Business Review*, May–June, p. 47.

3. French, Wendell L., and Cecil H. Bell, Jr. (1995). *Organizational Development: Behavioral Science Interventions for Organization Improvement*, 5th ed. Englewood Cliffs, NJ: Prentice-Hall.

4. For a more detailed description of the Achieving Styles Model, the underlying methodology, and the instruments for measuring both individual and organizational achieving styles, see Lipman-Blumen. (1996). *The Connective Edge: Leading in an Interdependent World*. San Francisco: Jossey-Bass, particularly Chapters 5–9. See also Lipman-Blumen, Jean, Alice Handley-Isaksen, and Harold J. Leavitt. (1983). "Achieving Styles in Men and Women: A Model, an Instrument, and Some Findings." In J. T. Spence (ed.). *Achievement and Achievement Motives: Psychological and Sociological Approaches*. San Francisco: W. H. Freeman, pp. 147–204.

5. Bennis, Warren G., and Philip E. Slater, op. cit.

6. Sproull, Lee, Stephen S. Weiner, and David Wolf. (1978). *Organizing an Anarchy: Belief, Bureaucracy, and Politics in the National Institute of Education*. Chicago: University of Chicago Press.

7. Giamatti, A. Bartlett. (1990). *Take Time for Paradise: Americans and Their Games*. New York: Summit Books.

8. Hegedus, C. and D.A. Pennebaker. (1993). "The War Room." Pennebaker Associates, Inc. and McEttinger Films, Inc.

9. WTTW/Chicago and Kurtis Productions. (1994). *The New Explorers: Skeletons in the Sand*.

10. Roberts, Nancy C., and P. J. King. (1996). *Transforming Public Policy: Dynamics of Policy Entrepreneurship and Innovation*. San Francisco: Jossey-Bass, pp. 132–133.

11. McGregor, Douglas. (1957). "An Uneasy Look at Performance Appraisals." *Harvard Business Review*, 35, 3, pp. 89–94.

12. Schellhardt, Timothy D. (1996). "It's Time to Evaluate Your Work and All Involved Are Groaning." *Wall Street Journal*, November 19, p. 1.

13. See, for example, Baker, Joe. (1988). *Causes of Failure in Performance Appraisal and Supervision*. New York: Quorum Books; and Mohrman, Allan M. (ed.). (1989). *Designing Performance Appraisal Systems: Aligning Appraisals and Organizational Realities*. San Francisco: Jossey-Bass.

14. Nulty, Peter. (1995). "Incentive Pay Can be Crippling." *Fortune*, November 13, p. 235.

15. Roberts and King, op. cit., pp. 131–32.

16. Bruck, Connie. (1989). *The Predators' Ball*. New York: Penguin.

17. McCord, Richard. (1996). *The Chain Gang: One Newspaper vs. the Gannett Empire*. Columbia, MO: University of Missouri Press.

18. WTTW/Chicago and Kurtis Productions, op. cit.

19. Ibid.

20. Ibid.

21. Potts, M. (1994). "Some Johnny Appleseeds Look Back at Their Mac." *Washington Post*, January 31–February 6, national weekly edition, pp. 20–21.

Chapter 5

1. Roberts and King, op. cit., p. 99.

2. Katzenbach, Jon R. and Douglas K. Smith. (1994). *The Wisdom of Teams.* New York: Harper Business, p. 66.

3. Pinchot, op. cit.

4. Rosenzweig's speech to the Stanford Historical Society is reported in Ray, Elaine. (1997). "Rosenzweig: Modern Universities Require Strong Leaders." *Stanford Report*, June 11, p. 5.

5. Lipman-Blumen (1996), op. cit.

6. Ibid.

7 de Tocqueville, Alexis. (1900). *Democracy in America*, rev. ed. New York: The Colonial Press.

8. Bennis, Warren G. (1997). *Organizing Genius: The Secrets of Creative Collaboration.* Reading, MA: Addison-Wesley, p. 22.

9. Weber, Max. (1946). *From Max Weber: Essays in Sociology.* Translated, edited, and with an introduction by H. H. Gerth and C. Wright Mills. New York: Oxford University Press.

10. Lipman-Blumen, Jean. (1973). "Role De-differentiation as a System Response to Crisis: Occupational and Political Roles of Women." *Sociological Inquiry*, 43, 2, pp. 105–29.

11. Wouk, Herman. (1952). *The Caine Mutiny.* Garden City, NY: Doubleday.

12. Lindblom, Charles. (1959). "The Science of Muddling Through." *Public Administration Review*, 19, pp. 79–99.

13. Lipman-Blumen (1996), op. cit.

14. Cyert, Richard M. and James G. March. (1992). *A Behavioral Theory of the Firm*, 2d ed. Cambridge, MA: Blackwell Business.

15. Lipman-Blumen (1996), op. cit.

16. Ibid.

Chapter 6

1.Popper, Micha. (1996). "Leadership in Military Combat Units and Business Organizations." *Journal of Managerial Psychology*, 11, 1, pp. 15–23.

2. *Straits Times* of Singapore. March 13, 1995.

3. Bailey, F. G. (1998). *Humbuggery and Manipulation: The Art of Leadership.* Ithaca, NY: Cornell University Press.

4. Kipling, Rudyard, "Gunga Din." In Untermeyer, Louis (1925). *Modern British Poetry: A Critical Anthology.* New York: Harcourt, Brace.

5. Gouldner, Alvin W. (1957). "Cosmopolitans and Locals: Toward an Analysis of Latent Social Roles." *Administrative Science Quarterly*, 2, pp. 281–306.

6. Shulman, Seth. (1996). "Code name: CORONA." *Technology Review*, 99, 7, October, pp. 23–24.

Chapter 7

1. *Harvard Business Review* (1992). "The Complex Case of Management Education," 70, 5, pp. 16–24.

2. Much of the best experimental and observational work on these issues was done in the 1950s and 1960s. See, for example, Cartwright, D. and A. Zander (eds.). (1960). *Group Dynamics: Research and Theory*, 2d ed. Evanston, IL: Row, Peterson.

3. Sherif, Muzafer. (1962). *Intergroup Relations and Leadership*. New York:Wiley. See also, for example, Fisher, Roger, Elizbeth Kopelman, and Andrea Schneider. (1994). *Beyond Machiavelli: Tools for Coping with Conflict*. Cambridge, MA: Harvard University Press.

4. Grove, Andrew S. (1997). *Only the Paranoid Survive*. New York: Harper-Collins.

5. Peters, Thomas J. (1987). *Thriving on Chaos*. New York: Knopf.

6. Cohen, M. D. and James G. March. (1974). *Leadership and Ambiguity: The American College President*. New York: McGraw-Hill.

7. See, for example, Churchman, C. West. (1968). *Challenge to Reason*. New York: McGraw-Hill.

8. McCann, Abbot Justin (trans.). (1952). *The Rule of St. Benedict*. Westminster, MD, p. 25.

Chapter 8

1. Leavitt, Harold J. (1951). "Some Effects of Certain Communication Patterns on Group Performance." *Journal of Abnormal and Social Psychology*, 46, pp. 38–50.

2. Endpaper, (1996). *New York Times Magazine*. September 29, p. 216.

3. Bennis and Slater (1968), op. cit.

4. The phrase was coined, we believe, by Eliot Jacques. See his (1983). *The Form of Time*. New York: Crane Russak.

5. That's the title of a paper by Lindblom, Charles. (1959). "The Science of Muddling Through." *Public Administration Review*, 19, pp. 79–99.

6. Grove, Andrew S. (1985). *High Output Management*. New York: Random House.

7. See O'Toole, James, and Warren Bennis. (1992). "Our Federalist Future: The Leadership Imperative." *California Management Review*, 34, 4, pp. 73–90, and Handy, Charles. (1992). "Balancing Corporate Power: A New Federalist Paper." *Harvard Business Review*, 70, 6, pp. 59–71.

8. Halal, W. E. (1994). "From Hierarchy to Enterprise: Internal Markets Are

the New Foundation of Management." November 1994, *Academy of Management Executive*, VIII, 4, pp. 69–83.

Chapter 9

1. Carvell, Tim. (1997). "Who Says They're Independent?" *Fortune*, April 14, pp. 27–28.

2. Cringely, Robert X. (1992). *Accidental Empires*. New York: HarperCollins, p. 189.

3. Ibid., pp. 80–81.

4. Ibid., pp. 82.

5. Ibid., p. 84.

6. Argyris, Chris. (1964). *Integrating the Individual and the Organization*. New York: Wiley.

7. Lipman-Blumen (1996), op. cit. See especially Chapter 8.

8. Ibid.

9. Kidder, T. (1981). *The Soul of a New Machine*. Boston: Little Brown.

Chapter 10

1. Both examples are adapted from a seminal paper by Ruth L. Love. (1989). "The Absorption of Protest." In Leavitt, H. J., and L. Pondy. (1989). *Readings in Managerial Psychology*, 4th ed. Chicago: University of Chicago Press, pp. 471–97.

2. Ibid.

3. Lesieur, F. G. (1958). *The Scanlon Plan*. Cambridge, MA: MIT Press.

4. Bruck, op. cit.

Chapter 12

1. Cooley, Charles H. (1902). *Human Nature and The Social Order*. New York: C. Scribner's Sons, Chapter 6.

2. Taylor, Frederick W. (1911). Letter to the Editor. *The American Magazine*, 72, 2, pp. 244–45.

3. Roethlisberger, Fritz J., and William J. Dickson. (1939). *Management and the Worker: An Account of a Research Program Conducted by the Western Electric Company, Hawthorne Works, Chicago*. Cambridge, MA: Harvard University Press.

4. McGregor, Douglas M. (1960). *The Human Side of Enterprise*. New York: McGraw-Hill.

5. Blake, Robert R., and Jane S. Mouton. (1962). *The Managerial Grid*. New York: Ronald.

6. Lesieur, op. cit.

7. Whyte, William H., op. cit.

8. Livingston, J. Sterling (1971). "The Myth of the Well-Educated Manager." *Harvard Business Review*, January/February 1971, pp, 79–89. See also Leavitt,

Harold J. (1975). "Beyond the Analytic Manager." *California Management Review.* 15, 3. 1975, pp. 5–21.

9. *Wall Street Journal.* "Work Week." February 11, 1997, p. 1.

10. For such a treatise, see Leavitt, Harold J., and Homa Bahrami. (1988). *Managerial Psychology.* 5th ed. Chicago: University of Chicago Press.

11. McClelland, David C. (1961). *The Achieving Society.* Princeton, NJ: Van Nostrand.

12. Maslow, Abraham H. (1954). *Motivation and Personality.* New York: Harper.

13. Csikszentmihalyi, Mihaly. (1990). *Flow: The Psychology of Optimal Experience.* New York: Harper & Row.

14. Ibid., p. 3.

15. Adams, Scott. (1996). *The Dilbert Principle.* New York: Harper Business.

16. Becker, Ernest. (1973). *The Denial of Death.* New York: Free Press Paperbacks. See also Lipman-Blumen (1996), op. cit., Chapter 12.

Chapter 13

1. *Wall Street Journal.* May 11, 1998. p. 1.

2. *Wall Street Journal.* May 12, 1998. p. 1.

3. For a re-analysis, see Garthoff, R. L. (1987). *Reflections on the Cuban Missile Crisis.* Washington, DC: The Brookings Institution.

4. Blight, James G. (1990). *The Shattered Crystal Ball: Fear and Learning in the Cuban Missile Crisis.* Savage, MD: Rowman & Littlefield.

5. See, for example, Pauchant, Thierry C., and Ian I. Mitroff. (1992). *Transforming the Crisis-Prone Organization.* San Francisco: Jossey-Bass.

Chapter 14

1. See Lipman-Blumen, Jean. (1998). "Connective Leadership: What Business Needs to Learn from Academe." *Change,* January/February, pp. 49–53.

2. See Bennis and Slater (1968), op. cit.

3. Personal communication, Pasadena, CA, June 1997.

4. Personal interview, Brentwood, CA, June 1997.

5. Personal interview, Pasadena, CA, April 1997.

Chapter 15

1. Portions of this chapter have been adapted from Leavitt, Harold J. (1996). "The Old Days, Hot Groups, and Managers' Lib." *Administrative Science Quarterly,* 41, pp. 288–300.

2. Dunlap, Albert J. (1996). *Mean Business: How I Save Bad Companies and Make Good Companies Great.* New York: Times Business.

3. Hancock, Jay. (1996). "'Chainsaw Al' Dunlap Just a Hack?" *Baltimore Sun.* Reprinted in *Portland* (Maine) *Press Herald,* December 1.

4. "New MBAs: Nasty by Nature." *Fortune.* February 17, 1997, p. 127.

5. Lipman-Blumen (1996), op. cit.

6. Harmon, Amy. (1996). "Maxis Saboteur Unhappy with Way Firm Had Him Programmed." *Los Angeles Times*, December 6, p. D1.

7. See, for example, Carson, Sune. (1951). *Executive Behavior.* Stockholm: Strombergs. See also Kotter, John. (1982). "What Effective General Managers Really Do." *Harvard Business Review.* November–December, pp. 156–167, and Mintzberg, Henry. (1973). *The Nature of Managerial Work.* New York: Harper and Row.

Chapter 16

1. Clark, Marcia, with Teresa Carpenter. (1997). *Without a Doubt.* New York: Viking Penguin, p. 32.

2. Halberstam, David. (1986). *The Reckoning.* New York: Avon, p. 218.

3. Bennis, Warren. (1993). *An Invented Life.* Reading, MA: Addison-Wesley, pp. 7–8.

4. "The Best B-Schools." *Business Week*, October 21, 1996, pp. 110–57.

5. Graham, Pauline (ed). (1996). *Mary Parker Follett — Prophet of Management.* Cambridge, MA: Harvard Business School Press.

6. Personal interview, Pasadena, CA, December, 1997.

7. Ibid.

8. Lipman-Blumen (1996), op. cit.

9. Foster, Richard N. (1986). *Innovation: The Attacker's Advantage.* New York: Summit Books.

Index